Facing Climate Collapse

This book was supported by the Council for World Mission (CWM) through its DARE Programme (Discernment and Radical Engagement).

Facing Climate Collapse

Ecology, Theology and Capitalocene

Luis Martínez Andrade
and Seforosa Carroll

scm press

© Editors and Contributors 2025

Published in 2025 by SCM Press
Editorial office
3rd Floor, Invicta House,
110 Golden Lane,
London EC1Y 0TG, UK
www.scmpress.co.uk

SCM Press is an imprint of Hymns Ancient & Modern Ltd
(a registered charity)

Hymns Ancient & Modern® is a registered trademark of
Hymns Ancient & Modern Ltd
13A Hellesdon Park Road, Norwich,
Norfolk NR6 5DR, UK

All rights reserved. No part of this publication may be reproduced,
stored in a retrieval system, or transmitted,
in any form or by any means, electronic, mechanical,
photocopying or otherwise, without the prior permission of
the publisher, SCM Press.

The Authors have asserted their right under the Copyright, Designs and
Patents Act 1988 to be identified as the Authors of this Work

Scripture quotations are from New Revised Standard Version Bible: Anglicized
Edition, copyright © 1989, 1995 National Council of the Churches of Christ in
the United States of America. Used by permission. All rights reserved worldwide.

British Library Cataloguing in Publication data

A catalogue record for this book is available
from the British Library

ISBN: 978-0-334-06633-0

EU GPSR Authorised Representative
LOGOS EUROPE, 9 rue Nicolas Poussin, 17000, LA ROCHELLE, France
E-mail: Contact@logoseurope.eu

Typeset by Regent Typesetting

Contents

About the Contributors — vii

Preface — xiii
Jooseop Keum

Introduction — 1
Luis Martínez Andrade and Seforosa Carroll

Part 1: Theology

1 Theology and Anticolonial Critical Theory in 'Capitalocene' — 7
   Luis Martínez Andrade

2 'Anthropocene' or 'Global Coloniality'? A Decolonial Theological Reflection — 22
   Hadje Cresencio Sadje

3 A Forgotten Body of War: Ecofeminist Theology in 'Militarycene' — 40
   Keun-joo Christine Pae

4 Salvation and Liturgy Reimagined through Earth-centred Worship in the Age of Anthropocene: What Has Salvation Got to Do with Mother Earth? — 56
   Lilian Cheelo Siwila

5 The 'Garden on Fire': An Ecological Reading of the Day of the Lord in the Old Testament — 69
   Nokcharenla

Part 2: Ecology

6 Taiwan Indigenous Women and Ecofeminism 87
  Wan Jou Lin

7 Upright Walk on a Habitable Earth in Anthropocene 103
  Beat Dietschy

8 'For the Life of the ... Animals': Christian Anthropology
  Revisited in Light of the Climate Crisis 119
  Nikolaos Asproulis

Part 3: Voices from the Global South

9 Ecojustice in Abya Yala: Decolonization and the Practice
  of 'Good Living' 135
  Yenny Delgado

10 Sustainable Anthropocene and Ecological Justice:
   Perspectives from the Ethos of the United Congregational
   Church of Southern Africa (UCCSA) 149
   Revd Xolani Maseko and Thandi Soko-de Jong

11 Out of the Closet and Out of the Tomb of Ecological Sins 163
   Suzana Moreira

Epilogue – Facing Climate Collapse: Ecology, Theology and
Capitalocene 177
Joerg Rieger

Index of Names and Subjects 183

About the Contributors

Luis Martínez Andrade received his PhD in Sociology from L'École des hautes études en sciences sociales (EHESS) in Paris. He currently holds the position of Scientific Collaborator at Université Catholique de Louvain, Belgium. Among his many books are *Religion without Redemption: Social Contradictions and Awakened Dreams in Latin America* (Pluto Press, 2015), *Ecología y Teología de la liberación: Crítica de la modernidad/colonialidad* (Herder, 2019). He is co-editor of *Decolonizing Liberation Theologies: Past, Present, and Future* (Palgrave Macmillan, 2023) and of *Indecentes e Indignadas: Teologías, Pedagogías y praxis de liberación en América Latina* (Laboratorio Educativo, 2024).

Seforosa Carroll is Academic Dean and Lecturer in Cross Cultural Ministry and Theology at United Theological College, Australia. She is an Australian Fiji-born Rotuman theologian who spent her formative years growing up in Lautoka, the western side of Viti Levu in Fiji. Seforosa received her PhD in Theology from Charles Sturt University in 2015. She is a Center of Theological Inquiry Fellow at Princeton University, United States, and was a resident member of the 2017–2018 Inquiry into Religion and Migration at the CTI. She is a Research Fellow of the Public and Contextual Theology Research Center (PaCT), Charles Sturt University, Australia.

Hadje Cresencio Sadje is a human rights activist and has experience working with local, regional, national and international organizations. He has also been dedicated to the effort of decolonizing Christian philosophical and theological perspectives. He is currently a PhD candidate at the University of Vienna in Austria. His publications include *Theology at the Border: Community Peacemaker Teams and the Refugee Crisis in Europe* (Canada: Pandora Press, 2022), and *Grassroots Asian Theologies: Doing Pentecostal Theology in the Philippine Context* (Ekpyrosis Press, 2022).

Keun-joo Christine Pae is Professor of Religion and Women's and Gender Studies and Chair of the Religion Department at Denison University, Granville, Ohio, United States, and Episcopal Priest. She is the author of *Transpacific Imagination of Theology, Ethics, and Spiritual Activism: Doing Feminist Ethics Transnationally* (Palgrave Macmillan, 2023) and co-editor of *Embodying Antiracist Christianity* (Palgrave Macmillan, 2023).

Lilian Cheelo Siwila is an Associate Professor in the School of Religion, Philosophy and Classics at the University of KwaZulu Natal. She is head of Systematic Theology and acting head of Gender, Religion and Health, Academic Leader – Community Engagement. She is involved in research activities with a number of ecumenical bodies such CWM, WMF and other research-related organizations. She is a member of the Circle of Concerned African Women Theologians. She has published widely in internationally recognized journals and books, including edited volumes.

Nokcharenla is from Dimapur, Nagaland (north-east India). She worked at Bishop's College, Kolkata, India, as an Assistant Professor of Old Testament for three years. Currently she is a PhD candidate at Aizawl Theological College, India. Her research interest lies in ecofeminist reading of stereotyped flat characters in the Old Testament for narrative reclamation and to foster conscious and deliberate actions towards a symbiotic relationship in the web of life.

Wan Jou Lin (林宛柔) is a PhD Candidate at the Department of Taiwan Culture, Languages and Literature at National Taiwan Normal University in Taipei. Lin focuses on ecofeminism and indigenous knowledge to study and criticize the world (dis)order imposed by neoliberal economic globalization. Her research interests include political ecology, postcolonialism, ethnic literature to dialectics between indigenization and globalization, especially female voices on traditional ecological knowledge and their resistance and resilience on climate crisis.

Beat Dietschy is a Swiss philosopher and theologian with an MTh and PhD from the University of Basel. He has been a collaborator with the German philosopher Ernst Bloch in Tübingen. He was Director of Swiss NGO Bread for All and President of NGOs such as Comundo (Lucerne). Currently, he is a member of the board of ECLOF International and the foundation Swisspeace. He is co-editor of various works by and about Bloch including the *Bloch Dictionary* (De Gruyter, 2012) and an article about Bloch's 'Alliance with Nature' in the *Historical-Critical Dictionary of Marxism* (Haymarket Books, 2024). He has published approximately 150 articles on development, globalization, theology of liberation, decolonial thinking, indigenous movements, political diakonia, right-wing populism and intercultural philosophy.

Nikolaos Asproulis is currently Deputy Director of the Volos Academy for Theological Studies, Volos, Greece, and Lecturer at the Hellenic Open University, Patras, Greece. He is also Chair of the *PanOrthodox Concern for Animals*. He graduated in Theology (University of Athens, 1997), and obtained MTh (2007) and PhD degrees (2016) in Theology at Hellenic Open University. Asproulis' research focuses on the history and development of contemporary Orthodox theology (twentieth–twenty-first century). His most recent publications include *Priests of Creation: John Zizioulas on Discerning an Ecological Ethos* (T&T Clark, 2021); he co-edited with John Chryssavgis, *Eastern Orthodox Christian Animal Theology: God, Animals and Creation in Dialogue* (Lexington Books, forthcoming 2025).

Yenny Delgado is a Theologian and Psychologist. She has worked with social movements, local churches and regional governments for over a decade, advocating for inclusive and decolonial education. Yenny is an active religious leader, ordained ruling elder, and member of the Advisory Committee on Social Witness Policy in the Presbyterian Church, United States. She is also the founder and director of Publica Theology and convener of Women Doing Theology in Abya Yala. She is a PhD candidate in the Psychology of Religion at the University of Lausanne, Switzerland.

Xolani Maseko is an ordained minister in the United Congregational Church of Southern Africa (UCCSA) and Reformed Theologian who has served the Church as a Pastor and 'Mission and Ministry Director' in charge of ministerial training processes, and mission programmes in more than seven countries where the UCCSA exists. He earned his PhD in Theology in 2021, specializing in Church History and Polity, from the University of Pretoria in South Africa. He has taught at the Catholic University of Zimbabwe as an Adjunct Lecturer (2017–22) and currently is a Research Associate at the University of Pretoria in the Systematic and Historical Theology department. His research interests and publications focus on Church History, Ecclesiology and Public

Theology. His latest publications include *Ecclesiological Response to Covid-19 and the Question of Meaning in Context* (South Africa: Studia Historiae Ecclesiasticae, 2022), and *Hagar's Spirituality Prior to and After Captivity: An African and Gendered Perspective* (South Africa: HTS Teologiese Studies/Theological Studies, 2024).

Thandi Soko-de Jong is a PhD candidate in Theology. She holds a Master of Theology in Theology and Development from the University of KwaZulu-Natal (Pietermaritzburg, South Africa) and a Research Master's in African studies from the African Studies Centre, Leiden University (Leiden, the Netherlands). She is also a research associate (Theology) at the University of Pretoria. Her research interests and publication projects focus on Intercultural Theology and the intersection between theology and social concerns such as ecology, gender, and the legacies of slavery and colonization. Her publications include *African Traditional Religion: Reclaiming the Sustainable Anthropocene* (co-author, ASEAN Journal of Religious and Cultural Research (2022)), and *God's Economy of Peace: Lessons from the Malawian Countryside* (*Gods economie van [salam/shalom]. Lessen over duurzaamheid vanaf platteland van Malawi*, in the Green Bible, the Netherlands: Netherlands Bible Society, 2018).

Suzana Moreira is a socio-environmental activist from Brazil. As a nomad theologian, she has been learning to deconstruct the white, cisheteronormative, colonial, and Eurocentric Catholic worldview in which she was born. Through her Master's degree in Systematic Pastoral Theology and Bachelor's degree in Theology from the Pontifical Catholic University of Rio de Janeiro, she discovered herself to be a bisexual, which helped her in the process of decolonizing her way of *sentipensar* theology and her (non)place inside the Catholic Church. She worked for over 10 years as a translator and interpreter in Portuguese, English and Spanish, and has published the translation of important Latin American theology works, such as *Teologia Latino-Americana: raízes e ramos* by Maria Clara Bingemer (Vozes, 2017). Since 2017, she has dedicated herself especially to climate activism, eco-theology, ecofeminist theology, Latin American liberation theology, and spends time playing music, contemplating nature, and dancing on stilts to keep her theology grounded in her body experience.

Joerg Rieger is distinguished Professor of Theology, Cal Turner Chancellor's Chair of Wesleyan Studies, and Director of the Wendland-Cook Program in Religion and Justice at Vanderbilt University. His books include *Jesus vs. Caesar: For People Tired of Serving the Wrong God* (Abingdom Press, 2018), *No Religion but Social Religion: Liberating Wesleyan Theology* (Wesley's Foundery Books, 2018), *Unified We Are a Force: How Faith and Labor Can Overcome America's Inequalities* (Chalice Press, 2016), *No Rising Tide: Theology, Economics, and the Future* (Fortress Press, 2009) and *Theology in the Capitalocene: Ecology, Identity, Class, and Solidarity* (Fortress Press, 2022).

Preface

This book is fruit of the work of the Council for World Mission (CWM). From its very beginning, the mission of CWM has extended beyond the confines of worship and faith communities, into public arenas where services relating to education, health, welfare and ecology are provided, assessed and re-envisioned. Since the 1970s, CWM has wrestled with how to decolonize mission globally and locally – its praxis, pedagogy and theory – and how to proclaim fullness of life at a time when all of life is threatened.

CWM is committed to radical discipleship and prophetic spirituality. Through the Discernment and Radical Engagement (DARE) Programme, CWM conveys its prophetic role in the present socio-political, economic, ecological and global landscapes. DARE is inspired by liberation theologies that have emerged from the diverse context of struggles, its praxis, pedagogies and theories; and it explores, shares, transforms and tries to make sense of divinities, scriptures, traditions, responsibilities, destinies, practices, experiences, biases. DARE is open to the signs of the times and committed to the mission from the margins. Engagement with the margins is the first step for mission, theology and the ecumenical movement to manifest their radical, liberating, decolonizing spirits.

DARE and liberation theologies are radically interdisciplinary, inter-religious and intersectional in their approach. This accompanies the shifts in academic trends, but transcends those trends to root DARE in praxis, pedagogies and theories of struggles for liberation, decolonization and counter-imperial testimonies. As DARE is one of the key priorities of CWM's missiological discernment, I hope this series of publications out of Global DARE Conferences will inspire, encourage and empower mission, theology and movements towards liberation and reconciliation!

Revd Dr Jooseop Keum
CWM General Secretary

Introduction

LUIS MARTÍNEZ ANDRADE
AND SEFOROSA CARROLL

In this new millennium, the survival of the human species is in danger. We observe, on the one hand, that the biophysical limits of the earth are no longer able to supply the consumption demands of a socio-economic system whose sole objective is the production of surplus-value. On the other hand, we are witnessing climate change caused by capitalism. While some researchers have proposed the term 'Anthropocene' to account for the new geological era, others have opted for the term 'Capitalocene'. Capitalocene unmasks the processes of domination (of the global North over the global South) and contemplates the role of exploitation.

From the trenches of the world of ideas, some theologians or philosophers have decided to take the floor in order to devise hypotheses that account for the current ecological crisis. However, it seems to us that the submission to the ideological and categorical frameworks in force on the part of the intellectuals of the global North has led them to devise notions and categories of a discourse closer to the 'Environmentalism of the Rich' than to that of the 'Environmentalism of the Poor'. For example, we think of that of 'L'écobiographie' proposed by the French philosopher Jean-Philippe Pierron or that of 'Dark Ecology' coined by the English philosopher Timothy Morton. Others, influenced by French philosopher Bruno Latour and interested in the elaboration of neologisms for the markets (both academic and editorial), act as promoters of the 'Environmentalism of the Rich' and, therefore, prefer to avoid addressing the conflicts linked to the dynamics of capitalist exploitation.

For Brazilian theologian Leonardo Boff there is a link between ecology and liberation theology because both are concerned with the two bleeding wounds: that of misery and that of the systematic aggression against nature. It is for this reason that Boff sees ecology as a 'cry of the oppressed'. This 'cry' is expressed both in global poverty and in the destruction of the environment. Boff affirms that the earth bleeds, especially in its most singular being, for the oppressed, the marginalized and the excluded, for all of them make up the great majorities of the planet. It is from them that we must think of the universal balance and the new ecological world order. This is why ecology and liberation theology are sensitive to the *cry of the victims* who demand freedom (Exodus 3.7), and the redemption not only of mankind but also of creation (Romans 8.22–23).

For over three decades, a line of research has been developing that combines the contributions of political ecology, eco-Marxism and liberation theology and emphasizes the ecological dimension in the struggles of the popular movements of the global South. 'Environmentalism of the Poor' (Joan Martínez Alier) is one of the epithets used to name the process of anti-hegemonic struggle and resistance of peoples and communities from the onslaught of capitalist modernity. Inspired by the struggles of the *seringeuiros* in Brazil (Chico Mendes), of the indigenous communities of the Mexican Southeast (neo-Zapatista movement) and of those who confront extractivism from Guatemala to Argentina, through the fierce opposition of the Nasa indigenous peoples to mining in Colombia, and ecofeminism (*Red Latinoamericana de Mujeres Defensoras, Red de Sanadoras Ancestrales Iximulew-Guatemala*, among others), the political ecology of this new millennium is from below and on the left.

Faced with the palpable climate chaos, a number of researchers from both the global North and the global South participated in the Discernment and Radical Engagement (DARE) global forum in Bangkok, hosted by the Council for World Missions (CWM) in September 2023. Proposals for papers were invited by DARE that interrogate the Anthropocene and imagine liberation on behalf of, and with, ecology. At this global forum, we set out not only to discuss the relevance of the term Anthropocene, but also to ponder the theoretical-political and theological proposals that are being constructed from popular resistance, from the rebellion of indigenous peoples and from the hope of the 'Wretched of the Earth'.

This book is a product of the Bangkok CWM DARE global forum gathering, bringing together the various voices of specialists from different disciplines (theology, philosophy, sociology, among others) who have addressed, from a critical-prophetic perspective, the link between theology, ecology and Anthropocene, with leanings towards the Capitalocene as a more appropriate term to describe the trek towards climate collapse. The chapters in this book are intersectional in method and analysis, with a liberational edge, as they attend to questions of justice, liberation and hope.

The book is comprised of three parts, and the chapters attempt to contribute to the debate on the crisis of civilization we are going through. Part 1 discusses some fundamental issues for contemporary theological and social thought. The themes of the five chapters in Part 1 (from Luis Martínez Andrade; Hadje Cresencio Sadje; Keun-joo Christine Pae; Lilian Cheelo Siwila; and Nokcharenla) range from the decolonial turn to ecofeminism, including the role of the churches in this climatic chaos. All the chapters are prophetic in mood, calling into account the role of theology and church in re-envisioning an alternative future in the face of climate collapse.

Part 2 of the book focuses mainly on the ecological dimension of certain currents of theological, philosophical and socio-anthropological thought. The three chapters in this part attend to the notion of ecology from their location, context and faith tradition bringing together an indigenous feminist perspective from Taiwan (Wan Jou Lin), a perspective from Europe (Beat Dietschy) and a perspective from the Greek Orthodox tradition (Nikolaos Asproulis).

The last section of the book, Part 3, presents voices from the global South. Each of these three chapters (from Yenny Delgado; Xolani Maseko and Thandi Soko-de Jong; and Suzana Regina Moreira) are context specific, exploring the wisdom of their cultures and faith traditions as well as challenging aspects of culture and tradition that inhibit liberation and justice. These three chapters also provide insight into praxis and implementation of practical activities by churches and communities that may continue to inspire hope (rather than hopelessness) in the reality of climate collapse that confronts us.

Finally, Joerg Reiger closes the book with an epilogue which brings together the intent and spirit of the Thailand DARE gathering with his own concluding reflections on the Capitalocene. This is a fitting close to both the Bangkok DARE global forum of September 2023 and this book.

PART I

Theology

I

Theology and Anticolonial Critical Theory in 'Capitalocene'

LUIS MARTÍNEZ ANDRADE

Introduction

Over the last three decades, we have become accustomed to heatwaves and drastic temperature changes. While some regions of the planet suffer frequent droughts, other regions are victims of heavy floods. At the end of 2015, we learned about the tragedy suffered by the city of Mariana, in the Brazilian region of Minas Gerais. Three years later, as a result of storm Friederike (Lessenich, 2019), it was the turn of some European cities. Although the contexts were different, the image was the same: houses and cars floating, people missing and dead bodies in the water, communities destroyed. Faced with this scenario, some researchers and academics have resorted to the term 'Anthropocene' (Crutzen, 2002) not only to replace the term 'Holocene', and thus refer to a new geological epoch, but also to indicate the influence and responsibility of human activities on climate change. While the term has been gaining increasing strength in some ecological currents (degrowth movement, deep ecology, adherents of collapsology), from other perspectives this term is problematic since it does not take into account class relations (eco-socialism), race (environmental justice) or gender (the different currents of ecofeminism of the global South) in the socio-historical structure of capitalist modernity. Hence, authors such as Jason W. Moore (2015), Andreas Malm (2016) Renán Vega Cantor (2019) and Joerg Rieger (2022) are inclined to use the term 'Capitalocene' to point out the responsibility of fossil capitalism in climate chaos.

From the *Dialectic of Enlightenment* (Horkheimer and Adorno, 2002) to *Living Well at Others' Expense: The Hidden Costs of Western Prosperity* (Lessenich, 2019), through the works of Walter Benjamin (1979) and Ernst Bloch (1996), Critical Theory has always underlined the necrophiliac character of capitalist modernity expressed in the domination over nature, the obsession with quantification, and the belief in the myth of progress (Löwy and Sayre, 2010). In this sense, the contributions of Critical Theory are of great value for an uncompromising diagnosis of the current social situation. Moreover, the tradition of Latin American and Caribbean critical thought has also elaborated concepts and categories that enable us, on the one hand, to understand the destructive dynamics of capitalist modernity and, on the other, to combat the Eurocentric dregs of political philosophical thought (Dussel, 2007; Montañez Pico, 2020; Grosfoguel, 2022).

Theology, churches and ecology

Since the 1970s, different reports from the Club of Rome have alerted us to the limits of growth. The 1972 report analyses five significant trends: accelerated industrialization, rapid population growth, widening undernutrition, the decay of non-renewable resources, and the degradation of the environment. This report warned of the terrible consequences of the continuation of this model of development. In terms of the position of the Church, French historian Olivier Landron (2008) considers that contemporary historians of Roman Catholicism have not sufficiently studied in depth the relationship between the Church and nature for two main reasons: 1) Because the relationship between God and humanity has been seen as privileged, and 2) as a result of the suspicion of pantheism. From the debates at the Second Vatican Council (1962–5), though, we see a repositioning of theology concerned with the creation and its different manifestations. In France, the theology of creation was deeply marked by Thomism, which had little interest in the relationship between the Creator and the universe. The 1988 French translation of *God in Creation: An Ecological Doctrine of Creation*, by German theologian Jürgen Moltmann (1993), marked a point of inflection in taking account of the ecological crisis through theological analysis. Equally, the figure of Pierre Teilhard de Chardin occupies an important place in contemporary thought around these matters, through theology (*Christogenesis*), philosophy (*holism*) and science (*palaeontology*). Moreover, we should point out that the Brazilian theologian Leonardo Boff (1997) integrates the 'noosphere' concept in his anti-hegemonic critique just as in his questioning of the capitalist system that destroys nature.

Frédéric Rognon (2020), Professor of Philosophy at the Faculty of Theology of the University of Strasbourg, argues that the ecological turn in French Protestantism is basically as a result of two factors: on the one hand, the weight of the ecclesial and academic agendas promoted by the Protestant Federation of France and, on the other, local initiatives (for example, the creation of the organization A Rocha in 1999 or the Bible and Creation network formed in 2006). Although French Protestantism has important figures for the development of an ecological sensitivity (Charles Gide, Albert Schweitzer, Wilfred Monod, Théodore Monod, Jean-Marc Prieur, Jacques Ellul, among others), for Frédéric Rognon, the weight of the Theology of the Cross has somewhat slowed down this development. In this regard, Rognon points out that the publication in 1989 of the collective book *L'agitation et le Rire. Contribution critique au débat Justice, Paix et Sauvegarde de la Création* expressed not only the rejection of inductive theologies but also the distrust of the theology of creation (Rognon, 2020, p. 87).

In *Church and Climate Justice*, theologian Vinod Wesley presents an overview of the development of the link between climate justice and Christian ethics. Starting from a perspective situated in south Asia, Wesley underlines the role of the Bible as the great ecological resource. Thus, the book of Genesis, the story of Noah and the Ark, the biblical concepts of Sabbath and Jubilee, are interpreted from an ecological perspective. In this regard, Vinod Wesley writes that:

> The book of Revelation is not God's vengeance story; rather, it is God's pronouncement of justices against the empire and its system destroying the world which is manifested as climate change today. This is story of [sic] God's redeeming act of the human and the non-human world, which is caught in the midst of destructive forces, causing climate change. Books like Revelation invite us to be aware of the climate crisis, encourage us to challenge the forces causing it, and to envision hope and life in the midst of catastrophes because the God of love still loves this world. (Wesley, 2020, p. 32)

Following the approaches of the theologian Cynthia Moe-Lobeda, Vinod Wesley recognizes the role of structural sin in the production of ecological injustices and proposes an 'ecological conversion' (Wesley, 2020, p. 53) aimed at a new social pact between human beings and nature. Wesley emphasizes the importance of the contributions of ecofeminism (Gabriel Dietrich, Aruna Gnanadason, Vandana Shiva, Ivy Singh, Melanie Harris, among others) and popular movements (the Chipko movement, for example) from the global South in the construction of the ethics of ecological justice.

In Latin America, the ecofeminist current and the current of liberation theology have been fundamental not only in denouncing structural sin but also in unveiling the ecocidal logic of capitalist modernity. One of the main representatives of the eco-theology of liberation is undoubtedly the Brazilian theologian Leonardo Boff (1997). A companion of social movements such as the Landless Workers' Movement in Brazil (Martínez Andrade, 2022), the reflections of Boff have been able to combine Franciscan spirituality with the struggle for social justice (Boff, 2008). Currently, Brazilian theologians Ivone Gebara (2000) and Nancy Cardoso (2022) are making valuable contributions in the field of eco-theology.

Ecocidal logic of modernity

In their recent work, Bruno Frère and Jean-Louis Laville (2022) recognize the contemporaneousness of Horkheimer and Adorno's diagnosis of the pathologies suffered by reason in all human activities. Frère and Laville (2022) maintain that Horkheimer and Adorno's *Dialectic of Enlightenment* is not only a radically new questioning of the celebrated imposing of disembodied rationality that allowed the planning of the Holocaust, but also a denunciation of the double capitalist exploitation of human beings and of nature. Thus, *Dialectic of Enlightenment* is indeed an excellent analysis of the tendency towards self-destruction of rationality expressed in the cult of quantification, in the submission to the total power of capital, in the obedience to social hierarchy and, of course, in the love–hate relationship with the body. According to Horkheimer and Adorno:

> The body cannot be turned back into the envelope of the soul. It remains a cadaver, no matter how trained and fit it may be. The transformation into dead matter, indicated by the affinity of corpus to corpse, was a part of the perennial process which turned nature into stuff, material. The achievements of civilization are a product of sublimation, of the acquired love–hate for body and earth, from which domination has violently severed all human beings. (Horkheimer and Adorno, 2002, p. 194)

While the myth of Enlightenment was being consolidated in bourgeois society, technical rationality was becoming a key element in the designs of both social control and domination over nature. However,

Max Horkheimer and Theodor Adorno also observed the deformation of the cult of nature by 'the fascists' pious love of animals, nature, and children' (Horkheimer and Adorno, 2002, p. 210). This observation seems important to us at a time when certain vegetarian or vegan currents assume a moral superiority over the feeding of carnivorous populations (peasants) or social classes (working class), but without questioning the capitalist model of production.

Perhaps the most radical criticism of capitalist civilization and the myth of progress was formulated by two peripheral members of the Frankfurt School, namely the German philosophers Ernst Bloch and Walter Benjamin. Founder of an ontology of the *not-yet* and a philosophy of process, Bloch (1996) strives to establish other non-capitalist forms of relationship with nature. For example, in *The Principle of Hope*, Bloch rehabilitates the role of utopias in the alliance between human beings and nature. His perspective emphasizes the co-productivity of nature as a subject with the human being and, therefore, diametrically opposed to the abstract technique of bourgeois society and the heuristic of fear, the concrete technique escapes the logic of accumulation and unlimited exploitation of nature. Hence the philosopher Arno Münster (2010, p. 163) argues that, even after Bloch's adherence to historical materialism, the author of *Atheism in Christianity* remained sensitive to the romantic and mystical exaltation of nature of the young Friedrich Schelling. Ernst Bloch continually accentuates the fabulous features of nature and throughout his encyclopedia of the forms of utopian consciousness we find reference to clouds, the sea, the starry sky, water, landscapes, gardens, Arcadia (Martínez Andrade, 2015). The Prius of nature is manifested, according to Bloch, in the elaboration of desiderative images since the utopian Totem embodied in the aesthetic and mystical terrain is not exhausted.

There is no doubt that the work of the German philosopher Walter Benjamin is one of the most interesting intellectual legacies of critical thought in terms of denouncing both the cultural expressions of modernity and its temporal structures (Löwy, 2019). In fact, his critique of the empty temporality of modernity (represented in the idea of progress) can be seen in one of his first writings, a lecture in Berlin from 1914 on 'The Life of the Students'. Subsequently, his conversion towards historical materialism, through the reading of Georg Lukács' *History and Class Consciousness* and his meeting with the Bolshevik Asja Lācis during the summer of 1924, only deepened his critique of capitalist modernity (Martínez Andrade, 2023). From his text *One-Way Street* (written before 1926 and published in 1928) to his theses *On the Concept of*

History, passing through his notes for *The Arcades Project* (*Passagenwerk*), we perceive the messianic-materialist dimension of his thought (Löwy, 2013). Benjamin, the author of *The Work of Art in the Age of Mechanical Reproduction*, was convinced that we must understand modernity as the age of hell (Benjamin, 1999). His thesis *On the Concept of History* represents the most radical critique of the ideology of progress. For Benjamin:

> ... the concept of progress must be grounded in the idea of catastrophe. That things are 'status quo' is catastrophe. It is not an ever-present possibility but what in each case is given. (Benjamin, 1999, p. 473)

Drawing on aspects of Jewish messianism (Franz Rosenzweig), romanticism (Friedrich Hölderlin, Johann Bachofen) and Marxism, Benjamin presented a concept of history as an open and indeterminate process, opposed to the evolutionist perspectives of his time (Löwy, 2001). Another important feature of Benjamin's thought was his denunciation of the destructive and exploitative relationship of modern capitalist society with nature. For Robert Sayre and Michael Löwy (Sayre and Löwy, 2020), in Benjamin's perspective we can identify anti-productivism and proto-ecological arguments of great significance.

Some years ago, the German philosopher and sociologist Axel Honneth (2017) indicated that it was essential to get rid of the vision of a rectilinear evolution typical of the nineteenth-century ideology of progress. Thus, the author of *The Struggle for Recognition: The Moral Grammar of Social Conflicts* suggested that it was necessary to update the idea of socialism by abjuring faith in progress. It is worth mentioning that these clues had already been pointed out in the 1930s by Walter Benjamin.

Currently, the German sociologist Stephan Lessenich (2019) has proposed the idea of externalization society to account not only for completely normal catastrophes (socio-environmental disasters) but also for the structural violence (economic inequality) that accompanies relations between the global North and the global South. It should be noted that Lessenich's perspective takes up some elements of the decolonial option (Walter Mignolo), feminist critique and world-system theory (Immanuel Wallerstein) in order to grasp the dependencies, the structures of global relations and the reciprocal repercussions. This is why the concept of externalization is linked to that of correlation. In order to understand the prosperity of some sectors of the countries of the global North, we must take into consideration the process of precariousness and pauperization of the populations of the global South.

Although many of these theses were already put forward by dependency theorists (André Gunder Frank, Ruy Mauro Marini, Vania Bambirra, Enzo Faletto, among others) in the 1960s, Lessenich's contribution lies in his attempt to move away from the Eurocentric perspective of some currents of thought.

We observe, then, that the double exploitation of capitalist modernity, that subjugates both human beings and nature, is a latent concern in the reflections of the members of the Frankfurt School. It is evident that the relationship with Marxism, on the part of the perspectives succinctly presented, has been different in each author. We think that these intellectuals recognize the ecocidal and productivity logic of capitalist modernity.

Anthropocene as an ideological move

The term 'Anthropocene' appeared at the beginning of 2002 to name a new geological epoch that resulted from the significant global impact that human activities have had on terrestrial ecosystems. Although there is no consensus on the date when the Anthropocene epoch originated, the chemist Paul Crutzen suggests that it dates from the late eighteenth century, specifically with the invention of the steam engine in 1784. This was the turning point in the expulsion of carbon dioxide on a planetary scale (Crutzen, 2002). Thus, one of the main causes is to be found in the period of the industrial revolution: the use of non-renewable fossil fuels. Although the notion of Anthropocene questions the excessive use of fossil fuels and the argument of industrial civilization, for thinkers such as Jason Moore (2015), Andreas Malm (2016), Renán Vega Cantor (2016) and Joerg Rieger (2022), this term is problematic because it holds all human beings responsible for environmental destruction. While, for some, the term erases European colonial history, for others it obliterates the logic of value inherent in the capitalist system of production/reproduction.

During the 1970s, in the context of the energy crisis of 1973 and 1974, some thinkers such as Manuel Sacristán, André Gorz and Raymond Williams reflected on the link between socialism and ecology and, consequently, laid the foundations of the eco-socialist or eco-communist project (Löwy, 2015). Beyond the divergences on some programmatic points, the eco-socialist thinkers reached the following conclusions: 1) the capitalist mode of production and consumption is ecocide, and 2) the ideology of progress is dangerous for the survival of the human species.

During the same period, very important criticisms emerged from ecofeminism (Mellor, 1997) and even from history (Crosby, 2003). Alfred W. Crosby's 1972 book examines the role of the discovery of the Americas and its consequences for the transformation of the environment. Some years later, this American historian published his work *Ecological Imperialism: The Biological Expansion of Europe, 900–1900*, giving the notion of ecological imperialism the right of citizenship and thus pointing out the importance of epidemics in the wars of conquest of the Americas. The work of Crosby laid the foundations for environmental history and, following this historian, researchers John R. McNeill and Charles Mann focused on the analysis of the socio-environmental consequences of the colonization of the Americas: the plantation culture (sugarcane) and large-scale monoculture, among others.

The sustainable rural development current, cultivated in the 1980s and influenced by the Narodnik tradition (Russian populists), also denounced both the eco-technocratic discourses and the technological optimism of the green revolution ideologues. The critique of development raised by Angel Palermo or Gustavo Esteva outlined an option for sustainable rural development for the poor. The environmentalism of the poor or popular ecology of Joan Martinez-Alier (2003) continued this line of research. During the 1990s, the work of Richard B. Norgaard (1994) was key to identifying a feature of bourgeois industrial civilization: the hydrocarbon society. Although R. Norgaard's approach did not draw from eco-Marxist sources, it at least had the merit of questioning the illusions of the ideology of progress.

For our part, we are convinced that the term Anthropocene hides more than it intends to reveal and, in this sense, it becomes problematic not only to point out those who are really responsible for climate chaos (transnational corporations, oil and mining consortiums, the value that is valued) but also to organize the pessimism of the victims of capitalist modernity. Consequently, we agree with theologian Joerg Rieger when he points out that:

> What is at the heart of the ecological devastations of our age is, therefore, both immanent and transcendent, material and immaterial, and all are shaped by the dynamics of capitalism, which is why it makes more sense to talk about the Capitalocene than the Anthropocene. (Rieger, 2022, p. 67)

Other theologians like George Zachariah not only question the term Anthropocene but also that of *Oikos* since both would respond to the universalist logic of the hegemonic discourse and, therefore, omit the different structures of domination and oppression: racism, patriarchalism, casteism, among others. *Oikos: Our Common Home* is a frequent theme and overarching metaphor of unity and universality in the theological reflections and writings on the ecological crisis and ecological restoration. This notion of *Oikos* is also informed and inspired by the logic of the necessity of universal categories and metanarratives to problematize and address global problems. Such problematizations are contested by the subaltern communities because blaming all human beings for the ecological crisis is a political strategy to perpetuate ecological injustice and ecological racism and casteism by absolving the ecological crimes of the dominant and the privileged communities and the corporations (Zachariah, 2022, p. 205).

Bio-coloniality of power

There is no doubt that the theses put forward by the Modernity/Coloniality/Decoloniality academic community (Restrepo and Rojas, 2010) have gained ground both in philosophy and in the social sciences. It is evident that, from the first texts of this academic community to its current approaches, not only the socio-political context has changed but also the intellectual relationship between some of its protagonists (Mignolo and Walsh, 2018). However, the outlines of this academic community remain influential: 1) There is no modernity without coloniality, since coloniality is an indispensable part of modernity (Mignolo, 2007, p. 18); 2) Modernity, capitalism and Latin America were born on the same day (Quijano, 1992, p. 3), The *ego conquiro* (I conquer) of Spanish–Lusitanian power laid the foundations of a new ontology that inferiorized non-Western peoples (Dussel, 2007, p. 4). Since 1492, the idea of race became a central element of the 'body politic of knowledge' of the project of modernity (Grosfoguel, 2022). We are convinced that the category of bio-coloniality of power elaborated by the Colombian researcher Juan Camilo Cajigas-Rotundo (2007) allows an articulation between the political ecology approach and the theoretical-methodological concerns of the modernity/coloniality research programme. Building on Arturo Escobar's hypothesis, for whom the project of modernity hides a colonial character, Cajigas-Rotundo (2007) proposes to understand, in the light of post-Fordist capitalism, the new tendencies of the coloniality of power present in the current formation of the production of nature – that is, the way nature is transformed and modified by the capitalist production system. In the early 1950s, biotechnology and genetic engineering inaugurated the post-natural era with the production and modification of organisms by multinational corporations. These biotechnological developments had a profound impact on both local economies and the health of the world's population. In addition, they also fostered the illegal appropriation of the knowledge of the indigenous populations of Latin America and the Caribbean. Although we agree with researcher Yilson Beltrán-Barrera (2019) when he argues that the author of the bio-coloniality of power has not developed a theoretical or methodological framework that incorporates the body-political in order to understand the new pattern of power over nature, we believe that this category allows us to account for the asymmetries, or structural heterogeneities, of the new pattern of power over the natural world.

One of the contributions of the modernity/coloniality research programme was to reinstate the importance of the role of the Americas in the configuration of both the capitalist system on a global scale and the idea of race. Indeed, during the sixteenth century, four phenomena unfolded in synchronic fashion: modernity, coloniality, capitalism and Eurocentrism. Within the frameworks of this new ontology, both black and indigenous populations and nature are conceived as *res extensa* (Dussel, 2008). The conquest, and later colonization, of the Americas implied the establishment of two ecocide modalities: 1) the plantation economy in which slave labour was articulated in the capitalist market, and 2) mining exploitation, expressed in the gold and silver cycles.

On the plantation economy, especially on the role of sugar through history, the work of American anthropologist Sidney W. Mintz (1986) stands out. He showed not only those plantations, as an economic form, were a European invention, but also that, after 1492, the Caribbean was trapped in the networks of imperial power. For Mintz, the sugarcane plantation should be understood as an industrial activity and, in this sense, we find some characteristic features of what is understood by industry: discipline, organization of the labour force, time, separation of production and consumption and, of course, separation of the worker from his work tools. It is true that Mintz was not the first researcher to have examined the link between the plantation economy and capitalism, as there were already works published (Montañez, 2020), especially those by Marxist authors such as Sergio Bagú, Eric Williams, D. Lloyd Best or George Beckford. However, Mintz was a pioneer in the study of the harmful implications of sugar consumption in the diet of the working class. Brought to the Caribbean by Christopher Columbus during his second voyage in 1493, sugarcane reshaped the global economy and, of course, our forms of socialization.

Regarding mining, where generations of indigenous people were immolated on the altar of capitalist modernity during the sixteenth and seventeenth centuries, the region's extractive projects are still in force. For Mexican researcher Aidée Tassinari (2018), the primary extractive accumulation model of capitalist logic causes territorial dispossession, environmental devastation and displacement of peoples and communities. Let us recall that, for Karl Marx (1967), the discovery of gold and silver deposits in the Americas, the extermination and enslavement of the indigenous population, the beginning of the conquest and plundering of the East Indies, and the conversion of the African continent into a hunting ground for black slaves were the events that marked the dawn of the era of capitalist production. Thus, these 'idyllic processes' represent other fundamental factors in the movement of original accumulation. Later, following Rosa Luxemburg's reflections, the Marxist geographer David Harvey (2005) will give an account of the actualization of the violence of primitive accumulation through the notion of accumulation by dispossession. It is important to note that even the so-called 'progressive' governments continue to be prisoners of the extractive model (Zibechi and Machado, 2022).

Indigenous communities, the first victims of this economic system, were in the vanguard of anticolonial and anti-capitalist struggles from the outset. Inspired by the revolts of their elders, indigenous-peasant movements such as the Neo-Zapatistas in Mexico and the Landless Workers' Movement in Brazil, MST are fighting not only against the antiquated structure of exploitation, but also against new forms of neoliberal domination (Vergara-Camus, 2014). In these movements, we can identify the role of a subversive spirituality in the tradition of liberation theology (McGeoch, 2018; Martínez Andrade, 2022). It goes without saying that the protagonists of these movements are racialized and gendered subjects for whom the defence of territory is linked to socio-political and environmental issues. Thus, their demands are not confined to the conservation of a lake or a single endangered species, but are aimed at a different paradigm of civilization.

As far as the link between political ecology and Marxism in Latin America is concerned, it's true that we can trace an ecological sensibility in the founders of Latin American and Caribbean Marxism such as Jean-Jacques Roumain, Jacques Stephen Alexis or José Carlos Mariátegui, but the ecological dimension begins to be more visible from the 1980s onwards. According to Mexican researcher Enrique Leff (2010), the appearance of *Capitalism, Nature, Socialism: A Journal of Socialist Ecology*, edited by James O'Connor in Santa Cruz, and other journals in Spain and Italy, contributed to the rise of political ecology in Latin America, based on a Marxist approach.

In the same vein, the *Centro Intercultural de Documentación* (CIDOC) founded in 1966 by Ivan Illich in the Mexican city of Cuernavaca has played a significant role in critiquing the structures of capitalist modernity. Among the *Centro*'s collaborators were Erich Fromm, Paulo Freire, Peter L. Berger and Susan Sontag, among others (González Gómez, 2021). In 1974, observes Christophe Fourel (2012), a certain André Gorz visited the CIDOC, returning with several articles for *Le Nouvel Observateur* and, above all, the material to write the collection *Écologie et politique*. Moreover, the figure of the Mexican bishop Sergio Méndez Arceo, in the tradition of liberation theology, is central to the development of CIDOC (Fazio, 1987).

The socio-environmental struggles waged by peasant and indigenous communities against illegal deforestation and the polluting activities of the extractive industry have shaped what Joan Martinez-Alier (2003) has called the 'environmentalism of the poor'. In Peru, one of the countries hit hardest by the mining industry, the struggle of Hugo Blanco, Trotskyist activist and director of the *Lucha Indígena Newspaper*, represents this link between political ecology and Marxism. In Brazil, liberation theologians Frei Betto, Marcelo Barros and Leonardo Boff have also claimed to be eco-socialists (Martínez Andrade, 2019)

Conclusion

Faced with the desolate situation in which we are living (civilizational crisis and climate chaos), it is necessary to recover the contributions of both the Critical Theory and the theologies of liberation to rethink and shape other forms of socialization. Precisely, the contributions of the critical theologies from the global South allow us to unveil the ideological power plays, including notions such as the Anthropocene that omit the role of exploitation. We are convinced that the term Anthropocene is politically sterilized, since it not only overlooks the weight of the society of externalization and the bio-coloniality of power, but also hides the dynamics of the value that is promoted. An Anticolonial Critical Theory must continue to denounce the sacrificial logic of the hegemonic social formation, but without detracting from the class perspective (Rieger, 2022, p. 95).

I would like to end this chapter with a message from the Brazilian theologian Leonardo Boff addressed to the Marxist philosopher Michael Löwy, which appears in his 'For an Ecosocialist "Great Transformation" – Fourteen Theses':

> The Anthropocene as a new geological era was not introduced by 'humanity' but by a capitalist mode of production, in its political version of a new liberalism, especially in its radical form (the schools of Vienna and Chicago). The absolute majority of humanity is the innocent victim of this system which can lead us to social-ecological Armageddon. For me this system cannot be reformed, but is so constituted as to lead us to the abyss, at the price of our lives. (Löwy, 2022, p. 328)

References

Beltrán-Barrera, Yilson, 2019, 'La biocolonialidad: una genealogía decolonial', *Nómadas* 50, pp. 77–91.

Benjamin, Walter, 1979, *One-way Street and Other Writings*, London: NLB Publishers.

Benjamin, Walter, 1999, *The Arcades Project*, Cambridge, MA: Harvard University Press.

Bloch, Ernst, 1996, *The Principle of Hope*, 3 vols, trans. Neville Plaice, Stephen Plaice and Paul Knight, Cambridge, MA: MIT Press.

Boff, Leonardo, 1997, *Cry of the Earth, Cry of the Poor*, New York: Orbis Books.

Boff, Leonardo, 2008, *Essential Care: An Ethics of Human Nature*, Waco, TX: Baylor University Press.

Cajigas-Rotundo, Juan Camilo, 2007, 'Anotaciones sobre la biocolonialidad del poder', *Revista Pensamiento Jurídico* 18, pp. 59–72.

Cardoso, Nancy, 2022, 'Land Lovers: From Agropornography to Agroecology' in L. Mendoza and G. Zachariah (eds), *Decolonizing Ecotheology: Indigenous and Subaltern Challenges*, Eugene, OR: Pickwick Publications, pp. 219–34.

Crosby, Alfred, 2003, *The Columbian Exchange: Biological and Cultural Consequences of 1492*, Westport, CT: Praeger Publishers.

Crutzen, Paul, 2002, 'Geology of Mankind', *Nature* 415.

Dussel, Enrique, 2007, *Política de la Liberación: Historia Mundial y Crítica*, Madrid: Trotta.

Dussel, Enrique, 2008, 'Meditaciones anti-cartesianas: sobre el origen del anti-discurso filosófico de la modernidad', *Tabula Rasa* 9, pp. 153–97.

Fazio, Carlos, 1987, *La cruz y el martillo*, México: Joaquín Mortiz.

Fourel, Christophe, 2012, *André Gorz, un penseur pour le XXIe siècle*, Paris: La découverte.

Frère, Bruno, and Laville, Jean-Louis, 2022, *La Fabrique de l'émancipation: Repenser la critique du capitalisme à partir des expériences démocratiques, écologiques et solidaires*, Paris: Seuil.

Gebara, Ivone, 2000, *Intuiciones Ecofeministas: Ensayos para Repensar el Conocimiento y la Religión*, Madrid: Trotta.
Gervais, Mathieu, 2020, *Nous, on se sauve nous-mêmes: sécularisation, identité paysanne et écologie*, Paris: Van Dieren.
González Gómez, Elias, 2021, *Convivencialidad y resistencia política desde abajo: la herencia de Iván Illich en México*, México: Universidad de Guadalajara.
Grosfoguel, Ramon, 2022, *De la Sociología de la Descolonización al Nuevo Antiimperialismo Decolonial*, Madrid: Akal.
Harvey, David, 2005, *The New Imperialism*, Oxford: Oxford University Press.
Honneth, Axel, 2017, *The Idea of Socialism: Towards a Renewal*, London: Polity Press.
Horkheimer, Max, and Adorno, Theodor W., 2002, *Dialectic of Enlightenment: Philosophical Fragments*, Stanford, CA: Stanford University Press.
Kocka, Jürgen, 2017, *Histoire du capitalisme*, Geneva: Markus Haller.
Landron, Olivier, 2008, *Le Catholicisme Vert: Histoire des Relations Entre l'Église et La Nature au XXe Siècle*, Paris: Cerf.
Leff, Enrique, 2010, *Ecología y capital: racionalidad ambiental, democracia participativa y desarrollo sustentable*, México: Siglo XXI.
Lessenich, Stephan, 2019, *Living Well at Others' Expense: The Hidden Costs of Western Prosperity*, London: Polity Press.
Löwy, Michael, 2001, *Walter Benjamin: Avertissement d'incendie: Une lecture des thèses «Sur le concept d'histoire»*, Paris: PUF.
Löwy, Michael, 2007, *El marxismo en América Latina: Antología, desde 1909 hasta nuestros días*, Santiago de Chile: LOM Ediciones.
Löwy, Michael, 2013, *On Changing the world: Essays in Political Philosophy, from Karl Marx to Walter Benjamin*, Chicago, IL: Haymarket Books.
Löwy, Michael, 2015, *Ecosocialism: A Radical Alternative to Capitalist Catastrophe*, Chicago, IL: Haymarket Books.
Löwy, Michael, 2019, *La révolution est le frein d'urgence: Essais sur Walter Benjamin*, Paris: L'éclat.
Löwy, Michael, 2022, 'For an Ecosocialist "Great Transformation" – Fourteen Theses' in W. Baier, E. Canepa and H. Golemis (eds), *Left Strategies in the Covid Pandemic and Its Aftermath*, London: Merlin Press, pp. 326–34.
Löwy, Michael and Sayre, Robert, 2010, *Esprits de Feu: Figures du romantisme anticapitaliste*, Paris: Sandre.
Malm, Andreas, 2016, *Fossil Capital: The Rise of Steam Power and the Roots of Global Warming*, London: Verso.
Martinez-Alier, Joan, 2003, *The Environmentalism of the Poor: A Study of Ecological Conflicts and Valuation*, UK: Edward Elgar Publishing.
Martínez Andrade, Luis, 2015, *Religion Without Redemption: Social Contradictions and Awakened Dreams in Latin America*, London: Pluto Press.
Martínez Andrade, Luis, 2017, 'Biocolonialité du pouvoir et mouvements sociaux dans l'Amérique latine', *Ecologie & Politique* 55, pp. 153–64.
Martínez Andrade, Luis, 2019, *Ecología y teología de la liberación: Critica de la modernidad/colonialidad*, Barcelona: Herder.
Martínez Andrade, Luis, 2022, 'Elective Affinities between Liberation Theology and Ecology in Latin America' in W. Goldstein and J. P. Reed (eds), *Religion in Rebellions, Revolutions, and Social Movements*, London: Routledge, pp. 219–30.

Martínez Andrade, Luis, 2023, *Teoría crítica anticolonial: Ensayos de historia intelectual*, Valencia: Tirant humanidades.

Marx, Karl, 1967, *Capital: A Critique of Political Economy*, New York: International Publishers.

McGeoch, Graham, 2018, 'Marxismo, mistica e o MST: Qual é o segredo do MST n aluta pela reforma agrarian no Brasil?', *Debates do NER* 3, pp. 174–96.

Mellor, Mary, 1997, *Feminism and Ecology*, London: Polity Press.

Mignolo, Walter, 2007, *La Idea de América Latina. La Herida Colonial y la Opción Decolonial*, Barcelona: Gedisa.

Mignolo, Walter, and Walsh, Catherine, 2018, *On Decoloniality: Concepts, Analytics, Praxis*, Durham, NC: Duke University Press.

Mintz, Sidney, 1986, *Sweetness and Power: The Place of Sugar in Modern History*, London: Penguin Books.

Moltmann, Jürgen, 1993, *God in Creation: A New Theology of Creation and the Spirit of God*, Minneapolis, MN: Fortress Press.

Montañez Pico, Daniel, 2020, *Marxismo Negro: Pensamiento descolonizador del Caribe anglófono*, México: Akal.

Moore, Jason, 2015, *Capitalism in the Web of Life: Ecology and the Accumulation of Capital*, London: Verso.

Münster, Arno, 2010, *Principe Responsabilité ou Principe Espérance?*, Paris: Le bord de l'eau.

Norgaard, Richard B., 1994, *Development Betrayed: The End of Progress and a Coevolutionary Revisioning of the Future*, London: Routledge.

Quijano, Aníbal, 1992, 'Colonialidad y Modernidad/Racionalidad', *Perú Indígena* 13, pp. 11–20.

Restrepo, Eduardo, and Rojas, Axel, 2010, *Inflexión Decolonial: Fuentes, Conceptos y Cuestionamientos*, Popayán: Universidad del Cauca.

Rieger, Joerg, 2022, *Theology in the Capitalocene: Ecology, Identity, Class, and Solidarity*, Minneapolis, MN: Fortress Press.

Rognon, Frédéric, 2020, 'Le chemin tortueux du protestantisme français vers la théologie verte', in C. Monnot and F. Rognon (eds), *Église et écologie. Une révolution à reculons*, Geneva: Labor et Fides, pp. 79–94.

Sayre, Robert, and Löwy, Michael, 2020, *Romantic Anti-capitalism and Nature: The Enchanted Garden*, New York: Routledge.

Tassinari, Aidée, 2018, *La nueva fiebre del oro*, México: UACM/Gedisa.

Vega Cantor, Renán, 2019, *El capitaloceno: crisis civilizatoria, imperialismo ecológico y límites naturales*, Bogotá: Teoría & Praxis.

Vergara-Camus, Leandro, 2014, *Land and Freedom: The MST, the Zapatistas and Peasant Alternatives to Neoliberalism*, London: Zed Books.

Wesley, Vinod, 2020, *Church and Climate Justice*, Delhi: Indian Society for Promoting Christian Knowledge (ISPCK).

Zachariah, George, 2022, 'Whose *Oikos* Is It Anyway? Towards a *Poromboke* Ecotheology of "Commoning"', in L. Mendoza and G. Zachariah (eds), *Decolonizing Ecotheology: Indigenous and Subaltern Challenges*, Eugene, OR: Pickwick Publications, pp. 201–18.

Zibechi, Raul, and Machado, Decio, 2022, *El Estado realmente existente: Del Estado de bienestar al Estado para el despojo*, Santander: La Vorágine.

2

'Anthropocene' or 'Global Coloniality'? A Decolonial Theological Reflection

HADJE CRESENCIO SADJE

Introduction

In 2016, Professor Chris Rapley, a British scientist and climate change expert, made the following public statement: 'The Anthropocene marks a new period in which our collective activities dominate the planetary machinery' (*Guardian*). This may appear ambitious, but Rapley, like other scientists today, believes that the 'Anthropocene' epoch, which describes the significance of human impact on the earth, has now become so profound that a new geological epoch – the 'age of humans' – must be declared. Despite its ambiguity, Rapley contends that it has had a significant impact on climate change and environmental debates (Malhi, 2017, pp. 77–104; Burdon, 2020, pp. 309–28). Moreover, according to American environmental scientist Erle Christopher Ellis, the concept of the Anthropocene contradicts conventional wisdom on environmental issues, environmental laws, and orthodox approaches to climate change (Ellis, 2015, pp. 171–9; Lewis and Maslin, 2015, pp. 171–9). As Ellis writes:

> The many heated controversies surrounding the Anthropocene make clear that there is far more at stake than just a new interval of geologic time. The significance of the Anthropocene resides in its role as a new lens through which age-old narratives and philosophical questions are being revisited and rewritten. The Anthropocene is both a new narrative relating humans and nature and a bold new scientific paradigm – a 'Second Copernican Revolution' – with the potential to radically revise the way we think of what it means to be human. (Ellis, 2018, p. 4)

Ellis suggests that the concept of the Anthropocene is critical in understanding human capacity to respond to environmental crises and climate change disasters. This has two implications. First, climate scientists believe that we are entering an era in which humans have complete control over the environment. Finally, humans have an absolute duty and responsibility to protect the environment.

However, critics argue that the Anthropocene, as a newly proposed geological epoch, spawned a new type of grand narrative that maintained Western knowledge's privileged status over non-Western knowledge, particularly in public policy debates about environmental policy and climate change. This makes the Anthropocene a contentious subject, especially within the humanities and social sciences. In fact, this new proposed geological epoch has received significant attention from a variety of disciplines, including philosophy (Polt and Wittrock, 2018, pp. ix–xviii), political science (Lövbrand et al., 2020, pp. 1–8), international relations (Rothe, Müller and Chandler, 2021, pp. 1–16), sociology, anthropology, history, science and technology (Zwier and Blok, 2017, pp. 222–42), and religious studies and theology (Deane-Drummond, Bergmann and Vogt, 2017, pp. 1–18; Thomas, Williams and Zalasiewicz, 2020, pp. 1–13). But the question remains: What exactly is the Anthropocene?

What is the Anthropocene?

Despite its promising contribution to the debates on key environmental issues, Anthropocene is also the subject of much criticism. It seems that proponents of the Anthropocene are trying to offer an explanation for every issue related to ecological and environmental catastrophes; in particular, the climate and ecosystems that have begun to be significantly impacted by human activity. Nevertheless, a number of scholars contend that the ecological epoch's suggested change is ambiguous, divisive, unresolved and hotly contested within the scientific community (Ellis, 2018, pp. 5–15; Schulz, 2017, pp. 46–62; Davies, 2016, pp. 15–68). One of the emerging questions is the exact meaning of the word 'Anthropocene'. As naturalists broadly construed, Anthropocene implies that human activity impacted and shaped the earth's geology and ecosystems (Ellis, 2018, pp. 5–15; Schulz, 2017, pp. 46–62; Davies, 2016, pp. 15–68). However, this literal interpretation of the Anthropocene as the '*Anthropos*' or 'Man' is rejected by other academics (Matthew, 2020, pp. 67–82). Scholars who contend the exact start date (interval of geologic time) and concept of the Anthropocene (age of humans) have arguably become the most discussed and provocative tendencies in Anglophone and Continental academic circles (Ellis, 2018, pp. 5–15; Latour, 2014, pp. 1–18).

To complicate things, in his book *Anthropocene: A Very Short Introduction*, Erle Ellis (2018, pp. 1–5) suggests that the idea of the Anthropocene poses a number of significant queries and challenges, such as: Does the age of humans mean the end of nature? Who is responsible for the Anthropocene? Homo sapiens? The farmers? Or affluent industrial-era consumers? Different advocates offered differing responses to these queries. Dipesh Chakrabarty's 'The Climate of History: Four Theses' is one of the earliest notable articles that critically addressed and evaluated the new hypothesized geological epoch (Chakrabarty, 2009, pp. 197–222). Chakrabarty does not view the Anthropocene as a bad thing. In fact, the 'Four Theses' is a foundational work for investigating and comprehending the newly postulated geological period (Chakrabarty, 2009, pp. 197–201). According to Chakrabarty, the Anthropocene pushes humans to share philosophical, moral, social, ethical and community responsibility for caring for nature (Chakrabarty, 2009, pp. 207–12). To put it simply, Chakrabarty insists that humanity as a whole is responsible for climate change (Boscov-Ellen, 2018, pp. 70–83). Despite Chakrabarty's diagnosis of climate change being very relevant, many critics are still not persuaded by his arguments (Boscov-Ellen, 2018, pp. 70–1). Many leftist scholars, for instance, contest that Chakrabarty's view failed to expose the social class conflict and political-economic factors in the debate of the Anthropocene (Boscov-Ellen, 2020b, pp. 72–6). Hence, critics observe that Chakrabarty's view of the Anthropocene is more or less political, which led to anti-political solutions (Boscov-Ellen, 2020b, pp. 77–81). For those critics, the incompleteness of Chakrabarty's view is problematic since it ignores power struggles in environmental problem and climate change issues. Within the discourse of the Anthropocene, the problematic politics of environmental issues and climate change must be recognized as harmful concerns.

Furthermore, in the essay 'Anthropocentrism: More than Just a Misunderstood Problem', Helen Kopnina, Haydn Washington, Bron Taylor and John Piccolo (2018, pp. 109–27) rejected the oversimplified notion of the Anthropocene (Kopnina et al., 2018, pp. 109–27; Hayward, 1997, pp. 49–63). Drawing on Tim Hayward's arguments, they contend that this narrow definition of the Anthropocene is misanthropic and detrimental to environmental conservation (Kopnina et al., 2018, pp. 111–20; Hayward, 1997, pp. 49–63). For them, speciesism and human chauvinism, not anthropocentrism, are the underlying causes of environmental problems and climate change catastrophes (Kopnina et al., 2018, pp. 111–20; Hayward, 1997, pp. 49–63). Similar arguments were put forward by Jeremy Davies. In his book *The Birth of the Anthropocene*, Davies (2016, pp. 1–14) clarifies what the Anthropocene actually means. For Davies, the scientific term 'Anthropocene' is a far simpler concept because there is no scientific consensus agreement on its start date (p. 8). Davies argues, 'In a word: no more clean breaks that put humans on one side and nature on the other and, thereby, merge each antagonist into a uniform blob' (p. 8). He further argues that the notion of the Anthropocene is neither a rhetorical device nor a shock tactic to expose the horror of human destructive capacity or place human agency at the centre of the physical world (p. 8).

Although human agency, according to Davies, is a primary driver of changes in the global system, human agency is by no means the master of the physical world (Davies, 2016, pp. 48–50, 57, 107–96). Instead, he argues that the new proposed geological epoch, the Anthropocene, offers a very different way of looking at the distant past (p. 27).

Anthropocene or Capitalocene?

Another criticism of the Anthropocene is that it overemphasizes human agency over social structure. In his book *Anthropocene or Capitalocene? Nature, History, and the Crisis of Capitalism*, Jason W. Moore argues that scholars must re-evaluate their understanding of the Anthropocene (Moore, 2016, pp. 1–13). By concentrating on the intersectionality between agency and social structures, the book was able to articulate how capital or money, power relations and nature varied from earlier views (Moore, 2016, p. 113). Moore identifies several reasons for the ecological disaster – for example, infinite greed, power relations, Cartesian (nature/culture) dualism, and a work-centred perspective. Capitalism (capitalist world-ecology), Moore and others argue, is closely intertwined with the system of cheap nature, and the endless accumulation of capital is the core cause of environmental problems or ecological disasters (Moore, 2016, pp. 78–153). Moore and others further argue that environmental and ecological challenges in general should be investigated in light of the tensions in living and social structures under a neoliberal global capitalist system. For instance, Daniel Hartley argues that these inconsistencies and exploitative social structures manifest themselves at political, economic, social, cultural and ideological levels, obscuring and disconnecting the problem from its structural sources and roots (Hartley, 2016, pp. 155–7). Like Moore, Hartley contends that the notion of Anthropocene posits five problematic discourses. First, an inadequate definition of humanity; second, an over-emphasis on technological determinism; third, a homogeneous time of linear succession of human history; fourth, human history wilfully blind to the history of mass urban poverty, gentrification and accumulation by dispossession; and, fifth, depoliticization of climate change and environmental issues that lead to technical and managerial solutions (Hartley, 2016, pp. 155–7). In short, Moore and Hartley argue that the new projected geological period is an inadequate conceptualization, abstraction and diverging language that conceals the core problem of the neoliberal global capitalist system.

Furthermore, in his popular book *The Great Derangement: Climate Change and the Unthinkable*, the well-known and prolific author Amitav Ghosh questioned the 'individual moral adventure' depicted in contemporary literary discourses that address and tackle the impacts of climate change and ecological disaster, whether scientific (apocalyptic) fiction and non-fiction at the same time (Ghosh, 2016, pp. 1–84). Ghosh emphasized how contemporary literature tends to favour individualistic explanations for climate change challenges and ecological catastrophes. Rather, he contends that in order to engender collective political and social action, climate change challenges and ecological disasters must be placed in an appropriate broader political, social and economic context (pp. 125–33). According to Ghosh, contemporary scientific (apocalyptic) literature has become a source of fear and anxiety, paralysing many from critically engaging in climate change debate and climate action (pp. 117–62).

Anthropocene as a colonial discourse

Other critics contend that the Anthropocene is yet another construction of the Western colonial discourse. A growing critical fascination with the new proposed geological epoch, the Anthropocene, appears to have led to a re-Westernization of debates and discourses about climate change and ecological catastrophe. The Anthropocene, according to many detractors, is simply another grand/meta narrative of the Western/Eurocentric scholarship that is attempting to sum it all up (Fiske, 2022, pp. 109–22). For instance, Michael Simpson's work, titled 'The Anthropocene as Colonial Discourse', challenges the prior intense disputes concerning the concept of the Anthropocene and the periodization of time. Simpson reveals the philosophical underpinnings of this category, particularly the Eurocentric and colonial understandings of modernity and its colonial 'other' that were acquired from the European Enlightenment, as well as the deployment of this knowledge (Simpson, 2020, pp. 53–71).

Simpson delves further into the nature of the Anthropocene, highlighting three strongly Eurocentric elements of the intellectual currents preceding the Anthropocene: first, the Anthropocene is a Western grand narrative about the gradual progression of human civilization (Simpson, 2020, pp. 53–5); second, the Anthropocene is when human cultures transition from a state of Nature or savagery to a state of Civilization, which implies exercising sovereign agency over nature (pp. 61–2); and third, the Anthropocene has a teleological trajectory (pp. 62–4). Simpson attempts to salvage the concept of the Anthropocene by contending that the primary contemporary challenge is to decolonize the Anthropocene's articulation. He maintains, however, that it is critical to point out that the issue of the new suggested geological epoch, the Anthropocene, cannot be discounted. Simpson succinctly writes:

> Moreover, so long as the concept of the Anthropocene continues to privilege Western scientific knowledge and remains a construct that is deeply invested in the ontoepistemological categories of Western philosophy, it will continue to exclude and silence ways of knowing that are considered beyond the bounds of the Western philosophical tradition. Regardless of whether the Anthropocene is to be conceptually salvaged or discarded, the task of decolonizing this discourse requires the destabilization of these categories, the provincializing of the Western imaginary, and the opening up of space for ways of knowing and being that offer counter-imaginaries and possibilities for rethinking how we might navigate these challenging times. Indeed, as Achille Mbembe has described, the 'decolonization project' has 'two sides' – the first of which is the deconstruction of 'epistemic coloniality,' while the second side is 'an attempt at imagining what the alternative to this model could look like' (2015, p. 18). My intention here is to contribute to the former – the critical dismantling of colonial structures of thought that discredit and suppress other ways of knowing and being. (Simpson, 2020, p. 67)

What does Anthropocene mean for Christian theologians today?

But what does the Anthropocene mean for Christian theologians today? In 1967, Lynn White, Jr's controversial seminal article 'The Historical Roots of Our Ecological Crisis' is one of the earliest scholarly works that discusses the connection between the study of religion and nature. White concludes that religions, particularly Western Christianity, are to blame for the environmental crisis (White, Jr, 1967, pp. 1–9). For White, religion pervades and influences human actions in all realms of human–nature relations (White, Jr, pp. 6–9). However, despite White's valuable insights on Christianity's contribution to the environmental crisis, his thoughts continue to be mirrored in modern debates, particularly in the environmental academic arena (van Urk, 2020, pp. 206–23).

Many Christian scholars believe that White actually misinterpreted Scripture. Nevertheless, scholars argue that his critique simply cannot be ignored or dismissed. As Charlee New writes:

> White's idea has gained currency and Christianity now faces the charge of carrying inherent problems with the environment. Namely, Christianity fosters an instrumentalist view of nature and animals, and promotes man's superiority in a way that is incompatible with attempting to live sustainably and compassionately on the planet. Christians must be quick to reflect honestly on such criticisms, however, it is also crucial to affirm that Christians do not need to shuffle shamefaced towards environmental activism, leaving their biblical thinking 'at the door'. (New, 2017)

In his encyclical letter titled *Laudato si'*, Pope Francis made similar remarks. He points out that an authentic ecological strategy must always be social – social ecology – incorporating themes of justice into public debates about the environmental problem and climate change (Francis, 2015, pp. 103–20).

Despite notable efforts to develop Christian eco-theology, many contemporary Christian eco-theological expressions and thoughts fall short of appropriately addressing the implications of climate change and the environmental catastrophe. Some progressive theologians argue that the underlying cause for this is that most mainstream Christian theologies do not reject a Christian theology of conquest and displacement. Lily Mendoza and George Zachariah provided this particular viewpoint. Mendoza and Zachariah write:

A deeper engagement with mainstream ecotheologies and religious environmentalism exposes their colonial and neo-liberal moorings. Creation theologies propagate the idea of the creation of the universe as the act of a sovereign and transcendent God creating 'out of nothing' (*ex nihilo*). The European colonial theology of conquest is founded on the Genesis narratives of primordial earth as 'void,' 'dark,' and 'deep,' and the Patristic creation theology of 'creation out of nothing,' legitimizing the vocation and mission of the chosen race to colonize the heathens and their lands. Human vocation, as prescribed in the first creation story of the Hebrew Bible, to 'subdue' the earth and to have 'dominion' over the rest of the creation offers theological legitimization to colonialization. The colonial doctrine of *terra nullius* (nobody's land) and the notion of 'private property' are deeply influenced by this creation theology. (Mendoza and Zachariah, 2022, pp. 1–3)

Given this context, one of the most difficult issues is to transform modern Christian theological thinking into very relevant critiques of climate change disputes and environmental problems. Mendoza and Zachariah argue that Christian theological expressions and reflections must be self-decolonizing first and foremost (Mendoza and Zachariah, pp. 1–3). For Mendoza and Zachariah, it is an excellent step to examine certain flawed theological narratives that justify and support European-American imperialism and colonialism, including resource exploitation and destruction (pp. 4–5). However, many fundamentalist Christians have much hesitation and doubt about whether this self-decolonizing task is at all appropriate and necessary.

Decoloniality and Christian theology/ies

In his book *On Decolonizing the Anthropocene: Disobedience via Plural Constitutions* (2021), Mark Jackson posed the critical question, 'Do we really need a new universal philosophical anthropology of humans, the impulse for which has been so problematic a part of modernity?' If so, he maintains that 'If an anthropology is necessary, let it be a radically decentring one' (Jackson, 2021, p. 699). But what did Jackson mean by 'radically decentring tone'? To avoid totalizing, hegemonic and controlling Anthropocene narratives, he claims that it is time to listen to and recognize various options, voices and perspectives (Jackson, 2021, p. 699). According to Jackson, this rejection stems from the belief that a newly universal philosophical anthropology of humans is subjective, biased, ideologically and politically motivated, and perpetuates a dominant Western ideology by marginalizing and suppressing alternative perspectives on environmental issues and climate action (Jackson, 2021, pp. 700–1; Hedges, 2021, pp. 410–16, 419–20, 538). He also contends that the Anthropocene concept is profoundly rooted in the privileged Western production of knowledge (Jackson, 2021, pp. 702–8). Jackson aims to confront the problematic notion of the Anthropocene by rejecting the recently suggested universal philosophical anthropology of humans. According to him, it makes room for alternate voices and viewpoints, particularly among indigenous groups from the global South who are most affected by climate change disasters (Jackson, 2021, pp. 702–8). He encourages people to be cautious and to challenge the power dynamics that underpin Western knowledge production and the depiction of climate change calamities. As a result, he believes that decolonizing how academics, public policymakers and stakeholders reformulate and reframe the concept of the Anthropocene is critical (Jackson, 2021, pp. 702–8).

According to Miguel De La Torre, a Christian theological discourse that seeks to completely abandon and reinterpret the Christian salvific narrative is thus revealed to be based on the wrong premise. It inevitably falls short when Christianity's historical contributions to environmental issues and climate change are ignored or minimized (Poole, 2020, pp. 47–73). As a result, Christianity in particular became the empire's primary vehicle (De La Torre, 2018, pp. 81–114). Decolonizing Christian theologies calls into question the Anthropocene's status as a single, authoritative narrative of human history or a final understanding of environmental concerns and climate action. They advocate for alternative religious motifs, and sources that are more liberal.

Anthropocene as global coloniality and the 'promise' of the decolonial option

The 'promise' of the decolonial option is to expose and oppose the colonial matrix of power-coloniality that is embedded in various discourses, including the new proposed geological epoch, the Anthropocene. But what exactly do decolonial thinkers mean when they talk about coloniality? According to Sabelo J. Ndlovu-Gatsheni, colonialism (Maldonado-Torres, 2007, pp. 240–70) is a power structure, an epochal condition, and an epistemological design that is central to the current world order

(Ndlovu-Gatsheni, 2013a, pp. 187–8; Ndlovu-Gatsheni, 2013a, pp. 3–44; Ndlovu-Gatsheni, 2021, pp. 167–77). According to Ndlovu-Gatsheni, coloniality is a racially hierarchized, imperialistic, colonialist, Euro-American-centric, Christian-centric, heteronormative, patriarchal, violent and modern world order that emerged after Christopher Columbus' so-called 'discovery' of the 'New World' (Ndlovu-Gatsheni, 2013a, pp. 3–44). It is explicitly Euro-American knowledge production that justifies and perpetuates global disparities, such as unequal distribution of resources, opportunities and power. Ndlovu-Gatsheni evokes the same line of argument made by Walter Mignolo:

> While the imperial vision seeks to impose, reproduce, and maintain dominant Euro-American hegemony over the world, 'the decolonial paradigm struggles to bring into intervening existence an-other interpretation that bring forward, on the one hand, a silenced view of the event and, on the other, shows the limits of imperial ideology disguised as the true (total) interpretation of the events'. (Ndlovu-Gatsheni, 2013b, p. 24)

He also claims that '... global coloniality is there to make sure the powerful Euro-North American powers remain powerful' (Ndlovu-Gatsheni, 2013a, p. 189). Rather than challenging global coloniality, he contends that it problematically reinforces dominance and colonial structure, endangering human flourishing (Ndlovu-Gatsheni, 2013c, pp. 196–9).

Following Simpson's case against Anthropocene as colonial discourse, it is demonstrated that Anthropocene is a form of colonial discourse – more specifically, as another form of the colonial matrix of power that conceals and fails to challenge the Western world's epistemic privilege and intellectual imperialism (Grosfoguel, 2011, pp. 1–37). For example, in the Anthropocene debates and discussions, non-Western 'people became represented as bystanders in human history deserving to be civilized by Europeans and educated by Europeans within a world constructed and configured by Europeans', in the words of Ndlovu-Gatsheni (2013a, p. 189). This practice was dubbed epistemic privilege by many decolonial thinkers (Ndlovu-Gatsheni, 2011, pp. 44–66). According to the concept of epistemic privilege, Western intellectuals enjoy a privileged position in terms of comprehending and describing 'how and why the universe works' – globally, rationally, logically and scientifically. However, decolonizing the notion of the Anthropocene can only be realized when the characteristics of these Euro-American epistemologies can be interrogated or examined.

Decoloniality provides a comprehensive analysis or intersectional perspective on climate change and ecological disasters (Kurtis and Adams, 2017, pp. 46–60). Rather than providing a precise explanation for specific human activity, decolonial scholars emphasized the interconnectedness of social realities such as knowledge systems, social systems, races, actors, institutions and ecological systems (Mignolo, 2011, pp. 175, 273–83; Ndlovu-Gatsheni, 2013c, pp. 3–44; Bhambra, 2014, pp. 115–21).

Second, decoloniality calls into question the foundation and control of hegemonic knowledge by drawing on indigenous sources (Mignolo, 2002, pp. 59–96). According to decolonial scholars, knowledge is defined and transmitted by a specific privileged and powerful group as a result of historical situations and events that are loosely related to a specific ideological and political agenda (de Sousa Santos, 2014, pp. 118–63).

Third, decoloniality rejects the idea that there is a single normativity ('orthodoxy') or 'Western canon of thought' that applies to all circumstances and civilizations (Leonardo, 2018, pp. 7–20; Afolabi, 2020, pp. 93–110). Fourth, decoloniality questions and challenges the global North's epistemologies, notably its epistemological model that promotes Western knowledge and subordinates non-Western knowledge (de Sousa Santos, 2014, pp. 118–63).

Finally, decoloniality holds that knowledge production necessitates pluralistic or participatory formations (particularly in the most vulnerable communities affected by climate change); thus, it rejects inferiorized (non-Western) 'Other' epistemologies, imposed categories and classifications of knowledge, but not engendered epistemological pluralism (de Sousa Santos, 2014, pp. 188–211). In short, it is not advocating that non-Western scholars throw the baby out with the bathwater or totally abandon the Western ways of seeing and knowing.

With this in mind, what can Christian theologians learn from decolonizing the Anthropocene concept? To begin with, any endeavour to rethink Christian theology must be broad, freeing and dedicated to the dismantling of Euro-American thinking, especially Christian theologies and one-size-fits-all narratives that justify and encourage environmental plunder and destruction. It calls into question the Western privilege model of theological thought and the Western framework that legitimizes the exploitation of nature. Second, any attempt to recreate Christian theological reflection must upend the current social order meant to keep neoliberalism in place (De La Torre, 2018, pp. 139–40). It must reveal the neoliberal mindset that supports over-exploitation of forest, minerals, land and water resources. Third, any theological study, academic framework, scientific perspective or theory development necessitates pluralistic voices, participatory formations, and acknowledgement of the importance of Indigenous Knowledge Systems and Practices (IKSPs) and non-Western ideas. It challenges Western theological paradigms while encouraging epistemic and theological plurality. Finally, Christian theological inquiry must remain critical and reject any one-size-fits-all narrative, such as the Anthropocene, while encouraging many narratives and realities.

Conclusion

To summarize, despite the confusion, there are four aspects of the arguments presented in this chapter that deserve attention. First, *climate change and environmental issues are among our most pressing concerns* (UN News Global Perspective Human Stories, 2023). Despite the obvious dangers of climate change, many wealthy countries continue to avoid taking action. Others deny climate change or the existence of solvable problems. Some have proposed a new geological epoch, the Anthropocene, to account for the effects of human activities on natural biodiversity. Others deny climate change or the existence of solvable problems. Although the concept of the Anthropocene has sparked debate and resulted in several alternative proposals, it could be argued that the Anthropocene remains a reasonable starting point for discussions about holding human agency accountable for climate change. However, emphasizing human responsibility over corporate greed or selfish elites does not clearly identify who is to blame. It may be inappropriate to emphasize personal responsibility, but greedy corporations refuse to accept responsibility for their significant role in the climate change disaster.

Second, *the idea of the Anthropocene is a perfectly intelligible one.* Moving away from global coloniality, decolonial epistemic freedom and critique is desperately needed. It must expose hegemonic Euro-American pronouncements that keep non-Western people as spectators in the global ecological catastrophe. This has been referred to as intellectual hegemony and epistemic injustice by decolonial scholars. Thus, it is also vital to ask, 'Whose Anthropocene?' Is another Western grand narrative required to define and explain our contemporary situation? By raising these crucial concerns, it pushes people from the global South to abandon their over-reliance on Western theory construction and knowledge production (Alatas, 2006, pp. 133–5).

Third, as many philosophers and social scientists have suggested, *in order to solve climate change or the ecological crisis, climate change and environmental issues must be placed in their right perspective*. The chapter demonstrates, through the decolonial lens, that the environmental disaster is a symptom, not the primary cause. Climate change, or the ecological disaster, needs political, social, cultural, economic, religious and theological investigation. I contend here that without a broader perspective or an intersectionality approach to climate change, any attempt to trace its root causes holistically, such as micro-meso-macro analysis, will fail because climate change requires an intersectionality analysis and a new decolonial global paradigm for humanity.

And finally, but importantly: *decolonized Christian eco-theology/ies demanded practical visibility that resulted in profound unity or 'deep solidarity' and widespread critical mass movement.* If the global society and stakeholders do not respond to the climate change catastrophe with 'deep solidarity' that incorporates mutual care and concern for environmental justice, humanity's future is lost. The prominent German-American theologian Joerg Rieger attempts to make sense of the need for 'deep solidarity' to survive in his outstanding book *Theology in the Capitalocene: Ecology, Identity, Class, and Solidarity.* As Rieger writes:

> In sum, deep solidarity accomplishes two unexpected things: not only is it built on a challenge of privilege and genuine appreciation of difference, but it also manages to employ differences for the common good and the power of resistance. These differences can be multiple, tied simultaneously to race, ethnicity, gender, sexuality, nationality, and even religion. Deep solidarity, therefore, amounts to a reversal of anything the Right might call solidarity. As the solidarity of the Right is guided by sameness and by privileged racial and religious identities, the solidarity of the Left is guided by experiences of economic exploitation that affect the working majority, compounded by race, ethnicity, gender, sexuality, and nationality. Significant guidance comes, therefore, from those who experience these compounded forms of exploitation, domination, and oppression in their own bodies because they are more existentially affected by the system than anyone else. Deep solidarity needs to start from below, which does not mean that the burden of the work should be on the shoulders of the proverbial 'least of these,' but vision and leadership have roots where the pressures are greatest. (Rieger, 2022, p. 175)

In addition, putting this into action involves the establishment of a critical mass movement as well as 'deep solidarity'. According to Rieger, deep solidarity entails not only bringing together Christian stakeholders concerned about climate change and ecological disasters, but also a willingness to collaborate constructively, resulting in concrete collective action or mass mobilization. This is consistent with decolonial theory, which claims it is not a metaphor. It was enacted, embodied and realized in the midst of social, cultural, economic and political transformation (Tuck and Yang, 2012, pp. 1–40; Fanon, 1963, pp. 1–51). As Franz Fanon pointed out:

> Decolonization, which sets out to change the order of the world, is, obviously, a program of complete disorder. But it cannot come as a result of magical practices, nor of a natural shock, nor of a friendly understanding. Decolonization, as we know, is a historical process: that is to say it cannot be understood, it cannot become intelligible nor clear to itself except in the exact measure that we can discern the movements which give it historical form and content. (Fanon, 1963, p. 36)

Amitav Ghosh observes that religious groups, particularly Christian churches, are oblivious to the issues posed by climate change. However, Ghosh contends that it is critical to see religious groups at the vanguard of the fight against climate change and for environmental justice. Ghosh, like other Western scholars, believes that these religious actors and groups serve as conduits for religious discourses to affect and alter people's daily lives (Ghosh, 2016, pp. 117–63; Wilson and Steger, 2013, pp. 481–95). Ghosh succinctly writes:

> If a significant breakthrough is to be achieved, if the securitization and corporatization of climate change is to be prevented, then already-existing communities and mass organizations will have to be in the forefront of the struggle. And of such organizations, those with religious affiliations possess the ability to mobilize people in far greater numbers than any others. Moreover, religious worldviews are not subject to the limitations that have made climate change such a challenge for our existing institutions of governance: they transcend nation states, and they all acknowledge intergenerational, long-term responsibilities; they do not partake of economistic ways of thinking and are therefore capable of imagining nonlinear change – catastrophe, in other words – in ways that are perhaps closed to the forms

of reason deployed by contemporary nation-states. Finally, it is impossible to see any way out of this crisis without an acceptance of limits and limitations, and this in turn is, I think, intimately related to the idea of the sacred, however one may wish to conceive of it. If religious groupings around the world can join hands with popular movements, they may well be able to provide the momentum that is needed for the world to move forward on drastically reducing emissions without sacrificing considerations of equity. That many climate activists are already proceeding in this direction is, to me, yet another sign of hope. (Ghosh, 2016, pp. 160–1)

References

Afolabi, Olugbemiga Samuel, 2020, 'Globalisation, Decoloniality and the Question of Knowledge Production in Africa', *Journal of Higher Education in Africa / Revue de l'enseignement supérieur en Afrique* 18/1, Special Issue on: The Politics of Knowledge Production in Africa (With selected papers from the 15th CODESRIA General Assembly) / Numéro spécial sur: La politique de production de connaissances en Afrique (Avec des articles issus de la 15e Assemblée générale du CODESRIA), pp. 93–110.

Alatas, Syed Farid, 2006, *Alternative Discourses in Asian Social Science: Responses to Eurocentrism*, New Delhi: Sage.

Bhambra, Gurminder K., 2014, 'Postcolonial and Decolonial Dialogues', *Postcolonial Studies* 17.2, pp. 115–21.

Boscov-Ellen, Dan, 2020a, '"Whose Universalism?" Dipesh Chakrabarty and the Anthropocene', *Capitalism Nature Socialism* 31.1, pp. 70–83, doi: 10.1080/10455752.2018.1514060 (accessed 21.12.2023).

Boscov-Ellen, D., 2020b, 'A Responsibility to Revolt? Climate Ethics in the Real World', *Environmental Values* 29.2, pp. 153, 174, https://doi.org/10.3197/096 327119X15579936382617.

Burdon, Peter D., 2020, 'Obligations in the Anthropocene', *Law Critique* 31, pp. 309–28.

Carrington, Damian, 2016, 'The Anthropocene Epoch: Scientists Declare Dawn of Human-influenced Age', *The Guardian*, https://www.theguardian.com/environment/2016/aug/29/declare-anthropocene-epoch-experts-urge-geological-congress-human-impact-earth (accessed 13.11.2023).

Chakrabarty, Dipesh, 2009, 'The Climate of History: Four Theses', *Critical Inquiry* 35.2, pp. 197–222.

Chakrabarty, Dipesh, 2015, 'The Human Condition in the Anthropocene: Roundtable Discussion', *YouTube*, 31 July, https://www.youtube.com/watch?v=1CcPq8qb-38 (accessed 12.12.2023).

Davies, Jeremy, 2016, *The Birth of the Anthropocene*, Berkeley, CA: University of California Press.

Deane-Drummond, Celia E., Bergmann, Sigurd B. and Vogt, Markus, 2017, *Religion in Anthropocene*, Cambridge: Lutterworth Press.

De La Torre, Miguel A., 2018, *Burying White Privilege: Resurrecting a Badass Christianity*, Grand Rapids, MI: William B. Eerdmans.

de Sousa Santos, Boaventura, 2014, *Epistemologies of the South: Justice Against Epistemicide*, New York: Routledge.

Ellis, E. C., 2018, *Anthropocene: A Very Short Introduction*, Oxford: Oxford University Press.

Ellis, E. C., Lewis, S. L. and Maslin, M. A., 2015, 'Defining the Anthropocene', *Nature* 519, pp. 171–9.

Emmett, Robert, and Lekan, Thomas, 2016, 'Foreword and Introduction', in *Whose Anthropocene? Revisiting Dipesh Chakrabarty's 'Four Theses'*, pp. 5–14.

Eva, L., Mobjork, M. and Soder, R., 2020, 'The Anthropocene and the Geopolitical Imagination: Re-writing Earth as Political Space', *Earth System Government* 4, pp. 1–8.

Fanon, Franz, 1963, *The Wretched of the Earth*, New York: Grove Press.

Fiske, Desirée, 2022, 'Towards an Anthropocene Narrative and a New Philosophy of Governance: Evolution of Global Environmental Discourse in the Man and the Biosphere Programme', *Journal of Environmental Policy & Planning* 24.1, pp. 109–22.

Francis, Pope, 2015, *Laudato si, mi Signore*, https://www.vatican.va/content/francesco/en/encyclicals/documents/papa-francesco_20150524_enciclica-laudato-si.html (accessed 25.12.2023).

Ghosh, Amitav, 2016, *The Great Derangement: Climate Change and the Unthinkable*, Chicago, IL: University of Chicago Press.

Grosfoguel, Ramon, 2011, 'Decolonizing Post-colonial Studies and Paradigms of Political-Economy: Transmodernity, Decolonial Thinking, and Global Coloniality', *Transmodernity: Journal of Peripheral Cultural Production of the Luso-Hispanic World* 1, pp. 1–37.

Hartley, D., 2016, 'Anthropocene, Capitalocene, and the Problem of Culture' in J. Moore (ed.), *Anthropocene or Capitalocene?: Nature, History, and the Crisis of Capitalism*, Dexter, OH: PM Press, pp. 154–65.

Hayward, Tim, 1997, 'Anthropocentrism: A Misunderstood Problem', *Environmental Values* 6.1, pp. 49–63.

Hedges, Paul, 2021, *Understanding Religion: Theories and Methods for Studying Religiously Diverse Societies*, Berkeley, CA: University of California Press.

International Institute for Environment and Development, 2023, 'Countries Missing Deadlines to Submit Climate Plans More than Half the Time', *International Institute for Environment and Development*, 19 November, https://www.iied.org/countries-missing-deadlines-submit-climate-plans-more-half-time (accessed 14.11.2023).

Jackson, Mark, 2021, *On Decolonizing the Anthropocene: Disobedience via Plural Constitutions*, London: Routledge.

Kopnina, Helen et al., 2018, 'Anthropocentrism: More than Just a Misunderstood Problem', *Journal of Agricultural and Environmental Ethics* 31, pp. 109–27, file:///C:/Users/hadje/Downloads/Anthropocentrism_More_than_Just_a_Misunderstood_Pr.df (accessed 13.11.2023).

Kurtiş, Tugce, and Adams, Glenn, 2017, 'Decolonial Intersectionality Implications for Theory, Research, and Pedagogy' in Kim A. Case (ed.), *Intersectional Pedagogy*, New York: Routledge, pp. 46–60.

Latour, Bruno, 2014, 'Agency in the Time of Anthropocene: New Literary', *History* 45.1, pp. 1–18.
Leonardo, Zeus, 2018, 'Dis-orienting Western Knowledge', *The Cambridge Journal of Anthropology: Canon Fire: Decolonizing the Curriculum* 36.2, pp. 7–20.
Lewis, Simon L., and Maslin, Mark A., 2015, 'Defining the Anthropocene', *Nature* 519, pp. 171–9.
Lövbrand, Eva, Mobjörk, Malin and Söder, Rickard, 2020, 'The Anthropocene and the Geo-political Imagination: Re-writing Earth as Political Space', *Earth System Governance* 4, 100051, 10.1016/j.esg.2020.10.
Maldonado-Torres, Nelson, 2007, 'On the Coloniality of Being: Contributions to the development of a concept', *Cultural Studies* 21.2–3 March/May, pp. 240–70, ISSN 0950-2386 print/ISSN 1466-4348 online (accessed 12.12.2023).
Malhi, Yadvinder, 2017, 'The Concept of the Anthropocene', *Annual Review of Environment and Resources* 42, pp. 77–104.
Matthew, Andrew S., 2020, 'Annual Review of Anthropology: Anthropology and the Anthropocene: Criticisms, Experiments, and Collaborations', 49, pp. 67–82, https://doi.org/10.1146/annurev-anthro-102218-011317 (accessed 16.12.2023).
Mbembe, A., 2015, 'Decolonizing Knowledge and the Question of the Archive', Public lecture series at the Wits Institute for Social and Economic Research (WISER), University of the Witwatersrand, Johannesburg.
McCarroll, Pamela R., 2023, 'This Changes Everything: Decolonizing Theo-Anthropology toward an Earth-Centered Approach to Pastoral Theology', *Journal of Pastoral Theology* 33.1, pp. 51–71, DOI: 10.1080/10649867.2023.2204277 (accessed 12.12.2023).
Mendoza, Lily, and Zachariah, George, 2022, *Decolonizing Ecotheology: Indigenous and Subaltern Challenges*, Eugene, OR: Pickwick Publications.
Mignolo, Walter, 2002, 'The Geopolitics of Knowledge and the Colonial Difference', *The South Atlantic Quarterly* 101, pp. 59–96.
Mignolo, Walter, 2011, 'Epistemic Disobedience and the Decolonial Option: Manifesto', *Transmodernity* 1.1, pp. 44–66.
Moore, Jason W., 2016, *Anthropocene or Capitalocene? Nature, History, and the Crisis of Capitalism*, San Francisco, CA: PM Press.
Ndlovu-Gatsheni, Sabelo, 2011, 'The World Cup, Vuvuzelas, Flag-Waving Patriots and the Burden of Building South Africa', *Third World Quarterly* 32, pp. 279–93, 10.1080/01436597.2011.560469.
Ndlovu-Gatsheni, Sabelo J., 2013a, *Empire, Global Coloniality, and African Subjectivity*, New York: Berghahn Books.
Ndlovu-Gatsheni, Sabelo J., 2013b, 'Perhaps, Decoloniality is the Answer? Critical Reflections on Development from a Decolonial Epistemic Perspective', *Africanus* 43, pp. 4–5.
Ndlovu-Gatsheni, Sabelo J., 2013c, 'Empire and Global Coloniality: Towards a Decolonial Turn' in *Empire, Global Coloniality and African Subjectivity*, 1st edn, New York: Berghahn Books, pp. 3–44.
Ndlovu-Gatsheni, Sabelo J., 2014, 'Global Coloniality and the Challenges of Creating African Futures', *Strategic Review for Southern Africa* 36.2, pp. 187–8.
Ndlovu-Gatsheni, Sabelo J., 2021, 'Epistemic Injustice' in Francisco J. Carillo and Günter Koch (eds), *Knowledge for the Anthropocene: A Multidisciplinary Approach*, Cheltenham: Edward Elgar Publishing, pp. 167–77.

New, Charlee, 2017, 'Is Christianity to Blame?', *Beyond Stewardship*, University of Exeter, https://humanities.exeter.ac.uk/theology/research/projects/beyond-stewardship/blame/ (accessed 12.12.2023).

Polt, Richard, and Wittrock, Jon, 2018, *The Task of Philosophy in the Anthropocene*, Lanham, MD: Rowman & Littlefield Publishers.

Poole, Kristen, 2020, *Christianity in a Time of Climate Change: To Give a Future with Hope*, Eugene, OR: Wipf and Stock.

Rieger, Joerg, 2022, *Theology in the Capitalocene: Ecology, Identity, Class, and Solidarity*, Minneapolis, MN: Fortress Press.

Rothe, Delf, Müller, Franziska and Chandler, David, 2021, *International Relations in the Anthropocene: New Agendas, New Agencies and New Approaches*, New York: Springer International Publishing.

Schulz, Karsten, 2017, *Decolonising the Anthropocene: The Mytho-Politics of Human Mastery*, in Marc Woons (ed.), *Critical Epistemologies of Global Politics*, E-International Relations Publishing, pp. 46–62.

Simpson, Michael, 2020, 'The Anthropocene as Colonial Discourse', *Environment and Planning D: Society and Space* 38.1, pp. 1–19.

Thomas, Julia Adeney, Williams, Mark and Zalasiewicz, Jan, 2020, *Anthropocene: A Multidisciplinary Approach*, Cambridge: Polity Press.

Tuck, Eva, and Yang, K. Wayne, 2012, 'Decolonization is Not a Metaphor', Decolonization: Indigeneity, *Education & Society* 1.1, pp. 1–40.

UN News Global Perspective Human Stories, 2023, *Impact of 'Failed Promises' on Climate Change, Evident in Antarctica: A UN Resident Coordinator blog*, https://news.un.org/en/story/2023/11/1144127 (accessed 12.11.2023).

Van Urk, Evan, 2020, 'Public Theology and the Anthropocene: Exploring Human–Animal Relations', *International Journal of Public Theology* 14, pp. 206–23.

White, Jr, Lynn, 1967, 'The Historical Roots of Our Ecological Crisis', *Science*, pp. 1–9, https://www.cmu.ca/faculty/gmatties/lynnwhiterootsofcrisis.pdf (accessed 12.11.2023).

Wilson, Erin K., and Steger, Manfred B., 2013, 'Religious Globalisms in the Post-Secular Age', *Globalizations* 10.3, pp. 481–95, https://doi.org/10.1080/14747731.2013.787774 (accessed 9.12.2023).

Zwier, Jochem and Blok, Vincent, 2017, 'Saving Earth: Encountering Heidegger's Philosophy of Technology in the Anthropocene', *Techné: Research in Philosophy and Technology* 21.2–3, pp. 222–42.

3

A Forgotten Body of War: Ecofeminist Theology in 'Militarycene'

KEUN-JOO CHRISTINE PAE

Introduction

For years, the US Department of Defense has called climate change a threat to national security, as 'effects like rising sea levels and catastrophic storms threaten both military and civilian infrastructure and can even affect migration patterns' (US Government Accountability Office, 2014). However, the USA has not viewed its military bases across the globe as being the most responsible for global pollution and, thus, climate change (Vine, 2015, pp. 162–78). Part of the reason is that these bases are believed necessary for worldwide peace and security. The hypocritical response of the USA to climate change only suggests that we live in an irony.[1] On the one hand, the world has been excessively militarized for peace and security – namely, our survival. On the other hand, the military industrial complex, war and military campaigns have killed both humans and non-human ecological beings on an expansive scale, making a large part of the world unliveable. If we, liberation theologians and ethicists, seriously consider the irony of the world we live in, how can we reveal the deadly politics of war and militarism that brings neither peace nor security but genocide and ecocide?

Taking 'militarism' as a lens to interrogate the ecological crisis in our time, this chapter critically interrogates war against nature or 'environcide'. Environcide refers to the intentional destruction of the intimately co-dependent relationship between humans and their surrounding environment. If over-consumption and over-killing of environmental beings are the everyday war against nature, the US-led militarization of the world is an invisible but steady war against nature. The staples of this invisible war include extracting natural resources until they become depleted, as well as polluting, deforesting and scorching the earth until nothing is liveable. Both wars are tied to 'disaster capitalism' that expands the libertarian/neoliberal market system in a war-torn or disaster-wreaked region as if a clean slate or an apocalyptic opportunity for a new creation emerged; in this case, a new creation for a profit-driven neoliberal market system to maximize capitalist interests. Disaster capitalism needs proper shocks to disorient the socio-ecological system and to suppress people's demand for justice and liberation. Indeed, natural disasters and wars are ideal shocks to disorient and re-orient livelihood and, more significantly, to dislocate people from their land and to interrupt their relationships with nature. Thus, it might be impossible to imagine justice-oriented eco-theology without disarming the world.

This chapter theologically reflects on the militarized destruction of nature and the unequal distribution of the ecological cost of war's aftershocks. A war against nature, for which the US-led militarization of the world is primarily responsible, is an everyday reality of earth – all living beings, including humans and non-humans. For this reason, I use the term 'Militarycene' instead of 'Anthropocene'. Anthropocene simplifies a war against nature (e.g. humans vs nature) while obfuscating the unequal distribution of, and responsibility for, environmental destruction. Critically analysing a visible and invisible war against nature and its impact on the global poor, my chapter searches for liberative ecofeminist theology for peace in Militarycene. More specifically, through Brazilian ecofeminist liberation theologian Ivone Gebara's concept of 'inter-relationality', I reconstruct anti-war ecofeminist theology. For this, the first part of the chapter revolves around the two keywords 'shock' and 'crisis' to analyse environcide caused by war and militarism. The second half of the chapter articulates anti-war ecofeminist theology as ways of resisting militarized deaths of human and non-human entities and reimagining environmental solidarity work creatively and audaciously.

A war against nature: shock and crisis

We live in the remains of the ruins of war and the world created by one war after another. While the dead bodies of humans can be a spectacle in any war, the death of non-human environmental beings is invisible and forgotten. Deforestation caused by war is less visible than wildfires, although we cannot differentiate scorched bodies and trees by wildfires from those resulting from uranium-depleted bombs. A war against nature – perhaps the longest war in which humans engage – is seen as a silo of a human-made war, if not the inevitable byproduct of it. In light of 'shock and crisis', let us interrogate how war against nature is operated (in)visibly and how it continues on a mass scale.

Shock

The shock doctrine is a military strategy known as the 'shock and awe' or the 'scorched earth' operation frequently used in theatres of war. To paralyse enemies' perception of the battlefield and destroy their will to fight, the shock doctrine advocates for the overwhelming use of military power (e.g. airstrikes, saturated bombing, etc.) and spectacular displays of force. The USA's wars in Korea, Vietnam, Iraq, Afghanistan and other places displayed the 'shock and awe' tactic that burnt large areas of villages and social infrastructures, deforested mountains and jungles, and killed combatants and non-combatants indiscriminately. The shock and awe tactic can easily lead to mass killing, genocide and ecocide.

What war destroys and interrupts the most is the human relationship with the environment. From the beginning of our time on earth, we humans have developed our livelihoods in relationships with our surrounding nature. These relationships have shaped our ways of living, such as religious rituals, culture, civilization, folk tales, food systems, crops, cattle, houses and roads. For this reason, historian Emmanuel Kreike (2021, p. 3) argues that humans and nature have co-created the 'environmental infrastructure', which constantly changes society and the environment simultaneously. War intentionally or unintentionally destroys the environmental infrastructure, 'increasing societies' vulnerability to human-made and natural disasters' (Kreike, 2021, p. 4). Instead of ecocide, Kreike (2021, p. 4) uses the concept of 'environcide' to emphasize war's episodic and spectacular or continuous and cumulative violence to debilitate the human–nature relationship. Environcide has been a military tactic from ancient warfare onwards. Furthermore, as biblical themes, God's curse on the earth and its inhabitants in the book of Isaiah (ch. 24), and the total destruction of the world plagued with famine, fires and disease in the book of Revelation, can be read as the description of environcide.

Wars in the Persian Gulf, driven by Western colonialism and militarized oil-dependent global capitalism, exemplify the long history of environcide marked with a negative impact on the livelihood in the region. These wars, waged by the British Empire and the United States for the last two centuries, combined bombing with drilling that radically reshaped and transformed the entire system of property rights in the region and its ecology (Picard and Beigi, 2022, p. 42). The destructive First Gulf War (1990–1) is remembered with the images of black smoke and endless fires in the deserts and the thick black oil blanket on top of the ocean that resulted from the burning of hundreds of Kuwaiti oil wells and the spillage of gallons of crude oil into the Gulf (Cusato, 2021, p. 5). The war contaminated neighbouring countries' air, water and land. Less known, the Gulf War syndrome has affected combatants and non-combatants long after the end of the war. It is estimated that as many as 175,000 Gulf War veterans in the USA have chronic illnesses, including debilitating fatigue, cognitive problems, psychiatric disorders, and more (Haley, 2013). The causes of the Gulf War syndrome are controversial. However, scholars and medical experts believe these veterans were exposed to harmful chemicals during the US-led Operation Desert Storm – aerial and carpet bombing over Iraqi chemical weapons storage sites, the explosion of depleted uranium used in ammunition, and burning oil gas. How many civilians in the Persian Gulf suffer from the Gulf War syndrome is unknown, let alone the effects from the contaminated land. In 2003, the Persian Gulf region re-experienced environcide, ecocide and genocide under Operation Shock and Awe.

The Persian Gulf region has suffered from militarized oil monies since the 1920s when the British Empire took over the area from the Ottoman Empire, and Western capitalism started relying heavily on oil. While 25 corporate and state producers are responsible for more than 70 per cent of industrial greenhouse gas emissions, oil pollution spreads horizontally among marginalized communities (Picard and Beigi, 2022, p. 41). From an eco-Marxist perspective, Michael Picard and Tina Beigi (2022, pp. 39–40) analyse the Western military capitalists' accumulation of oil wealth by contaminating the Persian region, known as the process of 'accumulation by contamination'. They explain:

> Accumulation by contamination encompasses the wartime act of polluting a territory to clear the way for exploitation and accumulating wealth by simultaneously disseminating waste on the conquered territory after major hostilities have ceased. (2022, p. 39)

Accumulation by contamination is found in the USA's many wars beyond the Gulf War. As a historical example, during the Korean War (1950–3) the USA tested napalm and Agent Orange, newly developed weapons to clear mountains and villages to shock the North Korean and Chinese allies and North Korean guerrillas. The Korean War allowed the USA to consolidate its power in East Asia and interrupt postcolonial countries' nation-building. Since the war ended as a truce, the US military has been indefinitely stationed in South Korea. These US bases in South Korea have contaminated local land and waterways as the bases store gasoline, test new weapons, and house thousands of soldiers and their families who produce more rubbish and waste than local Koreans. Radioactive materials, harmful chemicals, petroleum and green gas are the products of US military activities in Korea. When the US Armed Forces in Korea started returning the Yongsan garrison to the Korean government in 2018, Korean society learned that the entire area was contaminated with petroleum and chemicals. The Yongsan garrison in the heart of Seoul is environmentally hazardous. According to a Korean non-profit organization, Lawyers for a Demographic Society, garrison soil was burnt easily because of multiple oil spillages covered up by the US military and the South Korean government (2021). Unfortunately, the stories of Yongsan and the Persian Gulf are shared among people living around US bases across the globe.

Crisis

Climate change is undoubtedly a crisis for all humanity, and the US military is the world's largest polluter. Water and land contaminated by US bases impose a crisis on hosting countries, their environmental infrastructure, and non-human creatures. From a biopolitical perspective, war is the biggest threat to life. Various crises created by natural and human-made disasters are often met by other military campaigns and capitalist development that further alienate humans from nature or destroy already fragile ecosystems. The opening of the Yongsan Children's Garden is a prime example of the crisis met by governmental cover-ups and city development at the cost of Korean civilians' health and well-being.

Despite public concerns, in 2022 the Korean government transformed part of the former Yongsan garrison (100,000 m^2) into Yongsan Park. On 4 May 2023, the day before the Children's Day of Korea, the Korean government opened the Yongsan Children's Garden, which included part of Yongsan Park, which was heavily contaminated with disposed petroleum and cancer-causing chemicals such as lead, cadmium, dioxane and benzene. The Korean government put 15cm of topsoil and gables on the contaminated area and planted flowers and trees, claiming that visitors would not come into contact with harmful chemicals thanks to this new thick topsoil. Environmental organizations in Korea warned of the danger of opening the contaminated Yongsan garrison to the public without adequately cleaning out the base under the topsoil. The US Armed Forces in Korea refused to take responsibility for purifying the returned base. In the meantime, the Korean government prioritized US–Korean military allyship and economic relations over Korean civilians' health. Since the Korean government could not guarantee the safety of the returned Yongsan garrison, it used the name 'garden' instead of 'park' because the park requires higher safety regulations (Yim, 2023).

The Yongsan case shows what scholar Rob Nixon (2011, p. 2) calls 'slow violence' that occurs gradually and out of sight. Nixon's concept refers to the violence of delayed destruction dispersed across time and space. Attritional violence is typically not viewed as violence at all because violence is generally considered immediate, eruptive and explosive (Nixon, 2011, p. 2). Incremental and accretive environmental destruction is invisible and neglected violence, although its destructive power can be more harmful than any form of violence. For more than 70 years, North Korea has been defined as a threat to South Korea. As a result, the US Armed Forces in South Korea have justified their presence in the country for the sake of peace and security for South Korea and East Asia. However, the reality of the US base is 'slow violence' against Koreans and their environmental infrastructure, ecosystem and economy.

As of August 2023, in response to wildfires in Maui, one of the Hawai'ian islands, the US government declared a state of emergency in Hawai'i. The major news outlet reported that global climate change, prolonged drought on the Hawai'ian Islands, and high-speed wind caused by Hurricane Dora were significant causes of the ferocious wildfires in Maui. US coast guards and soldiers stationed in the Hawai'ian islands were quickly deployed to rescue people. However, Hawai'i has suffered from militarized slow violence since the US annexation in 1894, a violence and a silent war that has changed the Hawai'ian ecosystem and undermined indigenous people's livelihood and ecological knowledge. Many environmentalists, scholars and local antimilitary activists argue that US colonialism, settler colonialism, militarization, tourism and profit-driven agricultural business (i.e. sugar and pineapple plantations) are the major players of slow violence.

The US annexation into Hawai'i accelerated the transformation of traditional agriculture into highly profitable sugar and pineapple plantations, which required intense human labour and a large amount of fresh water. Since these plantations extracted water resources, soils became drier and vulnerable to drought and wildfires. Even after

Hawai'ian agriculture no longer relied on sugarcane, the agricultural landscape could not be returned to pre-European contact or be suitable for crops (Spencer et al., 2020, pp. 45–57). The slow violence of maximizing profitable mono-product over biodiversity alienated indigenous people from their ancestral land and accumulated wisdom about crops and food. As Hawai'i has been the US military's strategic outpost in the Pacific, the islands share similar militarized landscapes with Yongsan Park contaminated with disposed petroleum, radioactive emission, oil spillage in the drinking water system and the ocean, and more. In addition, tourism is a militarized project in the Pacific. Military personnel are key tourism markets on militarized islands from O'ahu to Guam and from Puerto Rico to Okinawa. Tourist amenities are viewed as necessary for attractive and harmless military sites (Davis, 2015, p. 91). Tourist facilities and soldiers' rescue missions hide ecological destruction accelerated by US bases and tourism, just as tourist facilities disguise militarized violence in US base towns and add friendly faces to these bases.

Developers and neoliberal capitalists are likely to perceive wildfires in Maui as an opportunity to gentrify the island. Wildfires shocked the already fragile ecosystem of Hawai'i and, simultaneously, are perceived to create a clean slate as if a new capitalist market could be implemented. Canadian journalist Naomi Klein (2007) details how disaster capitalism operates in regions where natural and human-made disasters and wars wreaked havoc, such as tsunami-torn areas in south-east Asia in 2004, Hurricane Katrina wreaking havoc on New Orleans in 2005, and war-torn Iraq. While multinational corporations and a small number of global capitalists have reaped lucrative profits from developing destroyed areas, local residents have been dispersed by disasters. These developers already had plans to gentrify tourist hotspots and oil-storage places. Analogous to the biblical apocalypse for a new world, disasters create opportunities to extract resources and enact their developmental plans without people's resistance and governmental regulations. The ecological system is slowly destroyed until catastrophe occurs and never recovers after crises. As a result of excessive tourism and the militarization of the island, Maui locals had suffered from housing shortages, skyrocketing rental prices, and high living costs even before the wildfires. We do not know whether they can return to their homes or find affordable houses after disaster capitalists 'redevelop' and 'reconstruct' the island on the remains of wildfire ruins.

Ecofeminist theology as anti-war feminist theology in the Age of Militarycene

Ferocious wildfires, drought, floods and heatwaves across the globe seem to demonstrate that Earth violently responds to humans' slow but steady violence against it. Rob Nixon's slow violence (Nixon, 2011) is helpful, but it may not capture ecological beings' experiences of sudden and violent death. In other words, slow violence is always direct and eruptive violence against non-human environmental beings. Nonetheless, slow violence is useful in consciously exploring various forms of death in the Militarycene. How can we name and resist deaths in the Militarycene? First, I want to answer this question by problematizing the term 'Anthropocene'.

Anthropocene simplifies the complex and multifaceted structural issues behind ecocide or environcide, as it groups all human beings against nature. Thus, the frame of Anthropocene delimits our analysis of who is genuinely responsible for climate change and who is paying for and suffering the cost of ecocide. To emphasize the unequal geopolitical distribution of responsibilities for and suffering from climate change, political theorist Jairus Grove proposes the term 'Eurocene' (Grove, 2019, p. 5). European colonialism, conquests, wars, global order and the spread of Western capitalist lifestyles have accelerated environcide, while the global poor clean up trash and lose their livelihood to climate change. Eurocene is Militarycene: US-led militarization of the world is responsible for maintaining the neocolonial global order.

In contrast, wars and armed conflicts are concentrated in global South and formerly colonized lands; military industrial complex across the globe is located in poverty-stricken rural areas; new weapons and military technology are tested on islands in the Pacific; nuclear waste is exported to economically struggling countries; oil pipes cross through indigenous lands. These realities testify that the global poor and people of colour, including those living in industrialized countries in Europe, North America and East Asia, exponentially pay for the price of ecological destruction and climate change. How can we bring the deaths of non-human environmental beings and the global poor to critical theological reflection? Brazilian ecofeminist theologian Ivone Gebara has some answers to offer.

Gebara's ecofeminist theology: naming death

Based on social feminism and holistic ecology, Brazilian ecofeminist theologian Ivone Gebara (1999, p. vii) combines liberation theology with feminist theology in what she calls 'urban ecofeminism'. By critically observing hierarchical forms of life in the overpopulated city, Gebara illuminates the proximity of macro-politics to micro-politics. Namely, global capitalism, militarism and climate change are manifested in the everyday lives of the urban poor, especially women living in environmentally hazardous places. The women clean out trash created by the rich. The urban poor are not responsible for producing most waste or green gas. Many are also forced to leave their homes and move from one place to another. As the systematic exclusion of the poor from political and economic decision-making takes place, their lands and homes in rural areas and urban slums are destroyed and militarized. Gebara's critical observation of the lives of the urban poor demonstrates 'accumulation by pollution' not only in the Middle East but also in Latin America – in fact, all over the world. Thus Gebara argues for an alternative perspective to comprehend the proximity of macro-politics to micro-politics or the international to the personal. This alternative perspective can be summarized as 'inter-relationality' or 'interconnectedness'. The concept first points out the interconnectedness of various social structures, such as politics, neoliberal capitalism, militarism, racism, classism, patriarchy and (neo)colonialism, maintained through international laws, treaties and global institutions (i.e. the World Trade Organization). Simultaneously, inter-relationality is the reality of human life: we are connected to one another and to non-human environmental beings. Here, God is only revealed through interconnectedness among all beings and these beings' yearning for wholeness.

Interconnectedness among various forms of oppression illuminates the fact that multiple forms of death are entangled. Namely, spectacular deaths in a regional war indicate slow deaths in other places or in the future. The US military's aerial spraying of Agent Orange over jungles in Vietnam, Cambodia and Laos during its war in Indochina exemplifies how militarized deaths in south-east Asia are entangled with those in the United States.

From January 1962 to January 1971, the United States conducted Operation Ranch Hand to scorch jungles and rice fields in South Vietnam. US cargo planes regularly sprayed chemical herbicides, including Agent Orange, Agent White and Agent Blue, over forests, cropland, roads and villages. At least 20 million gallons of herbicides were sprayed over 5 million acres of woods and fields, or over 10 per cent of South Vietnam (Cusato, 2021, p. 2). Between 2.1 million and 4.8 million Vietnamese were directly exposed to high levels of herbicides without knowing their harmful effects (Cusato, 2021, p. 3). Since Agent Orange did not kill humans immediately, affected people – including civilians and soldiers as well as their children and grandchildren – who would suffer and eventually succumb to death have not been included in so-called body counts during the war in south-east Asia. Women miscarried or gave birth to children with severe disabilities or body deformities. People experienced painful cancers, fatigue and many symptoms related to dioxin, which debilitated them. More than 365,000 Vietnam War veterans and their children in the USA and 116,000 veterans and their children in Korea have suffered from severe physical and psychological side effects of Agent Orange, and thus been drastically harmed (Kim, 2020). While killing enemies in Vietnam, American and Korean soldiers were killing themselves and their offspring. Hence, some scholars and activists argue that the US military's use of Agent Orange should be punished as a crime against humanity because of the incalculably long-term damage to humans and nature brought by it (Kreike, 2021).

Political theorist Jasbir Puar (2017, p. xviii) argues that the opposite of bio-politics is not necropolitics, but 'sovereignty's right to maim'. As French philosopher Michel Foucault (1991) argues, bio-politics refers to sovereignty's manifestation of its power by protecting its people through various social apparatus such as hospitals, prisons, and even war. In contrast, Cameroonian political theorist Achille Mbembe (2019, pp. 66–92) analyses how sovereignty manifests its power by exercising its right to kill. In colonial warfare, settler colonialism, Black and indigenous ghettos and reservations, occupied territories, and many other places, we can observe sovereignty's right to kill the politically vulnerable and globally disenfranchised peoples. Most of them are racially and sexually minoritized women, men and children. Since maimed and disabled bodies are not killed, sovereignty can avoid being morally blamed for killing its enemies or subjects (necropolitics). However, sovereignty intentionally maims bodies in order to debilitate their livelihood. Maimed bodies are pushed to the verge of death rather than life. Sovereignty's right to maim also applies to the environment. The ecological/environmental system severely contaminated with herbicides may not appear dead but is surely debilitated. In the long run, all living beings in that area succumb to painful (or unnatural) death, as we already saw in Indochina.

Chemical herbicides used in South Vietnam have been sprayed over Oregon forests in the United States. According to the 2021 documentary film *The People vs. Agent Orange*, timber companies have employed helicopter pilots to spray mutagenic herbicides over Oregon plantation forests to kill weeds, shrubs and other plants that compete with trees harvested by the lucrative timber industry. As in Vietnam, Oregon citizens living in the mountains were exposed to toxic chemicals without knowing their multi-generational impact on health and the ecosystem. Oregon local government authorities – and even professors at Oregon State University – sided with timber companies, covering up the danger of toxic chemicals and their causes of miscarriage, congenital disabilities, cancer, lung diseases and more. Harmful pesticides and herbicides have been widely used in the United States over state parks, farms, mountains and private lawns. Monsanto, one of the five chemical corporations contracted with the US government to produce Agent Orange, is still manufacturing herbicides and even running the food patent business. For over 30 years, Monsanto has patented seeds, including crops, corn, vegetables and fruits, and controls the world's agricultural industry (Klein, 2014, pp. 134–6, 195–6). Monsanto's threat to biodiversity and death-bound business have been possible because of the USA's wars in Asia.

Since 1976, Oregonians in the mountains have been fighting against timber and chemical companies and the Oregon state government. They see the parallel between the war in Vietnam and their lives in the mountains rich with precious wood (Adelson and Taverna, 2021). Slow deaths in Vietnam caused by the US military campaign have been replayed inside the United States. Vietnamese farmers and rural Oregonians are connected in their disposability from the eyes of sovereignty, the military industrial complex, and capitalists. Simultaneously, they are connected in their yearning for wholeness, environmental activism, and the pursuit of justice.

How can we resist militarized death across the globe? In order to resist the militarized deaths of human and non-human beings, we must name deaths, critically interrogating how these deaths are interconnected. Interconnected deaths also reveal that our lives are bound up with one another.

Resisting death

Gebara (1999, p. 83) understands 'inter-relationality' as the primary reality constitutive of all beings, a notion that goes beyond consciousness and Western rationality. We may comprehend interconnectedness or imagine ourselves in the vast web of interconnected lives only at a metaphysical or spiritual level. Thus, relatedness can be understood as 'a religious experience, a cosmic condition, and an experience of the Divine' (Gebara, 1999, pp. 91–2, 102). Her ecofeminist theology can help us courageously and audaciously imagine resisting death.

First, inter-relationality as a reality and spiritual experience challenges the apocalyptic analogy to wars and natural disasters (the spectacles of death) and, eventually, disaster capitalism. The purpose of war, as argued previously, is to create a clean slate to impose the conqueror's economic and political interests on conquered lands and people. Capitalists perceive natural disasters exacerbated by humans as a clean slate or an apocalyptic opportunity to develop the wreaked areas for profits rather than to rebuild the environmental infrastructure for local people's resettlement and ecological recovery. Here, alternative theological reflections on disasters and apocalypse are necessary to hijack developmental projects from the military and profit-driven corporations.

Apocalypse is not the end of the world. Instead, it is time for God's creatures to appreciate how their lives are bound up with one another not only through death and suffering, but also through life and yearning for life. In the book of Revelation, the apocalyptic moment is not God's punishment for earth but the fall of the Roman Empire constructed upon patriarchy and hierarchical power structures. So, Revelation could be read as a description of how the world based on heteropatriarchal military capitalism would look. Australian queer theorist R. W. Connell (2005, p. 67) argues that the growing destructiveness of military technology, the long-term degradation of the environment and economic inequality are representative trends of the defence of hegemonic masculinity based on patriarchal heterosexual normativity. What Connell (2005, p. 216) calls 'hegemonic masculinity' is fed by compulsory heterosexuality. As the dominant ideas and practices of masculinity or the 'real man', hegemonic masculinity maintains the hierarchical relationship not only with femininity but also with other forms of masculinity represented by minoritized men (i.e. men of colour, gay men, male immigrants, and Muslim men). Hegemonic masculinity, in fact, sustains the institutionalized military and environmental destruction.

Second, like Connell, Gebara criticizes patriarchal heterosexual normativity embedded in mainstream Christianity and society for accelerating the alienation of humans from nature and human domination over nature. Ecofeminist theology illuminates the parallel between gender-based violence in a patriarchal society and environmental destruction. In a patriarchal society, women, sexual minorities and minoritized men are treated in the same way that non-human environmental beings are treated. Furthermore, the military requires patriarchy for its efficiency based on the hierarchical ranking system and killing enemies by 'otherizing' them first. Feminizing enemies is a standard military tactic to boost morale and strengthen militarized masculinity so that masculinized soldiers feel superior to enemies. Feminist international studies scholar Cynthia Enloe explains 'militarized masculinity' as the feelings of 'power and superiority over women and willingness to inflict violence on anyone deemed inferior', including non-human creatures (Enloe, 1988, pp. 71–93).

Similarly, American feminist theologian Susan Thistlethwaite (2004, p. 121) argues that militarism is a product of, and support for, 'the agnosticizing tendency in Christianity to denigrate the body and sexuality and to exclude them from the realm of the spirit'. In this case, militarized masculinity depends on the intentional separation of the body from the spirit, just as war alienates humans from nature. Alienation of one's body from spirit, especially among disposable labourers (i.e. the urban poor in Gebara's ecofeminist theology), and treating nature as dispirited material beings, are inevitable in military capitalism.

However, inter-relationality resists the separation between the body and the spirit, humans and nature, men and women, and even life and death. Here, I read Gebara's notion of inter-relationality through transnational feminist scholar M. Jacqui Alexander's elaboration on interconnectedness to imagine cross-border solidarity for environmental peace and justice. Recognizing the self as interconnected to all living beings can be compared to spiritual reckoning with a rediscovered reality of being. A deep appreciation of interconnectedness helps us recognize our deep yearning for the sacred and to move beyond an oppositional politic. As Alexander (2005, p. 282) argues, the justice work should make room for the deep longing for wholeness expressed on a material, physical, existential and psychic level because the neoliberal global power has produced 'fragmentation and dismemberment at both the material and psychic levels'. Indeed, the logic of colonialism and neoliberal capitalism divides and conquers various oppositional political movements and popular resistance for justice and peace. In this context, solidarity across differences becomes challenging to practise and to imagine. For Alexander, the source of yearning for wholeness is our deep knowledge that 'we are in fact interdependent – neither separate nor autonomous' and have 'a sacred connection to one another' (pp. 282–3). Hence, an oppositional politic might be necessary to start a movement but it cannot sustain us since it contradicts our desires to express interdependence and to be embraced by it. Our movement towards wholeness, or what Alexander calls 'the work of spirit and journey', opens our very core to a fundamental truth: we are connected to the Divine (the Erotic and the Sacred) through our connections with one another (p. 283). Such spiritual interconnectedness prompts us to assemble and reassemble ourselves in the community while working for social justice.

Environmental justice work in resistance to slow, fast and spectacular deaths of living beings necessitates the embodied practice of interconnectedness. This practice requires our holistic approaches to activism: spiritual, physical and material work for solidarity. At the same time, we must find creative ways of practising solidarity with non-human environmental beings by critically observing the interconnection of global social systems beyond the conventional Christian practice of stewardship over God's creation. Seeing humans in the vast web of life and death requires an alternative spiritual practice, a renewed Christian theology, and spiritual exercise, overcoming anthropocentric Christian views on God's love, justice, redemption and salvation. Most of all, theologians deeply concerned about climate change must critically interrogate how the US-led militarization has destroyed God's creation and separated and fragmented the interconnectedness of all living beings.

Conclusion

In arguing that Anthropocene is Militarycene, this chapter has critically analysed war against nature or environcide. The US-led militarization of the world for global peace and justice has slowly killed both humans and non-human ecological beings and destroyed the environmental infrastructure co-created by humans and nature. While 'accumulation by pollution' through the war business benefits only a small number of global capitalists, the cost of ecological destruction is distributed horizontally. Therefore, life-and-justice-centred liberation theology in our time requires us to analyse the death-bound political and economic system that targets both nature and the global poor as disposable for profits. In the light of Ivone Gebara's social analytical and theo-spiritual concept of inter-relationality, I reconstructed anti-war ecofeminist theology in resistance to militarized death. As a social analytical concept, inter-relationality illustrates the complex intersection of various forms of death across the globe as a result of transnational militarism. As a theo-spiritual concept, inter-relationality reminds us that all living beings are interconnected to one another in yearning for wholeness and the Divine. The intentional embodiment of inter-relationality can help us resist militarized death everywhere by conscientizing slow violence against nature and our own bodies.

Christians in Bethlehem in the occupied territories of Palestine cancelled Christmas there because of the war in Gaza. As of December 2023, more than 20,000 Palestinians, mostly women and children, have been killed by the Israeli Defence Forces' (IDF) airstrikes and carpet bombing. In solidarity with Palestinian victims killed and debilitated during the war, Christians in Bethlehem cancelled festive Christmas services, accentuating the true meaning of Christmas. God took human form to come to earth, live among God's creatures, and share the joy and tears of all living beings. Gaza has become an unliveable space slowly and steadily. IDF's genocide and environcide have taken the opportunity to remember the birth of God in the human form from Christians. If we conscientize silent suffering and the slow death of ecological creatures not only in Palestine but also in many war zones, we should have cancelled Christmas every year.

Note

1 I borrow the term 'irony' from Reinhold Niebuhr. Niebuhr states that 'Irony consists of apparently fortuitous incongruities in life which are discovered, upon closer examination, to be not merely fortuitous ... the person involved in it [the ironic situation] bears some responsibility for it ... the responsibility is related to an unconscious weakness rather than to a conscious resolution' (Niebuhr, 2008, *The Irony of American History*, kindle).

References

Adelson, Alan, and Kate Taverna (dir.), 2021, *The People vs. Agent Orange*, New York: ITVS.
Alexander, M. Jacqui, 2005, *Pedagogies of Crossing: Meditations on Feminism, Sexual Politics, Memory, and the Sacred*, Durham, NC: Duke University Press.
Connell, R. W., 2005, *Masculinities*, Berkeley, CA: University of California Press.
Cusato, Eliana, 2021, *The Ecology of War and Peace: Marginalising Slow and Structural Violence in International Law*, Cambridge: Cambridge University Press.
Davis, Sasha, 2015, *The Empires' Edge: Militarization, Resistance, and Transcending Hegemony in the Pacific*, Athens, GA: University of Georgia Press.
Enloe, Cynthia, 1988, 'Beyond "Rambo": Women and the Varieties of Militarized Masculinity', in Eva Isaakson (ed.), *Women and the Military System*, New York: St Martin's Press, pp. 71–93; quoted in David Vine, 2015, *Base Nation:*

How U.S. Military Bases Abroad Harm America and The World, New York: Metropolitan Books.
Foucault, Michel, 1991, *Discipline and Punishment: The Birth of the Prison*, trans. Alan Sheridan, New York: Vintage Books.
Gebara, Ivone, 1999, *Longing for Running Water: Ecofeminism and Liberation*, trans. David Molineaux, Minneapolis, MN: Augsburg Fortress.
Grove, Jairus, 2019, *Savage Ecology: War and Geopolitics at the End of the World*, Durham, NC: Duke University Press.
Haley, Bob, 2017, 'Unlocking the Causes of Gulf War Illness', University of Texas Southwestern Medical Center, https://utswmed.org/medblog/gulf-war-illness-cause/ (accessed 31.01.2025).
Kim, Tae-gwon, 2020, 'Koreans Were Victims and Perpetrators at the Same Time: Vietnam War', *Hangyeorae Archive Project*, 17 November.
Klein, Naomi, 2007, *The Shock Doctrine: The Rise of Disaster Capitalism*, New York: Picador.
Klein, Naomi, 2014, *This Changes Everything: Capitalism vs. The Climate Change*, New York: Simon and Schuster.
Kreike, Emmanuel, 2021, *Scorched Earth: Environmental Warfare as a Crime against Humanity and Nature*, Princeton, NJ: Princeton University Press.
Mbembe, Achille, 2019, *Necropolitics*, trans. Steve Corcoran, Durham, NC: Duke University Press.
Minbyun – Lawyers for a Democratic Society, 'The Return of the Yongsan Garrison: Where Does It Stand Now?', http://minbyun.or.kr/wp-content/uploads/2021/08/용산기지-소책자최종_저용량.pdf
Niebuhr, Reinhold, 2008 (1952), *The Irony of American History*, Chicago, IL: University of Chicago Press, kindle.
Nixon, Rob, 2011, *Slow Violence and the Environmentalism of the Poor*, Cambridge, MA: Harvard University Press.
Picard, Michael Hennessy, and Beigi, Tina, 2022, 'A Postcolonial History of Accumulation by Contamination in the Gulf' in Alexander Dunlap and Andrea Brock (eds), *Enforcing Ecocide: Power, Policing, and Planetary Militarization*, New York: Palgrave Macmillan.
Puar, Jasbir, 2017, *The Right to Maim: Debility, Capacity, and Disability*, Durham, NC: Duke University Press.
Spencer, Michael et al., 2020, 'Environmental Justice, Indigenous Knowledge Systems, and Native Hawaiians and Other Pacific Islanders', *Human Biology* 92.1 (Winter), pp. 45–57.
Thistlethwaite, Susan, 2004 (1996), 'Militarism in North American Perspective' in Mary John Mananzan et al. (eds), *Women Resisting Violence: Spirituality for Life*, Eugene, OR: Wipf and Stock.
US Government Accountability Office (2014), 'National Security Snapshot: Climate Change Risks to National Security', https://www.gao.gov/products/gao-22-105830#:~:text=Climate%20change%20poses%20threats%20to,in%20this%20area%20since%202014 (accessed 3.01.2025).
Vine, David, 2015, *Base Nation: How U.S. Military Bases Abroad Harm America and the World*, New York: Metropolitan Books.
Yim, Seonghui, 2023, 'You Cannot Visit the Yongsan Children's Garden, If You Know What It Hides', *Green Korea*, https://www.greenkorea.org/activity/peace-and-ecology/army/99989/ (accessed 3.01.2025).

4

Salvation and Liturgy Reimagined through Earth-centred Worship in the Age of Anthropocene: What has Salvation Got to Do with Mother Earth?

LILIAN CHEELO SIWILA

Introduction

Climate change has become one of the trending themes in current global research. From a theological perspective, the topic has attracted many theories and theological reflections, not only on how to address the problem, but who to blame for the continued degradation of nature. This has led to the need to seek alternative ways of doing theology. The destruction of the created order with all its beauty and the groaning of Mother Earth is more audible now than it would have been a few years ago. One of the theories prominent in the field of eco-theology is that Christianity is one of the contributors to the exploitation of nature. This is evident through the anthropocentric interpretation of certain texts of the Bible and the presentation of doctrines such as the doctrine of salvation which in most cases is taught with a focus on the salvation of the soul more than the whole creation, while the Genesis story is accused of legitimatizing the domination of the earth. What is clear, though, is that at the centre of every theological reflection on climate change is the doctrine of creation.

In our current context it is right to say that the cry of the earth has become more evident now than before, such that a day does not pass without hearing news about a natural disaster that has claimed lives and caused destruction to nature. While this is going on, media reports on natural destruction tend to be biased towards the loss of human lives with less consideration on the loss suffered by nature and other forms of livestock. Among the most common evidence of climate change in Africa is increased environmental degradation leading to serious deforestation and species depletion. The rate at which practical measures to curb these catastrophes are taken by various stakeholders, including the Church, does not go unquestioned. The absence of more practical and contextual approaches to address the problem of climate change is among the challenges faced by both the Church and society. Lastly, a capitalist hierarchical model of addressing the problem which seems to favour one type of approach over others has also not made things any better for those trying to solve the problem of climate change. Hence the aim of this chapter is to propose alternative and innovative ways of doing liturgy that speaks to ecojustice. The eco-liturgical practices proposed in this chapter are also meant to conscientize the Church on the need to seek for transformative ways of responding to ecological crisis.

Reimagining the doctrine of salvation through the ecological lens

'When God is angry heaven breaks loose' – these are words we sometimes hear. I want to begin this discussion with a conversation I had with students in my 2022 class that focused on introductions to Christian doctrine. In this section we were looking at the doctrine of creation. While we were busy discussing the traditional worldviews on the doctrine of creation and interrogating the literature on the subject matter, part of our province experienced a torrential rainfall that resulted in flooding in most parts of the country. This flooding that took place in KwaZulu Natal province in South Africa in April 2022 claimed several people's lives, livestock were drowned and properties were destroyed (this included homes, shops and churches); all were swept away by the water, leaving thousands of people homeless. Although the place where this disaster happened is near the sea, and one would associate this with strong sea winds, some of those who witnessed this catastrophe confessed that they had not seen this kind of disaster in this area before. One of the students who was part of my class was among those affected by the floods. This student narrated a scenario of how when he arrived home from school he was greeted by the realities of climate change. The houses and churches standing when he left home that day were no more, and some of the people whom he had spoken to in the morning had been swept away by the floods and others were buried in the mud. The question he posed to the class following this loss was, 'Does it mean that when God is angry and the heavens break loose, then human beings and nature become the victims? If so, where is the grace and salvation of God?'

The subject of the doctrine of salvation and how creation and all its natural resources experience what is sometimes termed the 'wrath of God' is one area that needs to be constantly questioned, especially in the current context where human intelligence seems to be more favoured than the wisdom of God in addressing issues of climate change. In this age of Anthropocene, the salvation of nature is not well embraced in theological reflections as a result of capitalist ideologies and its greedy approaches. Looking at all these factors, this student was indeed vindicated in questioning the saving grace of God versus what he saw as the wrath of God on humanity and nature. Some of the questions that this chapter seeks to answer are: 'Is there any place for nature in the doctrine of salvation? And, if so, how can the doctrine of salvation as understood in the African context be used to develop liturgies that are ecofriendly?' Some scholars (e.g. Ruether, 2003; Northcott, 2007; Jenkins, 2008; and Conradie, 2010) have argued that the doctrine of salvation cannot be separated from the doctrine of creation. Powell (2003), discussing the connection between the doctrine of salvation and the doctrine of creation, argues that any attempt to expound the doctrine of creation that overlooks these connections will be led seriously astray. Therefore, the kind of liberation theology proposed in this chapter is one of soteriology and healing and fullness of life. Mathew Jayath develops this argument further stating that:

> The creation of the universe was understood as a preparation for the creation of human beings and once human beings appeared on the scene, the cosmos became a stage for the drama in which the only actors were human beings and God. The Fall of human beings ... initiated the process of the incarnation of the transcendent God in the person of Jesus ... The redemption as seen from this theological paradigm was essentially an otherworldly salvation of human persons. This world was the valley of tears through which human beings had to travel to reach their eternal home which is heaven. The function of the church was to assist people in their journey ... Fundamentally, this theological paradigm negates the intrinsic value of the material universe. (Jayath, 2001, p. 60)

This kind of debate on the doctrine of salvation has been going on throughout the history of Christianity. The doctrine itself is multi-layered with different theories developed at different times in history. These theories were developed by the early Church Fathers, most of whom worked within their contextual realities. It is from this background of imagination of the doctrine of salvation that most Western-oriented churches developed their own teachings and liturgies that focused on the salvation of the soul as opposed to the salvation of the whole creation. Songs such as 'This world is not my home, I'm just passing through, my treasures are laid up, somewhere beyond the blue ...' by Albert Brumley (1905–77) creates an impression that human beings should not be concerned about what happens to this present world because it's not their final destination – they are simply sojourners. They have a better home in heaven with better vegetation and one that is free from all forms of environmental crisis, a land flowing with milk and honey, whose streams never run dry, with pavements of gold. I have many times listened to sermons – especially in funerals – where the pastor would remind the mourners that the deceased has gone to a better place while speaking of the present world as a place of evil and sin. These sermons are accompanied by a couple of hymns and songs that seem to endorse this kind of teaching. While this is true from our traditional and biblical teachings, such theologies need to be revisited and reinterpreted in such a way that the present world can also be seen as a better place. If the present world is pained with sin and evil, then who is to blame for its decay? Can a loving God give us an evil and sinful world while enjoying this heaven flowing with milk and honey? Definitely not. Genesis 1.29–31 answers this question more clearly. In verses 29–30 we see God handing a blameless world to humankind and making them responsible for all creation. Then verse 31 states, 'God saw all that he had created, and it was very good.' Throughout the creation story, the Bible is very clear in stating that God created heaven and earth and each had its own beauty.

Instead of the Church preaching about these eschatological messages that only prepare people for a new home in heaven that is better than the earthly home, why can't the Church also preach messages of how to make earth a better place and make heaven on earth? If God handed us a good and blameless earth, there is a need to revisit these theologies and propose alternative ways of addressing the doctrine of salvation. The Church needs a model of the liturgy that is ecologically friendly and contextual, hymns that speak of a renewed earth that returns its original beauty as described in Genesis 1, and a challenge for humanity to return the lost glory and keep this beauty.

Throughout human history Christianity is known to be the religion of salvation. However, the way in which Christianity has presented salvation has to a larger extent contributed to humanity's domesticating of the doctrine. According to Snyder, the Bible presents salvation as a colossal divine plan for the redemption of all creation and the restoration of all things (Acts 3.21). The plan to bring all things both in heaven and on earth, both visible and invisible, into reconciliation with God under the leadership of Jesus Christ is reflected right from Genesis to Revelation (Ephesians 1.10). In God's project, the plan of redemption is as broad as the scope of creation and the depth of sin, for 'where sin abounded, grace [has] much more [abounded]' (Snyder, 2007, p. 9). Therefore, in our understanding of the doctrine of salvation, the death and resurrection of Jesus, the first born of all creation, should be associated with healing and the restoration of all creation – meaning humanity and nature, since salvation is for all creation. At the same time it is also imperative to recognize that salvation and liturgy cannot be separated, so at the centre of every theological reflection on salvation is the teaching on liturgy. This is because liturgy cannot be separated from the restoration of God's people to God. In this case liturgy becomes the link between a reconciled people and God the reconciler.

Salvation in the African context

Salvation as understood in the African context does not carry an eschatological approach that destines one to heaven. Instead, the salvation one attains has much more to do with the now; it is holistic and looks out for the salvation of the whole of creation. All must be saved – both nature and humanity. To be saved from any form of destruction, or kept out of danger, does not seem to be very different from the salvation of the soul for eternity. The presence of danger calls for salvation, and both creatures and nature need this salvation. Talking about the concept of salvation in Africa, Sakupapa argues that:

> As an African notion of being and Bantu concept of the world, the notion of vital force was first extensively dealt with by the Belgian Franciscan missionary (Placide Tempels, 1959) in his Bantu Philosophy. In his view, vital force is the unifying notion that underlies Bantu cosmology, ethics and ritual. He opined that the notion of vital force as found among the Bantu includes of necessity all beings, namely: God, the living dead, humans, animals, plants and minerals (Tempels, 1959, p. 36). It is understood in terms of potent life or life energy. 'Force, the potent life, vital energy' (Tempels, 1959, p. 31) argued, 'is the object of prayers and invocations to God, to the spirits and to the

dead, as well as of all that is usually called magic, sorcery or magical remedies'. (Sakupapa, 2012, p. 428)

The holistic approach to salvation also requires that we revisit the Bantu ontology and cosmology as articulated by Tempels (and reinterpreted, and appropriated by, African theologians), which indicates a strong sense of respect for life. Sakupapa (2012) further argues that a conceptual framework of vital force is one that highlights the centrality of life and the inter-relatedness of beings (community). Within such a framework, the whole of reality is understood as inter-related, without any separation. An African concept of salvation with its respect for life is required in the project of climate justice. The idea of only seeing life as important when associated with human beings needs to be rejected in our eco-theological reflection, because denying other species an opportunity to life and flourishing has in some cases contributed to climate change due to the fact that the web of life is incomplete.

An ecclesiastical eco-liturgical approach to ecojustice

In responding to the previous discussion on salvation and creation, this chapter proposes a formulation of liturgies that are going to help the Church to confess the sin of exploitation of nature that has contributed to climate change in the name of economic development. In most African societies nature is revered as the indwelling of the Supreme Being and ancestors. Yet, over the past few years, the continent has experienced an enormous loss of forests and other natural resources to first world investors and also local people driven by economic greed. Natural resources, such as forests, rivers and mountains, are all seen as sacred spaces. This is why when calamities such as floods and droughts befall a community, the people are quick to point to the anger of God for sin committed by the community. A study conducted by Siwila (2015) among the Tonga people of the Gwembe valley, and the construction of the Kariba dam by the World Bank, show that, years after the dam was constructed (through forceful removal of the indigenous people, thousands of whom perished in the floods that resulted from the opening up of the banks of the river Zambezi during construction), the walls of the dam began to develop cracks, threatening to explode. While the architects were busy with investigations into the problem and trying to establish what could have gone wrong with the dam, one of the chiefs in the area took to the media to report that the reason why the dam kept developing cracks was because the ancestors were angry at how the events of the forceful removal of the people unfolded. He also mentioned that *nyami nyami*, the god of the River Zambezi where the Kariba dam is constructed, was angry because when the waters were parted by the wall *nyami nyami* was separated from his wife whom he believed to be on the other side of the river. The chief said that once in a while *nyami nyami* has tried to break the walls of the dam in order to get to his wife, thereafter causing cracks in the dam. He further suggested that the government of Zambia and the World Bank needed to do a ritual peace offering in order to stop this occurrence, as otherwise the dam will continue to crack. This kind of thinking is just one among many narratives that one would find in Africa when people's natural resources are tampered with. The whole idea of humanity committing sin against nature entails that human beings have to continuously be reminded of the need to reconcile with nature through divine intervention. This reconciliation is done liturgically in the form of prayer, sacrifice or worship. Hence the need for the Church to embrace an earth-centred liturgical worship for this kind of reconciliation.

Developing an earth-centred liturgy in the present Church

Charles J. Fensham and Sarah Travis (2017, p. 12) argue that before the word 'liturgy' was coined in Judeo-Christian worship practice, the work of the worship of God's people was enacted in certain ways. For example, the ancient Hebrew liturgy was captured in the poems of Genesis 1 and 2. This liturgy names the human being 'Adam' in Hebrew terms, meaning earth, dust or mud (*Adamah*); the authors further state that human beings are thus both 'of and in' the earth as environment. This poetic narrative of Genesis 1 and 2 is also used in the African form of eco-liturgical worship. For example, in the rain-calling rituals of the Tonga people of Zambia, songs sung by the worshippers remind them that they are from the earth and that Creator God who made them out of the soil is the maker of rain. Although the worshippers do not quote the Genesis story directly, most of their songs are attributed to this biblical narrative. The Psalms are also imitated through the praise of the Creator. What is very significant in this rain-calling ritual is the symbolistic liturgy displayed by the members involved in the worship. The liturgy includes songs, clapping of hands, sitting in a particular liturgical form, and the eating of a meal together after the ceremony. All these activities take place at a shrine.

Another example that this chapter would like to highlight on the issue of an earth-centred approach to liturgical worship is from the work of Daneel (1991), whose tree-planting Eucharist project among the African Initiated Churches in Zimbabwe produced what one would call an indigenous environmental revolution in the region. Through this liturgical practice, members of churches included the planting of a tree in their Eucharist service as part of their confession to God for humanity's destruction of nature. During the Eucharist service, each member who participated in the Eucharist was given a tree to plant as part of the liturgical celebration. This kind of liturgical approach to the celebration of the Eucharist did not only benefit the members of this church but also created an environmental revolution by regenerating the forests through the trees planted by church members. This created a relationship where both creation and humanity experienced salvation and reconciliation. As Fensham and Travis (2017) would argue, liturgy is an 'on earth' practice enacted by human beings who are on and of the earth and always inhabiting a particular culture and context in a particular time and place.

What, then, can the present Church learn from this practice? Clearly, it needs to undergo a serious theological reflection on how its current liturgy can be modified to be more contextual and speak to the realities of climate change. Ecological justice should not only be mentioned in the prescribed formal liturgies of the Church and sermons, but it also needs to be lived out by the members through practical ways. Ruether (2003) and Northcott's (2007) theology of eco-salvation should be the driving agenda for the Church's liturgy today. The resurrection of Mother Earth should not be associated with the eschatological hope of afterlife, but something that should be of the now. In the African context, the mainline churches – especially those of the reformed tradition – have many traditional observances that they can adopt and turn into eco-Sunday where the church does some practical activities to help serve Mother Earth. For example, churches can have litter Sundays where the whole congregation goes out to do a clean-up campaign in order to reduce plastic waste that endangers the environment. A church can also adopt an earth-centred worship Sunday liturgy and Holy Communion service where all members of the church are brought into reconciliation with nature.

Ecofeminist theologians have argued that unless the Church gives voice to the silenced Mother Earth, creation will continue to suffer at the hands of powerful greedy forces. The call by ecofeminist theologians reminds us that God's work of salvation of humanity is not complete without the salvation of creation. Klaus Nürnberger argues:

> Deforestation feeds a cycle of death. Population growth leads to an increased impact on nature: forests are chopped down, grazing is overstocked, agricultural lands are over-utilised, footpaths change into gullies, soil erosion takes away the topsoil, and water is polluted. The deterioration of the natural resource base again increases misery, thus leading to further population growth, further pressure against the system, greater security needs of the system, greater impact on nature, and so forth [in] a vicious circle, or rather a vicious network. (Nürnberger, 1994, p. 29)

Although there seems to be a lot of activities on tree planting in most parts of the world the point I'm making here is that the Church needs to participate in these activities liturgically and be able to demonstrate the sacredness of the process and engage in serious theological reflections that will lead to inner transformation of the lives of its members.

Towards an ecological reformation of the twenty-first-century Church

In many parts of the world the Church has sought alternative ways to address climate change, activities ranging from the theoretical to the practical. Ernst Conradie (2010) argues that an ecological reformation of Christianity is needed to become deeply rooted in each Christian tradition. Tradition thus becomes the cardinal point to earth-keeping in each context. At the same time a holistic approach to responding to climate change needs to be taken into consideration because issues of climate change are holistic in nature, and all are affected. This challenges the religious and ecclesial divides.

Conradie further argues that:

> ... in the age of ecological destruction, the church liturgy needs to move away from the Eurocentric traditional approach which does not provide enough room for ecological liturgical practices that are contextual and closer to the crisis in hand. Worship proclamation service and fellowship all require further reflections on how inclusive and relevant, it is to the ecological liturgical practices that are life affirming. (Conradie, 2010, p. 11)

Following the statements above, it is also important to mention that it is not the aim of this chapter to discard our traditional mainline liturgy but rather to call for alternative ways of responding, doing liturgy that is life-affirming, practical and contextual as alluded to by Conradie (2010). The interpretation of the creation story and some of the Psalms that are cited in our church liturgy need to be revised and made to be more ecologically inclined and practical, emulating the African model of ecological liturgical practices observed by Daneel (1991). The creation story has components that would not only make ecological liturgy exciting but also real and contextual to people. Illustrations such as God walking in the garden of Eden as captured in the Genesis 3.8 story could make an exciting liturgy where members of the church can be advised to see the church premises as their garden of Eden. Through this imaginative activity, members of the church should be reminded to keep the garden clean knowing that God, the owner of the garden, walks around the grounds. This symbolic form of practical worship will help decrease the litter that leads to pollution. The members' familiarity with the church grounds will also create a sense of embodiment and ownership that will lead to corporate communal responsibility and also make them see the grounds as a sacred space that needs to be kept clean and holy. Another model that a church can adopt from the African ecological worship practices is that of divine intervention for rain. Our churches have songs from mission hymn books that point to the need to call on God for the provision of natural resources such as rain. In Africa, most countries depend on agriculture as their main economic activity, hence the need for rain at the right time and in the right season cannot be overemphasized. The Church in Africa is a very important force to reckon with, especially when it comes to social issues, hence the same people found at the shrine praying for rain are the same people found in church on Sunday. It becomes easier for a church to adopt some of these traditional liturgical practices in their worship as a way of responding to climate change. The Church's involvement in 'rain-calling rituals' embodied within their church traditions will create a form of contextual eco-theology. Rain-calling rituals are mainly attended by women, and in Africa women make up the majority in the Church. Women who are in most cultures the leaders in these sacred places of worship can be assigned by the Church to perform eco-feminist liturgy that is inclined towards divine interventions for a plentiful rainfall and a better harvest. Although these rain-calling rituals were undermined by the Eurocentric form of worship brought by missionaries, the current ecological destruction caused by climate change pushes us to look back to the past for any alternative liturgy that will help save Mother Earth. This is because in the era of ecological crisis the need to re-weave and re-visit these teachings cannot be overemphasized. Biblical stories such as the story of creation need to be re-told in a more contextualized manner which does not remove it from the realities on the ground. Instruments that are found in our cultures need to be analysed for their life-giving aspects and incorporated into church liturgy so as to make meaning of a more localized and contextualized liturgical practice.

Towards a liberation theology for Mother Earth

In my analysis of the kind of liberation theology that will be viable for the liberation of nature, I want to start with the analogy used in an edited volume by Susan Brooks Thistlethwaite and Mary Potter Engel (1998). Using the building metaphor to express the radical challenge of liberation theology, they argued that liberation theologies are not about rearranging the furniture in the house of theology, or redecorating or remodelling the house, but rather it is about rebuilding the foundation (method) and redesigning the floor plan. These to me are very cardinal points to consider as we move towards reflecting on climate change from a more radical and justice approach. For a long time now, whenever the Church had wanted to address a problem that is not life-affirming to humanity or nature there has been a temptation simply to scratch the surface of change by either moving the theological furniture around or redecorating the issue with some doctrinal teachings of the Church. In this era of climate crisis, the Church cannot afford to do that but instead it needs to enter a complete transformation on how to respond to the problem at hand using radical measures where possible. Any liberation theology proposed for this work needs to be holistic and contextually inclined. It has to move away from the classical academic framework to a more hands-on practical approach. The key to this kind of liberation theory should be transformation. Our liturgy needs to be renewed in order to be relevant to the current ecological crisis.

Conclusion

In most African countries, as in other third world nations, deforestation is hugely motivated by the large-scale destruction of forests by foreign organizations with a capitalist mindset in the name of economic development. Therefore, complexities of climate change that have led to environmental crisis in most African countries call for the Church to resist such concepts and call for the liberation of the earth by interrogating some of the historical indigenous ways of saving nature. The frequent flooding in some of the countries in parts of Southern Africa have left some African countries with high levels of poverty. In addition, heatwaves throughout Africa call for a rethinking of ways in which the Church can join in this battle of addressing these catastrophes through the use of alternative theologies. I want to end this discussion with a quote from Mathew Jayath, who argues that:

> An authentic ecological understanding of human fulfilment calls for 'a decentring and recentring of human beings' in the world. It would require abandoning the anthropocentric perspective of the Priestly account of human beings called to subjugate and dominate the Otherkind (Gen. 1), and accepting the essential human kinship with the earth as depicted in the Yahwist creation account (Gen. 2) ... Thus, the decentring will help us move away from an anthropocentric, hierarchical and dualistic view of human beings and their fulfilment, and the recentring will contribute to the recognition of our essential interrelationship and dependence as well as our shared destiny. (Jayath, 2001, p. 72)

This is because the effects of climate change have not only affected our physical and material well-being, but have to a larger extend challenged our understanding of God.

References

Conradie, M. Ernst, 2010, 'The Salvation of the Earth from Anthropogenic Destruction: In Search of Appropriate Soteriological Concepts in an Age of Ecological Destruction' *Worldviews* 14.2–3, pp. 111–140.
Daneel, L, Marthnus, 1991, 'The liberation of creation: African traditional church perspectives', *Missionalia* 19:2, pp. 99–121.
Fensham, Charles J., and Travis, Sarah, 2017, 'What on Earth is Liturgy (Leitourgia)? Liturgy and Ecology', in C. W. Ayre and E. M. Conradie (eds), *The Church in God's Household: Protestant Perspective on Ecclesiology and Ecology*, Pietermaritzburg: Cluster Publications.
Jayath, Mathew, 2001, 'Ecologization of Eschatology: An Eco Theological Understanding of Human Longing and Fulfillment', *International Journal on Philosophy* (Disputatio Philosophica) 3, pp. 55–74.
Jenkins, Willis, 2008, *Ecologies of Grace: Environmental Ethics and Christian Theology*, Oxford: Oxford University Press.
Northcott, Michael, 2007, *A Moral Climate: The Ethics of Global Warming*, Maryknoll, NY: Orbis Books.

Nürnberger, Klaus, 1994, 'Towards a New Heaven and a New Earth' in John W. De Gruchy and Charles Villa-Vicencio (eds), *Doing Theology in Context: South African Perspectives*, Cape Town: David Philip, pp. 139–51.

Powell, Samuel, 2003, 'Introduction to the Doctrine of Creation in its Historical Developments', *Participating in God: Creation and Trinity*, Minneapolis, MN: Fortress Press.

Ruether, R., 2003, 'Ecological Theology: Roots in Tradition, Liturgical and Ethical Practice for Today' *Dialog* 42, pp. 226–34, https://doi.org/10.1111/1540-6385.00162 (accessed 6.01.2025).

Sakupapa, Teddy Chalwe, 2012, 'Spirit and Ecology in the context of African Theology', *Scriptura* 111.3, pp. 422–30.

Siwila, Lilian Cheelo, 2015, 'An Encroachment of Ecological Sacred Sites and its Threat to the Interconnectedness of Sacred Rituals: A Case Study of the Tonga People in the Gwembe Valley', *Journal for the Study of Religion* 28.2, pp. 138–53.

Snyder, Howard, 2007, 'Salvation Means Creation Healed: Creation, Cross, Kingdom, and Mission', *The Asbury Journal* 62.1 (Spring 2007), pp. 9–47.

Tauli, Corpuz, 1996, 'Reclaiming Earth Based Spirituality, Indigenous Women in the Cordillera' in Rosemary R. Ruether (ed.), *Women Healing Earth: Third World Women on Ecology, Feminism, and Religion*, Maryknoll, NY: Orbis Books.

Thistlethwaite, Susan Brooks, and Engel, Potter Mary (eds), 1998, *Lift Every Voice: Constructing Christian Theologies from the Underside*, Maryknoll, NY: Orbis Books.

5

The 'Garden on Fire': An Ecological Reading of the Day of the Lord in the Old Testament

NOKCHARENLA

Introduction

The world today is marked as the Sixth Mass Extinction; this is a mass extinction project whereby humans are recognized as being the major drivers in leading our entire creation into extinction. The ecological crisis has come to stay because we have caused it to arrive at the point where it is. In the face of this crisis, theology cannot stay silent and follow the multiple interpretations of the Bible that support the activities of the ecological crisis. Qualitative interpretation through socio-historical analysis for the liberation of creation is the need of the hour. Such is the concept of the 'Day of the Lord' in the Old Testament, a profound theme that holds great spiritual and ecological implications. Rooted in ancient Hebrew prophetic literature, it has been interpreted in various ways. It is often associated with divine intervention, judgement and representing a time of reckoning and restoration.

This chapter explores the deep ecological interpretation of this concept, emphasizing the urgent need for a paradigm shift in our perception of nature. This is done by comparing *forest*, which is a self-sustaining ecosystem, with *urban areas and cities*, a creation influenced by human activities, through the lens of ecology. An attempt is made to show how this concept can act on the frantic call made towards anthropogenic activities, just like the prophets of this concept cherished. An analysis on the effects of interpretation upon nature will be the basis for a call to action towards the 'Anthropogenic' ecological crisis.

Forest, a self-sustaining mechanism

Forest is sacred; forest is the heart of nature. It is intricately tied to the existence of the land and the people. It is a natural vegetation/reservoir supporting a variety of biodiversity, forming a complex ecosystem (Bhargava et al., 2019, p. 48). Forest has a profound influence on the structure and function of the human habitat (Salim and Ullsten, 1999, p. 2). It is a complex ecosystem, and its cycles indicate a self-sustaining quality of forests and life (Jhariya, Meenah and Banerjee, 2021, p. 150). *Forest is wisdom.* It teaches us about the cycle of life. When the leaves fall it becomes humus and soil that protects the earth, recycling nutrition and water, revitalizing springs, wells and streams.

Speaking from the indigenous and tribal community, there is always a deep sense of connection or a culture of conscious conservation which recognizes the fundamental interdependence of all phenomena. The rationale of attributing sacredness to forest by the indigenous tribal communities is a cultural conservative response to civilization that perceives nature/forests as merely a dead raw material. For the indigenous communities, forest is not merely a timber mine, but it is like an umbilical cord that connects the mother and the infant and implies the power of sustenance (Shiva, 2015, p. 78). The attribution of sacredness to forests in itself was, and is, an action plan of assembling the entire community for the sustainable use of forest resources. However, with the intensification of the expansion of human activities, the sacredness has been ripped off from the forest. The objective valuation of forest has triggered the varieties of biodiversity it supports. And the result is chaos – chaos for the entire creation, a space not liveable for God's created order.

The relationship between urban development (garden) and nature

As mentioned in the introduction of this chapter, the world today is experiencing the Sixth Mass Extinction. The created order is hypernatural, meaning that everything created by God, which was meant to function as a symbiotic existence, is now caused to behave in uncertain ways. To this catastrophic reality, one major point of reference to understand this reality comes from John Dryzek, one of the first social scientists to document the core features and implications of modern ecological problems. Dryzek suggested that there is an increasing realization that ecosystems interact with other ecosystems. Also, ecosystems have emergent properties, meaning their behaviour is not reducible to knowledge of their constituent parts. This he further explained by stating that:

> Ecosystems self-regulate on the basis of feedback loops within their component systems. As a result of these properties, environmental problems display a range of characteristics. They are non-reducible, which means that resolution cannot be guaranteed by resolving only a part of the problem. They are highly variable in a temporal and spatial sense, which means that the extent of the problem or the seriousness of it might not be the same in different places and at different points in time. (Huitema et al., 2014, p. 124)

Dryzek's explanation on connectivity and variability exhibits the urban-city struggle with the extreme uncertain ecological crisis that has been created by human beings. It is the feedback loops from the other related components in the ecosystem that require utmost care and attention. The feedback loops can be the unsustainable use of minerals, like unsustainable mining projects that negatively impact the territorial and aquatic ecosystem. When the negative impacts are not regulated, it results in more complex ecological crises to the extent of bio-accumulation of toxins in the entire food chain of creation. The neglected factors of unsustainable use of natural resources for a long period of time has led to most humans complaining about climate change today, which is another feedback loop. There is a striking resemblance between urban conurbations and 'garden'. Unlike forest, garden by nature is an anthropogenic creation. To be more specific, in the words of Joerg Rieger (2022, p. 3), garden can be referred to as a creation of Capitalocene, where the economic interests of a small and privileged group of people rule both people and the planet. Jason W. Moore also understands it as a system of power, profit and re/production in the web of life (2017, pp. 549–630). The human tendency to encroach is championed by Capitalocene, where the biblical concept of care for creation, including human beings, is buried under the ground.

Gardens are intentionally cultivated spaces, purposefully designed, and may contain a limited selection of plants. Comparing the garden, which is an anthropogenic creation, to that of our cities, which is also a human-built space, it is clear that the crisis is not 'natural' but instead a by-product of excessive greed. Rieger (2022, p. 3) rightly points out that theology can no longer limit itself to the religious, but neither can it limit itself to religion and politics without considering the economic flows of power in a global context. Doing theology that is liberative includes considering the feedback loops in all these areas. It is so because the anthropogenic spaces are no longer a space to look for life; instead, it has become a gas chamber – but one filled with the elite who want to claim the whole anthropogenic garden more than any animal in the jungle. Cities are burning in line with the ecological crisis and cannot be spoken of without understanding Capitalocene. McBrien describes Capitalocene as a 'Necrocene', a system that not only accumulates capital, but drives people to extinction (McBrien, 2016, pp. 116–37). For extinction to happen, natural resources need to be extracted beyond their limits. The minority that comprises the Capitalocene has pushed this agenda to its climax.

The development of urban areas involves the *extraction of land* to convert into urban spaces. The land stripped off from the native inhabitants becomes the home of the urban elite, where there is no space for the indigenous people of the land. The few who hold the lion's share create the urban spaces with the most lucrative lifestyle and standards. There is mass migration from the rural areas to the urban ones. However, this is exactly the agenda of Capitalocene. Mustafa Ergen rightly points to the agenda: a reduced rural population becomes the most favoured reason for urban developers in identifying the left-behind rural areas as ripe for development ones (Ergen, 2016, p. 89). Just as a planted garden is not well-adapted to the local climate and soil, requiring human maintenance to survive, to meet the needs of this, urban developers focus on economy and attribute 'value' to forest/nature. The defining factor in terms of the relationship between forest and garden (urban space) is human design, and cities are built on the basis of the policy of selective human preferences and values (Aronson et al., 2016, pp. 2952–63).

Urban cities as anthropogenic gardens in crisis

In the creation narrative, the primal mandate for the whole of creation was to establish a creative partnership, which is generative for all. However, care for creation is replaced by the politics of selective development of the gardens (urban spaces) by looting from the forest. When speaking of the habit of looting, the topic of colonialism cannot be left untouched. To loot freely comes with a certain commission of power. This is followed by a sense of privileged rights: that nature can be used however and whenever. This is followed by the excessive accumulation of wealth in the hands of the few. This chain reaction is perfectly explained by Vandana Shiva in a podcast called 'Covid, Capitalism, Climate: The Way Forward' (Rabble Radio). Shiva defines the purpose of colonialism as being commerce. But this commerce was brought about by force and further sanctioned by letters patent (Fenner and Budhu, 2021). Letters patent in the period of colonialism were issued by kings and queens, presidents or heads of state. Such letters sanctioned the searching out of 'heathen' and 'barbarous' lands, then to have, hold, occupy and enjoy them. In practice, this meant colonizers lived in these lands, building there and fortifying the structures, and suppressing the so-called 'heathen' and 'barbarous' people. The Queen of England at this time, Elizabeth I, issued letters patent from time to time to her subordinates. These sanctioned the taking of others' land in faraway countries in the manner described above (Willis, 2019, p. 20). This echoes Genesis 1.28: to fill the earth and to subdue and have dominion. But this role was replaced by monarchs during colonialization, with their sole aim being to discover, conquer and subdue. Shiva opines that the difference between that colonization and modern-day Capitalocene is, today, the billionaires are the gods. Such billionaires include the popes; they define Roman Catholicism. Billionaires are also kings and queens. They rule huge swathes of the world. And they are also the merchant adventurers whose private jets are flying around the world, while most people's mobility has been curtailed (Fenner and Budhu, 2021). The context was once the Covid-19 pandemic, but this observation still holds true today. Because of this licence to loot, ecological crisis has come to stay. Because the feedback loop of the interconnectedness was not the primary concern for the looters, the consequences have accumulated just as such people have accumulated wealth. Enriching the Capitalocene garden with the fruits from the jungle is absolutely a colonial mindset. But the people looted from have to pay the price and experience the uncertain change in the cycle of nature. For humans to save what is left of nature, ecological crisis should be the basic necessity for economics. But today, urban development has taken centre stage and nature continues to be neglected. The garden is 'on fire' for a number of reasons:

1 The focus of urban development is driven by Gross Domestic Product (GDP); this is the market value of all final goods and services produced in a country in a given time. But it does not say anything about the damage caused to forest/nature as a result of the production of those goods and services.
2 Aimed at connecting people, urban conglomerations have created more spaces for vehicles than for people, adding to the ever-increasing

global temperature. NASA concluded that July 2023 was hotter than any other month in the global temperature record as a result of heatwaves.
3 Building of so-called 'residential areas' on the margins of cities still requires proximity to that city. Hence vehicles create extensive and stable zones of pollution.
4 Demand for food for a rapidly growing population has led to dependency on chemical-intensive farming. This affects our limited water resources and leads to drought and the desertification of large areas.
5 People travel from the garden of their houses to the garden of their workplace while being in the back seat of a car, train or bus, focusing on their phones and ignoring all the garbage and homeless people filling the streets.
6 Temperature increase is experienced drastically as a result of the construction of apartments and large buildings (Sujathamma, 2019, pp. 579–82); cities built around coastal areas experience major flooding. The year 2023 has seen extreme and lethal flooding all over the globe, including severe landslides. Humans, the most vulnerable in the web of life, end up dead or missing.
7 Climate crisis in 2023 has unleashed disasters in an intensified form. Floods continue to be one of the most devastating results, where the poor pay the cost of the climate crisis contributed to by multinational corporations and the rich elite. Bangladesh, the home of labour exploitation is, for instance, one of the many countries that faced heavy rainfall leading to major flooding in 2023. The UNOSAT FloodAI Monitoring Dashboard on Bangladesh reported a total exposed population of 2.4 million in the four districts between 5 and 10 August 2023, with 1.3 million people affected. Of this 1.3 million, 630,000 women and 480,000 children (0–19 years old) were affected (Bangladesh: Floods and Landslides – August 2023). Tea garden workers in Bangladesh are mainly women; they are one of the most marginalized groups in the country with limited access to education for their children because their areas get affected extensively by floods.

Vandana Shiva aptly connects these crises, or the mindset of colonialism (to loot), to the mindset of corporate capitalism because the core for both is private monopolized maximization of commerce. Shiva laments the lost value of ecological balance and social justice as intrinsic to the right to a livelihood. She further gives a warning as to what the eco-imperialist would respond to the existing climate crisis by saying the following:

The eco-imperialist response to the climate crisis is to grab the remaining resources of the planet, close the remaining spaces of freedom, and use the worst form of militarized violence to exterminate people's rights and people themselves when they get in the way of an insatiable economy's resource appropriation, driven by the insatiable greed of corporations. (Shiva, 2009, pp. 19–23)

All these factors prove humans have demonstrated themselves to be clever *ecosystem engineers,* but incompetent ones because the common denominator for all this urbanization is *ecological recession* and *extermination of the vulnerable,* which is the total opposite of what forest provides (Adams, 2013, p. 230). Hence there is a need to counter the culture of carelessness, and this chapter tries to understand the concept of the Day of the Lord in the Old Testament in terms of interpretation towards realizing the urgency of the world in crisis.

'Day of the Lord' in the Old Testament: prophetic voice for ecojustice

Climate crisis intersects many areas of social justice because in the web of life defined by Fritjof Capra, all created order was intended to participate cohesively. When the symbiotic relationship is altered to a parasitic relation, there enters the issue of intersectionality, with each one affecting the other. Hence the Old Testament prophetic movement held justice and righteousness, the twin emblem of God the Creator, to the highest degree. This twin emblem was the founding principle upon which prophets in the Old Testament pioneered the prophetic movement. God's justice sensitizes us to the needs of others and impassions us to seek justice, especially for the poor and vulnerable. Justice, in the words of Dawn M. Nothwehr (2012, p. 279), is then the 'work of love brought to the social and public realm, placing the needs and interests of all in proper balance for the common good'. This understating of justice was put forward by the prophets of the Old Testament by analysing the social structures and systems developed by the elite few of their times.

The theme of the Day of Yahweh/Lord was a counter-culture employed by the prophets of the Old Testament, in the context of liberating the oppressed and the vulnerable. However, over a period of time, this theme has given more licence to the looters of nature and enslaver of humans to continue to do what they love to do. The liberating aspect of the Day of the Lord became a letter patent to conquer and rule. Old

Testament scholars have tried to give their explanation on the theme. Scholars such as Hermann Gunkel and Hugo Gressmann believed that the Yom YHWH (Day of the Lord) is the starting point of Hebrew eschatology, which is the study of the end times or the final events in history (Gunkel, 1901, p. 242). Gerhard von Rad (von Rad, 2001, p. 119) calls it 'the very heart of prophetic eschatology' that consists of two aspects: (a) as an event when God will unify Israel and Judah and restore creation; however, this will also bring punishment and judgement; (b) a time in the future when God will judge the entire nation. However, historically, this day has seen partial fulfilment, affecting not only Israel's enemies but also Israel itself.

Historical interpretation can be found in the work of some Old Testament scholars such as Gerhard von Rad who described the Day as a day of Yahweh's battle: when Yahweh routed his enemies on the battlefield and gave victory to Israel – or, rather, the day on which Yahweh would do so in the future (Barton, 2012, p. 64). John M. P. Smith interpreted the Day as being the time or desired period when an era of great glory and prosperity would be inaugurated for Israel, as a special nation with a divine mission. This hope for a great future was fostered by the traditional conception of a *God-ordained commission* (Udoekpo, 2010, p. 45). H. H. Rowley (1956, p. 177) maintains that although most of the predictions of the prophets concerned issues of their own times and contexts, these passages were also of the future, pointing to the time when God's wrath will consume all that is evil, and usher in the age of bliss.

However, if we read the texts where the Day of the Lord is the prophets, 'time' was not the primary focus. Be it in terms of an event in the future that is overly emphasized, or a past fulfilled event, there is one thing in common – that is, *prophetic cautions through a social lens*. The theme was used as a prophetic formula, to create a sense of moral and ethical values towards the entire created order, not only humans. The Day of the Lord brings the underlying reality of Capitalocene society. This is a society best described by Leonard Boff (2009, p. 235) as being a society *not* founded on principles of life, communal well-being, shared involvement or mutual support among individuals. Instead, it is rooted in economic considerations, leveraging power and mechanisms that generate prosperity by depleting natural resources and exploiting human labour. The prophetic caution through this theme was: the economic system of the elite few aims for boundless expansion in the quickest timeframe, requiring minimal investment while maximizing profits. Those who can thrive in this dynamic and adhere to this rationale will amass capital and attain affluence, albeit through an ongoing process of exploitation.

Though the Day of the Lord imageries are used mostly in metaphor form, it has real-life events. Metaphors per se can be used without harm, but when the metaphors become a real-life issue threatening the lives of people at risk, that is where the problem lies. Though the prophets in the Old Testament might not have used the language of intersectionality, their voices echo the concept. Prophets were ecologists who understood how the entire creation is inter-related. An apt example of prophetic intersectionality can be found in the words of Dr Martin Luther King, Jr that 'No one is free until we are all free.' Justice was the crux of the prophets because climate crisis impacts all of us. To address the issue of impacting lives, systems of power and oppression need to be addressed continuously. The connect made between urban areas as 'anthropogenic gardens on fire' calls for the pyramid of oppression to be challenged and dismantled; and to dismantle it, the people who are the most affected by 'global boiling' need to be addressed by the elites. The existence of a high-risk population further points to current social inequalities. The increased frequency of extreme weather events like floods, wildfires and droughts endanger the lives of people at the periphery. Multiple examples can be found in the Old Testament on the relationship between land, people and capitalists.

Joel

The book of Joel and the locust invasion is mostly read metaphorically as the Day of the Lord, when an army in the form of locusts will come to attack Jerusalem and Judah. The historical interpretation does not allow for an ecological reading; however, the social location of the text allows for a real-time ecological disaster. Joel can be referred to as an ecological prophet who knew the impact of anthropogenic activities upon the earth.

The plausible social location of the book is the Persian Empire of the fifth century BCE when wine was the royal currency. To make wine the royal currency, monoculture was introduced in the form of viticulture. This stripped the land of multiple crop patterns to one single crop/seed. From an economic point of view this seems progressive, but from an entomological point of view this is disastrous – the reason being that single species of crop increases the potential for a host of insects to breed. This relationship allows for a real-life locust invasion to happen in real time, not metaphorically. The locust invasion impacted the farming community the most, not the Persian royalty. This further pushed the farmers into poverty and hunger, adding to an already heavy yoke. Joel speaks of the Day again in the form of cosmic destruction like 'darkness and gloom, clouds and thick darkness' (Joel 2) which can today be recognized as the ever-increasing carbon emissions – which in the ecological reality is called the Dark Horse of Climate Change Drivers. From an urbanization point of view, the footprints of any empire are not those of lush green grass, but that of carbon footprints. Joel says, 'Before them the land is like the garden of Eden, but after them a desolate wilderness' (2.3). This is a clear parallel to the larger scale clear-felling of forests for agriculture or mining, like a destructive army moving across the landscape.

Amos

Israel at the time of the prophet Amos expected the Day of the Lord to be a time of national triumph, as a day of light. But in Amos 5.16–18 the Day of the Lord is described as a day where 'In all the squares there shall be wailing; and in all the streets they shall say, "Alas! alas!" They shall call the farmers to mourning, and those skilled in lamentation, to wailing; in all the vineyards there shall be wailing, for I will pass through the midst of you, says the LORD. Alas for you who desire the day of the LORD! Why do you want the day of the LORD? It is darkness, not light' because of Israel's crimes against justice and against God's righteousness (Armerding, 2001, p. 188).

This imagery shows how ecological crisis intersects class, resources and poverty, but this imagery is lived out by those people who are affected the most by climate crisis. Amos could see the social and ecological crisis arising out of the eighth century BCE economic extravagance yet social disparity to the level of buying 'the needy for a pair of sandals'. The upper class was a minority made up of the king, royal family and the aristocratic nobility, who accumulated wealth while the poor lower class was starving and extorted. The import/export trade of Israel and Judah during this period was extravagant. Imports of luxury goods, military material, and the monumental architecture benefited the elite few, who constituted less than 2 per cent of the total population. The foodstuffs and fibre exported to pay for these imports were produced by the peasant majority. Peasant producers could not consume what was exported; what they consumed, conversely, could not be exported. Land-grabbing was the order of the day.

Hence, the crisis that arises from an economy aimed at large-scale production at the cost of the peasant community is aptly described in Amos 5.19. It explains the gravity of the day as 'like someone who runs from a lion, and meets a bear, or like someone who goes into his house and puts his hand on the wall, and then is bitten by a snake.' It is the peasant population, women and children, who are most affected during a human-induced natural disaster. The workforce of the economy is neglected when disaster hits, leaving the vulnerable with nothing to rely upon.

The prophetic dimension of an unfulfilled future found in the eschatological beliefs in terms of interpretations allows for the present ecological crisis. The future is so disconnected from the present. It overlooks the prophetic call to the urban elite to amend their ways by showing how God is transparently revealed in the present laments and cries of nature and the people (Gottlieb, 2004). Hence, the Day of the Lord is not about a 'life after' but 'life itself'. Our responsibility is to participate as finite interconnected created beings with metanoic consciousness (Kearns and Keller, 2007, p. 409). Bruce Waltke's bifocal vision of both the future and the present is the vision we should wear to understand our ongoing crisis (Waltke, 2007, pp. 806–7). The goal is to be realistic about the tragedy of existence and to the interpretation of the present anthropogenic crisis.

The prophetic wisdom that arises from the Day of the Lord from an ecological point of view prompts readers in the direction of the concept of intersectionality. Taking the cue from the Day of the Lord, the prophetic call to ecological consciousness was not without its social aspect.

Interpretation towards symbiotic and intentional culture

Interpretation towards an intentional culture seems to be unachievable based on the ecological crisis we humans have created. But 'imagination', which Walter Brueggemann in his book *Prophetic Imagination* uses as a tool to counter dominant consciousness, allows for that unachievable ideology to become concrete actions. This tool from the point of view of the Day of the Lord from an ecological paradigm will begin by considering the following paths of justice and liberation.

'Hyper-natural', not as natural calamities

Justice to nature and the vulnerable will occur when the media stops defining ecological crisis as a natural disaster. *Hyper-natural* (Fretheim, 1991, pp. 385–96) means nature in excess or creation not functioning as it was created to be by God. We must begin to interpret nature not functioning as God intended, rather than a *natural calamity*. We find these *hyper-natural* warnings in the Day of the Lord as an introduction to the theme. Malachi speaks of the Day as 'burning like an oven': the Day would burn in such a way that it will leave them 'neither root nor branch' (Malachi 4.1–2). Though these things are being used metaphorically, we can see parallels today in the form of heatwaves, which affects health in the form of heatstroke, heat-exhaustion and similar. Issues on impacts of disasters are discussed globally, but under the umbrella term 'natural disaster'. This effectively shifts the accountability for the damage, death and cost of a calamity to 'nature' or 'acts of God'. We must begin by acknowledging that in almost every instance there are fundamental human-induced factors to the crisis that urban areas are experiencing. In terms of ecological crises, most of us assume that they are 'unexpected', but we must realize that they are a 'predictable result' of interactions between the physical environment, the built environment and communities experiencing them (Puttick, Bosher and Chmutina, 2018, pp. 118–20).

The anthropocentric valuation of nature must be eliminated

Aldo Leopold (1989, p. 204) rightly opined that, 'the role of *Homo sapiens* has to be changed from "conqueror" of the land community to plain member and citizen of it in the web of life'. The profit-oriented motive towards nature promoted by multinational corporations must be revoked, because the world that we live in today has become a conditional world of 'if'. If we do not amend our ways in nurturing creation, it will be the equivalent to falling into the trap we have made for ourselves.

Recognizing indigenous ecological wisdom

Chaos is the definition of our society today and we are facing the consequences of our own making. There is no doubt that technological advancement cannot be ignored. Instead, it should be improved. There should be a point of convergence where the indigenous practices and technological advancements meet in order to save what is left of nature.

We cannot abruptly stop consuming; instead, the low-impact practices of utilizing natural resources that the indigenous communities have always followed can be merged with technological inventions. It should be regenerative not extractive, leading to the development of an economy that is not linear or extractive, but a circular economy of fostering the web of life.

Personal engagement with nature

A sense of personal responsibility needs to be established with ecological crisis. There needs to be a shift in the focus on environmental news. At present, the focus on ecological crisis is still on the devastating impact on humanity. For instance, climate news mainly focuses on extreme weather events such as wildfires, hurricanes, cyclones and heatwaves, the direct 'threats to human lives, loss of property and infrastructure'. We focus on the rise in sea levels as a result of melting glaciers which pose a significant threat to coastal communities, leading to 'human and vulnerable displacement of the population'. But the understanding that humans were never at the centre should be realized.

Conclusion

Interpreting the Day of the Lord in the Old Testament from an ecological perspective underscores the ethical and moral imperativeness protecting and caring for the natural world. Anthropogenic crisis highlights the fact that the ecological crisis we face today is the result of anthropogenic activities or – to be more precise – the specific activities of the elite few. Recognizing our role in these issues means acknowledging our responsibility to address and reverse the damage.

We must re-evaluate our values, behaviours and societal systems to create a symbiotic relationship with nature. Hope for today and for the entire creation is not a white man coming in clouds and restoring it. Hope is engaging in stressful situations or, to be more precise, facing the ecological crisis but not being pessimistic or denying reality. Hope is to keep striving for justice in the midst of the impossible. The call to action to protect and save what is left of creation for present and future generations is a crucial message at hand that we must all press hard for.

References

Adams, William Mark, 2013, *Against Extinction: The Story of Conservation*, Earthscan.
Armerding, Carl E., 2001, *A Guide to Biblical Prophecy*, Eugene, OR: Wipf and Stock.
Aronson, M. F. J., Nilon, Charles H., Lepczyk, Christopher A. et al., 2016, 'Hierarchical Filters Determine Community Assembly of Urban Species Pools', *Ecology* 97.11, pp. 2952–63.
Barton, John, 2012, *The Theology of the Book of Amos*, Cambridge: Cambridge University Press.
Bhargava, R. N., Rajaram, V., Olson, Keith and Tiede, Lynn, 2019, *Ecology and Environment*, New York: CRC Press.
Boff, Leonardo, 2009, 'Social Ecology: Poverty and Misery' in David G. Hallman (ed.), *Ecotheology: Voices from South and North*, Eugene, OR: Wipf and Stock, p. 235.
Ergen, Mustafa, 2016, 'Relationship between Population and Agricultural Land in Amasya' in Mohamad Samer (ed.), *Urban Agriculture*, Croatia: InTech, p. 89.
Fenner, Victoria, and Budhu, Resh, 2021, 'COVID, Capitalism, Climate: The Way Forward', *Rabble Radio*, 30 June, https://rabble.ca/podcast/covid-capitalism-climate-the-way-forward/ (accessed 30.06.2021).
Fretheim, Terence E., 1991, 'The Plagues as Ecological Signs of Historical Disaster', *Journal of Biblical Literature* 110.3, pp. 385–96.
Gottlieb, Roger S., 2004, *This Sacred Earth: Religion, Nature, Environment*, London: Routledge.
Gunkel, H., 1901, *Genesis*, Gottingen: Vandenhoeck und Ruprecht.
Huitema, Dave, Jordan, Andrew, van Asselt, Harro and Patterson, James, 2019, 'Polycentric Governance and Climate Change' in Victor Galaz (ed.), *Global Challenges, Governance, and Complexity: Applications and Frontiers*, Cheltenham: Edward Elgar Publishing, p. 124.
Jhariya, Manoj Kumar, Meenah, Ram Swaroop and Banerjee, Arnab, 2021, *Ecological Intensification of Natural Resources for Sustainable Agriculture*, Singapore: Springer Nature Singapore.
Kearns, Laurel, and Keller, Catherine, 2007, *Ecospirit: Religions and Philosophies for the Earth*, New York: Fordham University Press.
Leopold, Aldo, 1989, *A Sand County Almanac, and Sketches Here and There*, New York: Oxford University Press.
McBrien, J., 2016, 'Accumulating Extinction' in J. W. Moore (ed.), *Anthropocene or Capitalocene?*, Oakland, CA: PM Press, pp. 116–37.
Moore, Jason W., 2017, 'The Capitalocene, Part I: On the Nature and Origins of our Ecological Crisis', *The Journal of Peasant Studies*, pp. 549–630.
Nothwehr, Dawn M., 2012, *Ecological Footprints: An Essential Franciscan Guide for Faith and Sustainable Living*, Minneapolis, MN: Liturgical Press.
Puttick, Steve, Bosher, Lee and Chmutina, Ksenia, 2018, 'Disasters Are Not Natural', *Teaching Geography*, 43.3 (Autumn), pp. 118–20.
Reliefweb, 2023, 'Bangladesh: Floods and Landslides – Aug 2023' and 'Chattogram Division Flash Flood and Monsoon Rain 2023 – Situation Report No. 0', https://reliefweb.int/disaster/fl-2023-000157-bgd (accessed 11.09.2023).

Rieger, Joerg, 2022, *Theology in the Capitalocene: Ecology, Identity, Class, and Solidarity*, Minneapolis, MN: Fortress Press.

Rowley, H. H., 1956, *The Faith of Israel: Aspects of Old Testament Thought*, London: SCM Press.

Salim, Emil, and Ola Ullsten, 1999, *Our Forests, Our Future: World Commission on Forests and Sustainable Development*, Cambridge: Cambridge University Press.

Shiva, Vandana, 2009, 'Soil Not Oil Environmental Justice in an Age of Climate Crisis', *Alternatives Journal*, pp. 19–23.

Shiva, Vandana, 2015, *The Vandana Shiva Reader*, Lexington, KY: University Press of Kentucky.

Sujathamma, C., 2019, 'Environmental Issues of Urban Areas and Wellness', *International Journal of Scientific Development and Research (IJSDR)* 4.5, pp. 579–82.

Udoekpo, Michael Ufok, 2010, *Re-thinking the Day of YHWH and Restoration of Fortunes in the Prophet Zephaniah: An Exegetical and Theological Study of 1:14–18; 3:14–20*, Switzerland: International Academic Publisher.

von Rad, Gerhard, 2001, *Old Testament Theology, Vol. 2*, Louisville, KY: John Knox Press.

Waltke, Bruce K., 2007, *An Old Testament Theology: An Exegetical, Canonical, and Thematic Approach*, Grand Rapids, MI: Zondervan.

Willis, John Dudley, 2019, *Our Violent World and the Ethics of Jesus*, Lulu Publishing Services.

PART 2
Ecology

6

Taiwan Indigenous Women and Ecofeminism

WAN JOU LIN

Introduction: construction of subaltern knowledge

Taiwan is embarking on a new phase in the reconstruction of its subjectivity, particularly in relation to a diverse and multicultural society within Taiwan, east Asia, and beyond. Following the lifting of Martial Law in 1987, Taiwan has reshaped its focus towards indigenized epistemology. The holistic worldview inherent in the epistemology of indigenous peoples has emerged as a central force in the recreation of Taiwan's subjecthood. This serves as an inspiration in addressing the disorder imposed by neoliberal economic globalization on a global scale.

Indigenous communities, possessing an intricate understanding of the natural environment, have cultivated a profound respect and wealth of knowledge. Upon examining the prevailing knowledge systems, one transitions to mainstream knowledge systems, which often reflect a dominance of Western and male subjective experiences. Consequently, certain perspectives, particularly those of females and indigenous individuals, tend to be marginalized. Indigenous epistemology, deeply intertwined with all living beings sharing their land, stands in contrast to Western epistemology that frequently perceives humans as separate and dominant over nature.

Similar to indigenous men, indigenous women have faced repression, enduring not only colonial violence but also patriarchal dominance. Thus, indigenous women's epistemology can encompass subaltern momentums to counteract various forms of repression stemming from Western male dominance and a growth-based economic system prioritizing profit over life. This chapter explores indigenous literature and ecological epistemology through the lens of ecofeminism, aiming to elucidate how, under the influence of neocolonialism, female wisdom and traditional values have been eroded. It reflects on the indigenous experiences in Taiwan.

Indigenous women have traditionally been regarded as the keepers of the home, concerned with body, mind, spiritual and emotional health, leaders of faith and rituals, and the souls of ecosystems. From the perspective of ecofeminism, diverse social, economic and cultural traditions exhibit distinct patterns for biologically different groups, thereby influencing the knowledge systems they develop. Indigenous knowledge, deeply connected to the collective memory of indigenous communities, remains rooted in its cultural matrix. Consequently, the reconstruction of cultural memories plays a crucial role in regenerating knowledge, facilitating the continued practice of ecological knowledge in contemporary settings.

The Education Act for Indigenous Peoples underwent a comprehensive amendment on 19 June 2019 in Taiwan, incorporating Article 5. This article underscores the development and enrichment of indigenous knowledge systems. It mandates that the central indigenous authority collaborate with other governing bodies responsible for education, technology, culture, and more, to establish long-term plans for constructing indigenous knowledge systems. Furthermore, it encourages and rewards academic research and knowledge studies conducted by indigenous peoples, marking the initiation of a more inclusive development of indigenous knowledge systems in Taiwan.

Pei-Lun Chang (張培倫), in his works from 2008 and 2009, was among the pioneers in identifying three key backgrounds for the reconstruction of indigenous knowledge systems: the heightened autonomy of indigenous peoples, the pressing need for ethnic education systems, and the rapid transformations occurring in their living environment. This undertaking specifically addresses methodology, epistemology and systems theory. The construction of indigenous knowledge systems is fundamentally perceived as a critical strategy for decolonization. This involves not only compensating for deficiencies in mainstream knowledge systems but also reconstructing indigenous identity through indigenous knowledge subjectivity, thereby achieving equality in power and resource allocation. Chang emphasized the holistic worldview and indigenous philosophy as core categorical knowledge. Moreover, he envisioned potential pathways for the transformation of indigenous knowledge.

These ideas were subsequently employed to assess contemporary indigenous education (Pei-Lun Chang, 2008). Chang drew inspiration from Linda Tuhiwai Smith's indigenous research agenda, which centres on the survival, recovery, development and self-determination of indigenous peoples, striving in four directions: decolonization, healing, transformation and mobilization. Tibusungu 'e Vayayana, in his research on Cou traditional domain resource management knowledge, categorized knowledge into three types: social, historical and spatial. He endeavoured to outline the framework of Cou knowledge systems using a three-dimensional spatial approach, enhancing the clarity of the overall image.

The indigenous peoples' movement in Taiwan began in the 1980s and transitioned into the 'post-indigenous movement' after 1990. Subsequently, it actively participated in grassroots cultural reconstruction efforts by consistently 'returning to the homeland'. The post-indigenous movement and the contemporary construction of indigenous knowledge systems can be viewed as parallel endeavours, with both seeking to construct indigenous identity, culture and knowledge as the subject.

Women and nature revisited

The term 'ecofeminism' was coined by Françoise d'Eaubonne in 1974. It describes the potential of women to influence environmental changes, aiming to draw attention to the role women play in initiating an ecological revolution. In ecofeminism, several key tenets emerge:

1 There is a clear connection between the oppression of women and the oppression of nature.
2 Understanding the characteristics that link these two forms of oppression is crucial for a proper comprehension of both.
3 Feminist theories and methodologies must incorporate an ecological perspective.
4 Solving ecological issues necessitates considering feminist viewpoints.

Ecofeminism challenges traditional feminism by re-examining the relationship between humans and non-human nature. The capacity of ecofeminism to reveal the interconnectedness of environmental and social injustice makes it an urgent and timely field of inquiry for the current issues of the Capitalocene. Ecofeminism arises out of the need to address challenges such as climate change, land degradation, species extinction, and the disproportionate effects of these changes on specific communities of women and their livelihoods. It highlights the contradiction between the human causes of environmental destruction and the human capacity to protect and care for the biosphere. The expansion of capitalism, particularly with the industrial revolution, connects technological advancement, changes in political economy, and the enabling of unprecedented exploitation of the natural world. Ecofeminism critiques global capitalism for its accompanying exploitation of 'others' – women, the poor, the colonized, and the non-human. It underscores the interconnectedness of environmental injustice and social injustice, particularly gendered social injustice.

Indian ecofeminist Vandana Shiva stands as one of the most prominent female thinkers and activists in the global South. Together with many scholars from the global South, she emphasizes that non-Western feminism does not solely stem from Western 'advanced' countries, but grows from local contexts with their struggles and nourishments. Mainstream ecofeminism faces criticism for being 'too Western' and 'too white', making it imperative to consider local contexts of anti-colonializations and resistance to capitalist invasion to balance, and ideally subvert, the Eurocentrism and economism inherent in modern perspectives. Decolonizing knowledge is a central concern in non-Western feminist movements.

For a considerable period, Shiva has been involved in seed conservation and the self-reliance of small-scale organic farming in India. She emphasizes that nature is not lifeless but possesses creative and dynamic forces. The organic processes between natural life and human life continue to shape our local and global ecology. Shiva essentially redefines the concepts of democracy, freedom and rights, traditionally European political concepts, from an ecological and life perspective. The concept of earth democracy is particularly meaningful, reimagining the political concept of 'democracy' to include all inhabitants of the earth, considering equal value for all. This value is intimately related to the processes of life, encompassing both organic life processes and geological processes within the earth. Shiva points out that the genetic modification and patenting of life by transnational capital continue the legacy of colonial capitalism and represent a dual 'biopiracy' against the creativity of people and nature in the global South. Thus, the significance of protecting seeds extends beyond the freedom of seeds themselves to encompass the freedom of farmers and the land that co-evolve with the seeds.

Shiva is not the only thinker expanding the concept of democracy to the non-human realm, and many contemporary cross-species perspectives are heading in this direction. Australian ecofeminist Val Plumwood's critique of Western scientific rationalism, rooted in her situated knowledge, aims to achieve a culturally significant critique through philosophical writing. Plumwood, involved in environmental conservation as a white Australian, offered a thorough critique of the Western binary opposition of rationality. She argued that the 'hyper separation' between culture and nature has long led to a crisis of reason, exacerbating the ecological crisis. Plumwood emphasizes the roots of this crisis within the mind–body dualism of Western tradition, advocating for 'ecological humanities perspectives' to establish an 'ecologically rational society'. Later, she turned to the intellectual resources of Australian indigenous wisdom, advocating for 'animist materialism' or philosophical animism. Plumwood believes that animist materialism helps reconcile science and faith, prompting science to reimagine materiality in a richer way, steering clear of the mind–body dualism presupposed by reductionist scientism and God-created perspectives.

Plumwood and Shiva, despite different starting points of knowledge and specific concerns, resonate deeply in their ecological political agendas. Plumwood advocates placing humans back within the ecology while including non-humans in an ethical community, essentially referred to as society. Her new cultural project is an ecological political image, akin to Shiva incorporating non-human existence and the entire earth system into a political blueprint of democracy, freedom, rights and participation.

A revisit to Taiwan indigenous literature from an ecofeminist perspective

Taiwanese indigenous female writers occupy a significant and evolving position within the broader context of indigenous literature in Taiwan. Their work delves into themes of identity, gender, cultural preservation, and the relationship between indigenous communities and the broader society in Taiwan. Indigenous women engage with issues of cultural preservation, revitalization and transformation, reflecting efforts to maintain traditional practices, languages and worldviews, as well as adaptations to contemporary realities. The intersections of gender with ethnicity, class and other aspects of identity remain crucial. How do female indigenous authors navigate these intersections, and how do they address issues such as gender-based violence, discrimination and inequality within indigenous communities? In their work, how they address environmental concerns and the relationship between their communities and the natural world differ from their counterparts, engaging with postcolonial themes that address the historical impact of colonization on indigenous communities and the ongoing effects of colonialism. We also find that female indigenous authors portray the survival of their communities, cultures and languages in the context of modernization and globalization.

Ecofeminist voices provide numerous narratives affirming our human and material connections with place, community and others. Like a pebble tossed in water, ecofeminism's ripples continue to expand, touching wider circles of narrative, culture and history. Ecofeminism's postcolonial perspective, present from the start and strongly expressed in the anti-capitalist critiques of Val Plumwood, Vandana Shiva and Maria Mies, has gained clear articulation. Ecofeminism's postcolonial perspective is permanent in explorations comparing indigenous writers from diverse colonial histories. Initially expressed through colony invasions, conquest of land, enslavement of humans and animals, exploitation of ecologies, and annihilation of culture through the imposition of religion, language and lifestyle, the enterprises and operations of colonialism are perpetuated by today's multinational corporations and the economics of industrial capitalism.

Taiwan indigenous literature processes a worldview that highlights the association between women, motherhood and nature, portraying women as nurturers and caregivers of the environment. This perspective draws parallels between the exploitation of women's bodies and the exploitation of the earth. Particularly under this perspective, indigenous female writers in Taiwan critique unsustainable models of development and question the costs of rapid economic development on both indigenous communities and the environment. In Taiwan indigenous literature, female writers often expose the spiritual dimensions, involving an examination of how women's spiritual experiences connect with ecological concerns and contribute to a deeper understanding of human–nature relationships. Female writers provide a nuanced understanding of how ecofeminism is manifested in Taiwanese indigenous literature, shedding light on the ways in which literature becomes a powerful medium for exploring the intricate connections between gender, nature, culture and society in the Taiwanese context.

Ecofeminism addresses a range of ecological and gender-related issues that are pertinent to the island's social, cultural and ecological landscape. Taiwan's indigenous cultures have a deep connection with the land, and ecofeminism in this context recognizes the vital role of indigenous women in traditional ecological knowledge and stewardship. Indigenous women's knowledge of medicinal plants, sustainable agriculture and natural resource management is a critical aspect of ecofeminist analysis.

It delves into how colonization disrupted indigenous communities' relationships with the environment and how indigenous women have resisted and adapted in the postcolonial era. It examines how women in Taiwan's indigenous communities demonstrate resilience and adaptability in the face of environmental changes, such as natural disasters or shifts in land use.

In the 1990s, following a shift from social activism to literary construction within the indigenous movement, there emerged a profound reconnection with the concept of indigenous identity, traditional indigenous civilizations, and the natural landscape – a sort of return to the roots. The literary works could exemplify a genre of writing that exposes social injustice in the present world. Meanwhile, the development of indigenous Mandarin literature among Taiwan's indigenous peoples began in the 1980s, and during this period the category of 'indigenous literature' underwent a meticulous clarification and definition, accompanied by a substantial accumulation of high-quality literary achievements. The development of contemporary indigenous Taiwanese women's literature has occurred primarily within the past two decades. Several notable authors have emerged, here in chronological order of their publications, including Lyiking Yuma (Atayal 1954–), *Inheritance – Stepping Out of Accusation* (prose, poetry, 1996); Liglav A-wu (Paiwan 1969–), *Who Wears the Beautiful Clothes Woven by Me* (prose, 1996); Remuy Aki (Atayal 1962–), *Mountain Flute and Sound* (prose, fiction, 2001); Ah Chi Gu (Amis 1983–), with *Anna, Taboo, Gate* (fiction, 2002); Faisu mukunana (Tsou 1942–), with *My Dear Aki, Please Don't Be Upset* (prose, 2003); Dadelavan Ibau (Paiwan 1967–), *Goodbye Eagle* (prose, 2004); Yulan Toyuw (Atayal 1968–), *Atayal Shadowweaver* (prose, criticism, 2004); Dong Shu-ming (Han and Pinuyumayan 1971–), *Souvenir* (poetry, 2007); and Min-ghsia Lisin Micyang (Amis 1976–), *She and Her Poetic Life* (prose, poetry, 2007). The development of contemporary indigenous Taiwanese women's literature is a relatively recent phenomenon spanning nearly two decades. Lyiking Yuma from Atayal published *Inheritance – Stepping Out of Accusation*, which encompasses cultural discourse, societal critique, ethnic historical memory, personal memories recollections, and several modern poems. Liglav A-wu's *Who Wears the Beautiful Clothes Woven by Me* explores family life memories, the life images of indigenous women, and broadly engages with aspects of ethnicity, gender, class and various facets of Taiwan's history. These works by Lyiking Yuma and Liglav A-wu represent the birth of a writing community within Taiwanese indigenous literature, particularly as indigenous women's literature.

In Yang Tsui's 楊翠 book *Minorities Speaks*, distinctive for its portrayal of minority discourse within indigenous women's writing, is the most extensive and comprehensive study of Taiwanese indigenous women's literature. *Minorities Speaks* employs a macroscopic view, family history narrative, subject identity, and diaspora classifications to analyse the works and discuss their aesthetic styles. Furthermore, Lin Yu-hsin's 林瑜馨 'Atypical Phenomena in indigenous Literature: A Case Study of Dadelavan Ibau, Dong Shu-ming, and Ah Chi Gu Explores Non-traditional Aspects of Indigenous Literature', refers the term 'non-traditional' to writing phenomena that do not primarily focus on indigenous activist themes. It engages in dialogue with the literary phenomena and styles found in the works of three female authors.

In Taiwanese indigenous literature, female writers have shown proficiency in writing about returning to their homeland, reinterpreting traditional culture, and expressing their unique perspective on land and nature, which differs from the mountain and sea writing often found in the works of indigenous male writers. Liglav A-wu refers to a residential community of indigenous people as a '部落 bùluò' (community), connecting this community through geographic, ceremonial, traditional domains, and various other connections. For instance, in the case of 'Liglav', the term does not denote a familial surname but rather the name of the slate-roofed houses in the community to which A-wu belongs. Female writers portray the land and nature as the roots of indigenous culture, simultaneously emphasizing the detrimental impact of modern economic development on the natural environment. Indigenous female authors remain a marginalized minority within Taiwanese indigenous literature.

What brought us forward: indigenous female voices in literary work

When compared to their female counterparts, indigenous male authors have already established a patriarchal cultural lineage within the natural space through their writings. With a particular focus on the literature of writing about land and the natural environment, when we face climate collapse we must aim to explore the distinct spatial imagination and bodily experiences within the writings of indigenous women.

Rimuy Aki's *Homeland of Mountain Cherry Blossoms* portrays the experiences of the Bona family, members of the Tayal people, who migrated from northern Hsinchu to Sanmin Township in Kaohsiung for cultivation in the 1960s. Written in the third person, the narrative expands indigenous stories and mountain ecology by incorporating elder tales into historical spaces, describing the true Tayal spirit (Tayal balay) that constructs the subjectivity of the Tayal tribe. The migration process of the Tayal people connects local spaces of Paiwan, Bunun and Kanakanavu peoples, revealing differences, conflicts and assimilation among ethnic groups. The Tayal people's ecological concepts in cultivation and hunting grounds reflect the significance of hunter taboos and traditional knowledge in modern ecological balance. Rimuy Aki's writing also emphasizes cultural ecological feminism, highlighting women's positive traits in nurturing, caring and intuition while rejecting the notion of the inferiority of women and nature compared to men and culture. The construction of traditional ecological knowledge among indigenous people also indicates that the connection between men and culture is a mistaken binary world in Western male philosophy and destruction.

In the environmental ecology of indigenous traditional ecological knowledge, Rimuy Aki's *Homeland of Mountain Cherry Blossoms* primarily focuses on the Tayal people's migratory cultivation and hunting process. Agriculture is the main occupation for the Tayal people, with forest activities equivalent to a vegetable garden, making agriculture the core of life, while hunting serves as the pillar of spirituality (Rimuy Aki, 2002, pp. 113–14). Rimuy Aki explains the distinctive features of the Tayal people's migratory cultivation, highlighting that if tribal population density becomes too high, both cultivation and hunting activities are affected. Opinion leaders (*mrhuw*) and elders (*bnkis*) in the tribe would propose migration and cultivation. Among Taiwan's indigenous groups, the Tayal people have the broadest traditional territory, with development patterns divided into vertical and horizontal development. These two patterns intertwine after migration, forming natural development phenomena within the natural trajectory.

During the cultivation process, Tayal people and the mountains, rivers and forests have a peaceful coexistence known as '*gaga*'. The Tayal people believe that humans nurture life from the mountains and forests' land and would never deplete the land and forests' life. Regardless of population density or cultivation methods, there are natural regulations:

> The cultivation of a piece of land usually does not exceed three years, and on average, it will be abandoned after two years to let the land rest. Before leaving, people will plant alder trees (iboh) in that piece of land to allow the land to rejuvenate. Alder trees can adapt to any

barren environment and can be used to grow mushrooms, or to build structures. Most importantly, alder trees are excellent soil improvers. The mycorrhizal fungi parasitic on their roots can absorb nitrogen from the air, having a nitrogen-fixing effect to improve soil quality. Of course, Tayal ancestors probably did not know about 'mycorrhizal fungi' or 'nitrogen'. The habit of planting alder trees on used land is the result of generations living together with nature. (Rimuy Aki, 2010, pp. 82–3)

Without an effective way to possess and transmit a rich 'traditional knowledge system', how could the Tayal people find harmony with nature? This 'traditional knowledge system' maintains natural energy and equips human survival conditions. The indigenous people's utilization of mountain and forest land reflects the inheritance of traditional ecological wisdom. Rimuy Aki, in *Homeland of Mountain Cherry Blossoms*, writes about the Tayal tribe's environmental ethics, placing humans in mutual dependence within the natural ecology. As a female author, Rimuy Aki vividly depicts the Tayal tribe's hunting culture and their keen environmental observations. Warren (1987) points out that ecological feminist ethics are contextualist ethics, encouraging people to tell various stories about their relationships, an approach that specifically elucidates their relationships with humans, non-human creatures and nature. The essence of ecological feminism is to redefine genuine humanity and make ethical decisions.

We are on indigenous land: situating the female indigenous knowledge

Taiwan's indigenous peoples possess what is known as 'Traditional Ecological Knowledge' (TEK). Guan Dawei 官大偉 explains that Western scholars have different interpretations of indigenous ecological knowledge, defining it as 'knowledge produced by people referred to as indigenous due to their unique interaction with the land' (2013, p. 74). Since the 1980s, there has been a flourishing trend in the study of indigenous traditional ecological knowledge, primarily as a result of conflicts between Western-dominated ecological conservation methods and the development of local indigenous communities. These conflicts arise both in relation to biodiversity and cultural diversity and in the increasing number of voices of indigenous peoples worldwide advocating for their rights. Therefore, conservationists, indigenous activists, local indigenous communities and national government agencies find it inevitable to address the relevance of traditional ecological knowledge to environmental conservation and local development. Consequently, the implications of traditional ecological knowledge and its applicability in social development have become significant research topics.

The traditional gender roles within indigenous communities related to environmental knowledge and cultural preservation perform their duties; this implies a certain division of power, and ethnic taboos. If traditional culture can only be inherited by its gender, order is the crucial issue. These roles may support or conflict with ecofeminist principles, and the role of indigenous women as keepers of ecological knowledge and their contributions to the preservation of biodiversity, sustainable agriculture and knowledge of medicinal plants.

Ecofeminist activists collaborate with, and support, indigenous communities in environmental protection and advocacy; the challenges and successes of such collaborations are discussed here. In the Australian ecofeminist perspectives, land rights play a practical and crucial context, which Australian indigenous women intersect with indigenous struggles for land rights, and territorial sovereignty reflects their unique perspectives on land ownership.

Ecofeminism speaks of indigenous resistance, which ecofeminist principles of the gender dynamics of such resistance efforts inform indigenous resistance to environmental exploitation, including logging, mining and large-scale development projects. Colonial histories and ongoing neocolonial practices intersect with ecofeminism in indigenous contexts and can be seen in the effects of land appropriation and environmental degradation on indigenous women and communities. After the 1980s indigenous movement, indigenous activists returned to their home community in order to seek indigenous subjectivity. Indigenous women especially inform resource management practices and efforts to regain control over traditional foods and agriculture from an ecofeminist approach.

Based on the research of 'Indigenous Peoples' Traditional Knowledge and Ecofeminism', Jolan Hsieh 謝若蘭 discussed the customary practices of the Amis: women traditionally take responsibility for the cultivation and harvest of fields, while men primarily engage in fishing and hunting. Although this appears to be a division of labour based on gender, it is in essence an established rule closely related to their social system. In the contemporary context of Cirakayan (Amis) people engaging in organic farming, the division of labour between women and men involves mutual respect and assistance. Despite specific roles assigned to men and women, they primarily share the workload. Agriculture is, in fact, the accumulation of results from various detailed tasks, and each step is crucial and cannot be overlooked or executed incorrectly. Especially in the cultivation process of organic farming, meticulous attention is required. Therefore, in many minor details, women and men have distinct but careful divisions of labour, aiming to ensure the complete protection of each step.

This differs significantly from past Amis practices in agriculture and hunting, where women entrusted certain tasks to men – such as operating large machinery because of their acquisition of technical skills. In the handling of different details for various crops, women share their experience and knowledge with men and work together – in activities such as using specific techniques to deal with pests. However, when it comes to sharing experiences and narrating their trial processes to others, men tend to be the primary voices. While not intentionally ignoring women's voices, it appears that women have become accustomed to this dynamic. From the perspective of ecofeminism, socio-economic and cultural traditions impose different socialization patterns on both genders. Men and women play distinct roles and possess different ecological wisdom in society. However, there is a tendency to provide opportunities for men to voice their opinions while overlooking the crucial contributions of women. This parallels the way discussions on resource development often focus on ecological balance and sustainable development, akin to civilizations relying on various traditional knowledge within the environment. In doing so, the importance of the partnership roles played by the two genders in the ecological sphere is frequently overlooked. In the case of the Cirakayan people, most of the agricultural work is carried out by women, which is somewhat related to the division of labour within families from an early age. Most women are trained in agricultural work from a young age, starting when they are still referred to as 'young women'. The primary focus is on producing the household's food source and maintaining the daily activities under a self-sufficiency model. This work includes not only growing vegetables and rice, but also animal husbandry, forming a comprehensive production mechanism. With the rapid changes in the environment and production patterns, the later work became somewhat disconnected from agriculture. Eventually, there was a return to agricultural work, primarily focusing on organic cultivation, establishing a communal farm in the tribe, and producing mainly organic fruit and vegetables. But today the scope of women's agricultural work has narrowed down to cultivating just a few vegetables and a few fruits. Traditional knowledge in the division of labour is intricate because each vegetable and fruit has different planting and care requirements. Usually, no single person possesses all the knowledge; it is distributed among individuals. Therefore, in this manner, cooperation and the exchange of knowledge become crucial (Hsieh, p. 92).

In the context of the Cirakayang tribe, the majority of farm work is carried out by women, influenced by the familial division of labour that began in childhood. Most women are trained to engage in agricultural work from a young age. Women's experiences in agricultural labour start from their early years as 'misses', mainly producing food for the household and maintaining a self-sufficient daily routine, involving not only vegetable and rice cultivation but also animal husbandry. As environmental and production patterns rapidly change, their later work becomes somewhat detached from agriculture, but with a return to organic farming being the primary focus, thus forming a communal farm. As noted, women's agricultural work narrows down to vegetable cultivation and the growing of some fruits. Traditional knowledge division is meticulous, as different species have various planting and care requirements. In this manner, cooperation and knowledge exchange become crucial.

If viewed from an ecological feminist perspective, there are different socialization patterns for men and women in society, influenced by social, economic and cultural traditions. Men and women play different roles and possess different ecological wisdom. However, opportunities for women to express themselves are often overlooked, mirroring the tendency in discussions of resource development based on traditional knowledge to focus on ecological balance and sustainable development, neglecting the crucial partner relationship between men and women in the ecological sphere.

Beyond ecofeminism in a Taiwan indigenous context

From the Cirakayan (Amis) people, we recognized Cirakayan men and women possessed different but unique knowledge based on their gender roles that had developed through traditional custom. The Cirakayan traditional custom has experienced capitalist modernization since Japanese colonization; assimilation policies undertaken by the government of the Republic of China and the mainstream culture of Han immigration, gender roles, and its (re)construction of knowledge have been falling into the trap of the male viewpoint being dominant. Rimuy Aki, in *Homeland of Mountain Cherry Blossoms*, writes about the Tayal people's environmental ethics, placing humans in mutual dependence within the natural ecology. Ecological feminists Maria Mies and Vandana Shiva noted that people under the capitalist patriarchy often feel alienated from everything. The lifestyle and endless consumption patterns of neoliberal economics lead people towards limitless consumer desires. Mies and Shiva point out that everyone should recognize and accept our commonality as humans, including our bodies and materiality, our carnality, and mortality.

From Taiwan indigenous women contexts, their experiences inspire us to accept that feminism doesn't necessarily need to perpetuate gender metaphors related to nature, but ecological issues must encompass conceptual, political, ethical and practical concerns, including gender stereotypes; moreover, we must transcend these gender stereotypes. As women, they are not trying to highlight how their experiences with nature are superior to those of men. We also find that even in the absence of specific female characteristics, with a connection to nature, when these activists become nurturers and protectors of life they can further contribute to a more holistic justice in the world. In this era of climate collapse in Capitalocene, who are we, what are we, what can we do, what should we do, and even what can we hope for, and all quests appear more urgent than ever before.

References (Chinese)

王秋今Chiu-Chin Wang,〈生態智慧：里慕伊・阿紀《山櫻花的故鄉》的三維生態學〉,《台灣原住民族研究》,第15卷第1期,頁281-311,2022年6月。

伐依絲・牟固那那Faisu. mukunana,《親愛的A'ki,請您不要生氣》,女書,2003年

利格拉樂・阿媩Liglav A-wu,《紅嘴巴的VuVu》,晨星出版,1997年。

利格拉樂・阿媩Liglav A-wu,《誰來穿我織的美麗衣裳》,晨星出版,1997年。

汪明輝 Tibusungu'e Vavayana (Ming-Huey Wang),〈台灣原住民族知識論之建構—以鄒族傳統領域資源管理知識為例〉發表於台灣原住民教授學會、東華大學原住民民族學院主辦「第一屆原住民族知識體系研討會」。壽豐,東華大學原住民民族學院國際會議廳,5月15-16日,2009年。

里慕伊・阿紀Rimuy Aki,《山野笛聲》,晨星出版,2001年。

里慕伊・阿紀Rimuy Aki,《山櫻花的故鄉》*Homeland of Mountain Cherry Blossoms*,麥田出版,2010年。

里慕伊・阿紀Rimuy Aki,《彩虹橋的審判》,新自然主義出版,2002年。

官大偉GuanDawei,2013,〈原住民生態知識與流域治理:以泰雅族Mrqwang群之人河關係為例〉,《地理學報》,70 期:頁 69-105。doi:10.6161/jgs.2013.70.04

明夏 禮幸・蜜薔Min-ghsia Lisin Micyang《她及她的詩生活》，白象文化，2007年。

林瑜馨Yuxin Lin，《原住民族文學的非典型現象- 以達德拉凡·伊苞、董恕明以及阿綺骨為例》Atypical Phenomena in Indigenous Literature: A Case Study of Dadelavan Ibau, Dong Shu-ming, and Ah Chi Gu explores non-traditional aspects of Indigenous literature，秀威資訊2015年。

阿綺骨Ah Chi Gu,《安娜、禁忌、門》，小知堂，2002年。

張培倫Pei-Lun Chang，〈建構台灣原住民族知識體系之規劃研究」計劃〉（未刊稿），2008年。

張培倫Pei-Lun Chang，〈關於原住民族知識研究的一些反思〉《台灣原住民研究論叢》5期，頁25-53，2009年。

張培倫Pei-Lun Chang, 2010。〈原住民族教育改革與原住民族知識〉《台灣原住民研究論叢》8 期，頁 1-27。

悠蘭・多又YulanToyuw《泰雅織影》，稻鄉，2004年。

楊翠Yang Tsui，《少數說話：台灣原住民女性文學的多重視域》*Minorities Speaks*（上、下），玉山社2018年。

董恕明Dong Shu-ming,《紀念品》，秀威資訊，2007年。

達德拉凡・伊苞Dadelavan Ibau《老鷹，再見》，大塊文化，2004年。

謝若蘭Jolan Hsieh、吳慧馨Hui-Hsin Wu，〈從生態女性主義觀點談原住民族傳統知識與習慣〉(Indigenous Peoples' Traditional Knowledge and Ecofeminism) 《臺東大學人文學報》第7卷第1期，頁73-98，2017年6月。

麗依京・尤瑪Lyiking Yuma，〈哭泣的土地〉，收於氏著，《傳承—走出控訴》，玉山社出版，1996年。

麗依京・尤瑪Lyiking Yuma，〈無休止符的悲歌〉，收於氏著，《傳承—走出控訴》，玉山社出版，1996年。

References (English)

Crutzen, Paul J., and Stoermer, Eugene F., 2000, 'The Anthropocene', *IGBP Newsletter* 41, pp. 17-18.

Ford, James D. et al., 2020, 'The Resilience of Indigenous Peoples to Environmental Change', *One Earth* 2 (June), pp. 531-43.

Foucault, Michel, 1972, *The Archaeology of Knowledge and the Discourse on Language*, trans. A. M. Sheridan Smith, New York: Pantheon Books.

Griffin, Susan, 1978, *Women and Nature: The Roaring Inside Her*, New York: Harper & Row.

Griffin, Susan, 1981, *Pornography and Silence: Culture's Revenge Against Nature*, New York: Harper & Row.

Grusin, Richard, 2017, *The Anthropocene Feminism*, Minneapolis, MN: University of Minnesota Press.

Harding, Sandra, 1998, *Is Science Multi-Cultural? Postcolonialisms, Feminisms, and Epistemologies*, Indianapolis, IN: Indiana University Press.

Hogan, Linda, 2008, *People of the Whale*, New York: Norton.

Hogan, Linda, and Peterson, Brenda, 2002, *Sightings: The Gray Whale's Mysterious Journey*, Washington, DC: National Geographic.

Kapoor, D., and Shizha, E. (eds), 2010, *Indigenous Knowledge and Learning in*

Asia/Pacific and Africa: Perspectives on Development, Education and Culture, London: Palgrave Macmillan.

Mies, Maria, 1993, 'The Need for a New Version: The Subsistence Perspective' in Maria Mies and Vandana Shiva (eds), *Ecofeminism*, London: Zed Books.

Mies, Maria, and Shiva, Vandana, 1993, *Ecofeminism*, London: Zed Books.

Mooney, Pat, 1988, 'From Cabbages to Kings', *Development Dialogue*, pp. 1–2.

Mooney, Pat, 1989, Proceeding of the Conference on Patenting of Life Forms, Brussels: ICDA.

Plumwood, Val, 2002, *Environmental Culture: The Ecological Crisis of Reason*, New York: Routledge.

Rose, Deborah Bird, 2011, *Wild Dog Dreaming: Love and Extinction*, Charlottesville, VA: University of Virginia Press.

Rose, Deborah Bird, 2013, 'Val Plumwood's Philosophical Animism: Attentive Interactions in the Sentient World', *Environmental Humanities* 3, pp. 93–109.

Shiva, Vandana, 1997, *Biopiracy: The Plunder of Nature and Knowledge*, Cambridge, MA: South End Books.

Shiva, Vandana, 2005, *Earth Democracy: Justice, Sustainability, and Peace*, Minneapolis, MN: Consortium.

Shiva, Vandana, 2016a, *Who Really Feeds the World?: The Failure of Agribusiness and the Promise of Agroecology*, Berkeley, CA: North Atlantic Books.

Shiva, Vandana, 2016b, 'The New Nature', *Boston Review: A Political and Literary Forum*, 4 January, https://www.bostonreview.net/forum/jedediah-purdy-nature-anthropocene/ (accessed 10.03.2025).

Shiva, Vandana, 2020, *Reclaiming the Commons: Biodiversity, Traditional Knowledge and the Rights of Mother Earth*, London: Synergetic Press.

Stevens, Lara, Tait, Peta and Varney, Denise (eds), 2017, *Feminist Ecologies: Changing Environments in the Anthropocene*, London: Palgrave Macmillan.

Taylor, Marcus, 2017, *The Political Ecology of Climate Change Adaption*, London: Routledge.

Warren, Karen, 1987, 'Feminism and Ecology', *Environmental Review* 9.1, Spring, pp. 3–20.

Warren, Karen, 1996, 'The Power and the Promise of Ecological Feminism' in Karen J. Warren (ed.), *Ecological Feminist Philosophies*, Bloomington, IN: Indiana University Press.

Warren, Karen, 2015 (2014), 'Feminist Environmental Philosophy', *Stanford Encyclopedia of Philosophy*, https://plato.stanford.edu/entries/feminism-environmental (accessed 16.01.2025).

7

Upright Walk on a Habitable Earth in Anthropocene

BEAT DIETSCHY

The creatures, too, must become free. (Thomas Müntzer, 1524)

Age of men?

The millennium had barely begun when it was proposed to name the new earth-historical epoch we are living in 'Anthropocene'. In February 2000, at a meeting of the United Nations Geosphere-Biosphere Programme held in Mexico, the atmospheric chemist Paul. J. Crutzen made the following proposal:

> Considering ... [the] major and still growing impacts of human activities on earth and atmosphere, and at all, including global, scales, it seems to us more than appropriate ... to use the term 'anthropocene' for the current geological epoch. (Crutzen and Stoermer, 2000, p. 17)

The proposal made by Crutzen and marine biologist Eugene F. Stoermer triggered an extensive scientific debate that continues to this day. This is surprising at first glance, as for many of the main proponents of the Anthropocene the idea of a human era is not necessarily a threatening scenario. So, what is this dispute about? The controversy is not so much about the fact and extent of human impact on the earth. That is nothing new. Buffon already wrote that 'the entire face of the Earth today bears the imprint of human power' (Buffon, 1778, p. 237, cited by Bonneuil and Fressoz, 2016, pp. 133–4). This was around the time when James Watt designed the steam engine and when, according to Crutzen, the Anthropocene may have started.

Criticism has been levelled at what the proposed epoch name does not say. So, Jason Moore asks:

> The motive force behind this epochal shift? In two words: coal and steam. The driving force behind coal and steam? Not class. Not capital. Not imperialism. Not even culture. But ... you guessed it: the Anthropos: Humanity as an undifferentiated whole. (Moore, 2017, p. 595)

Other authors see the intention of naming a geological epoch after ourselves as a dubious vision aimed at becoming managers of the planet: 'Stopping our assault on the earth is necessary for long-term human flourishing, but this sort of extreme planetary management is not' (Hettinger, 2021, p. 80). According to Hettinger, this planetary management project is based on an 'Age of Man Environmentalism'. Its rationale is simple: nature is everywhere, but it is not pristine wilderness and we do change it, so 'we can make more nature'; in short, 'We are already running the whole Earth, whether we admit it or not' (Marris, 2011, pp. 56, 2).

Crutzen and Schwägerl (2011) also speak openly of a human seizure of power: 'Albeit clumsily, we are taking control of the realm of Nature, from climate to DNA.' They do not hide the fact that this would mean the extinction of countless species and that our actions have already shaped the planet for thousands of years. But thanks to gene technology and soon also synthetic biology, new living beings would be created. It is no longer a question of an opposition between humans and nature: 'It's we who decide what nature is and what it will be.' This humanly dressed-up power grab is presented as a much needed 'eco-optimism' for our societies:

> Teaching students that we are living in the Anthropocene, the Age of Men, could be of great help. Rather than representing yet another sign of human hubris, this name change would stress the enormity of humanity's responsibility as stewards of the Earth. It would highlight the immense power of our intellect and our creativity, and the opportunities they offer for shaping the future. (Crutzen and Schwägerl, 2011)

'Nanotechnology: Shaping the World Atom by Atom' is the much-quoted title of a report by the US National Science and Technology Council. It states: 'Nanotechnology has given us the tools ... to play with the ultimate toy box of nature – atoms and molecules ... The possibilities to create new things appear limitless' (NSTC, 1999, p. 1). 'Shaping our future' is clearly the promise of Technoscience and big business. It is not surprising that for the protagonists of Anthropocene thinking humanity should urgently develop 'large-scale geoengineering projects, for instance to "optimize" climate' (Crutzen, 2002, p. 23). Crutzen's vision, commented Elmar Altvater, 'commits the error that Albert Einstein asked us to avoid: to think that humanity can resolve problems by applying the same methods that caused them' (Altvater, 2016, p. 140).

Nevertheless, such technologies can be interpreted as an expression of biophilia (Keith, 2013). This fits very well with modern capitalism which includes not only state and geopolitical power but also geopower. This geopower 'emerges at the nexus of big science, big states and technologies of power that make territory and the biosphere accessible, legible, knowable, and utilizable' (Moore, 2018, p. 245).

Given these circumstances, it is probably not far-fetched to assume that anthropogenic arguments contribute to obscure capitalogenic realities. By focusing on humanity and measuring human impacts on the planet the concept of an Age of Man conceals what are the main causes of ecological devastation in modern times. Altvater makes the point:

> Precapitalist social formations brought about major changes in culture and politics, in the economy and in techno-structures; but earth systems have been overstretched only under capitalist conditions ... Modern capitalism thus is more than a social formation ... The earth is changed, a new era has begun. (Altvater, 2016, pp. 144, 150)

Industrial capitalism has – by 'tapping (and depleting) the planet's energy and mineral reserves' – created a completely 'new global socio-ecological reality' (Altvater, 2016, pp. 145–6). The term Capitalocene refers therefore to this system of capitalist modernity in which 'nature' has been transformed into a capital asset. Following capitalist rationality 'the complexity of nature is reduced to a simple, fetishized category: natural capital', and 'reshaped as a provider of resources and a dumping site for emissions' (pp. 149–50).

Jason Moore argues in a similar way. According to him, the great transformations concerning landscape and property, labour productivity, and the technics of global appropriation 'suggest a way of thinking capitalist crisis world-ecologically'. This leads him to comprehend not only cheap labour (like care work), but also cheap nature 'as a system of domination, appropriation and exploitation' that is 'necessary to capitalist development but not directly valorised ("paid") through the money economy' (Moore, 2017, p. 620). Nancy Fraser (2022, p. xiv) describes the drastic consequences of this system of over-exploitation respectively extractivism as 'cannibalism'. She shows how capitalism is about 'to devour the social, political, and natural bases of its own existence'. Speaking of an age of humans is, then, at least a cynical statement that obscures the fact that the society we are living in should be seen 'as an institutionalized feeding frenzy – in which the main course is us'. In the same manner 'the earth's capacity to support life and renew itself' becomes another object of 'cannibalization' (Fraser, 2022, p. 11).

The rise and acceptance of such a project, in which genocide and ecocide are tolerated and even welcomed, cannot be explained by its economic success alone. Underlying it, says Amitav Ghosh in his 'Nutmeg's Curse: Parables for a Planet in Crisis', is 'a conception of the world, and of historical time, that sees the Earth not as a nurturer or a life-giver, but as dead weight whose enveloping ties must be escaped if Man is to rise to a higher stage of being' (Ghosh, 2021, p. 82). This higher purpose is at least in the room when the question is raised: 'Are Humans Now Overwhelming the Great Forces of Nature?' (Steffen et al., 2007). It is answered by authors like Mark Lynas (2011, p. 8) who says without hesitation: 'Nature no longer runs the Earth. We do.' For Hettinger this 'manifests an anthropocentric narcissism that is blind to the ongoing agency of nature' (2021, p. 76). In any case, it presupposes a Cartesian separation of humans from the rest of nature.

Feminist environmentalist Eileen Crist (2016, p. 15) recognizes in all this the centrepiece of a discourse that advocates a further expansion 'of a human species-supremacist planetary politics'. With the proclamation of the Anthropocene, 'we witness history's projected drive to keep moving forward as history's conquest not only of geographical space but now of geological time as well' (p. 17). Even more, by 'affirming the centrality of man – as both causal force and subject of concern – the Anthropocene shrinks the discursive space for challenging the domination of the biosphere, offering instead a techno-scientific pitch for its rationalization' (p. 25). In the end, says Crist, 'The discourse subjects us to the time-honoured narrative of human ascent into a distinguished species' (p. 24), with a godlike power, but without achieving anything other than 'the paltry view of the planet as an assortment of "resources" (or "natural capital," "ecosystem services," "working landscapes," and the like)' (p. 29). Crist's own vision is quite different. It is reminiscent of ecotheologian Thomas Berry, who propagated a future non-anthropocentric epoch called the 'Ecozoic Age': 'a period when humans would dwell upon the Earth in a mutually enhancing manner'.

'Anthropos' and the alterity of the planet

'Who is Anthropos?' asks philosopher Isabelle Stengers (2014, p. 149). Giving the name 'Anthropocene' to 'our' geological epoch, doesn't this mean that responsibility for the ecological devastation of the planet is being imposed on an abstract and anonymous universal subject of humanity? Stengers is not looking for an instance that would be to blame for climate change. She speaks of 'the intrusion of Gaia'. But Gaia is not a person who wants something from us. By bringing her into play she tries to evoke a 'we' into the picture where anonymity reigns – we have indeed to face the situation and take responsibility.

We are dealing so far mostly with socio-historical questions which are usually negotiated as political, ethical or justice issues. However, when Anil Agarwal and Sunita Narain talk, in the title of their 1991 book about global warming in an unequal world, they are referring to quite disparate – but related – phenomena (Agarwal and Narain, 1991). Geopolitical and geophysical problems should not be confused. 'At the same time, a new geological and geopolitical era has begun,' says Altvater (2016, p. 139). It is to the credit of Dipesh Chakrabarty that he draws attention to this. He, the historian of humanity and author of books such as *Humanism in an Age of Globalization*, is concerned with 'an awareness of the planet and its geo-biological history' (Chakrabarty, 2021, p. 1). In doing so, he confronts us with what the German philosopher Ernst Bloch called the non-contemporaneity of the contemporaneous. In Chakrabarty's words, it is apparent,

> ... that as humans we presently live in two different kinds of 'now-time' ... simultaneously: in our own awareness of ourselves, the 'now' of human history has become entangled with the long 'now' of geological and biological timescales, something that has never happened before in the history of humanity. (Chakrabarty, 2021, p. 7).

The process of change in nature – the gradual erosion of a mountain, for example – is generally perceived 'as a constant, unchanging background to human stories' (p. 7). Even though our activities affect the bio- and lithosphere, the longue durée of geological processes eludes them. According to Chakrabarty, attending to this gap between human time and the 'deeper, longer temporal rhythms of geobiological processes' (p. 65) is one of the main challenges for politics in the Anthropocene.

So, we are facing a crucial test: 'The crisis of climate change calls for thinking simultaneously on both registers, to mix together the immiscible chronologies of capital and species history' (p. 42). This fundamental alterity must be considered: 'It speaks to a growing divergence in our consciousness between the global – a singularly human story – and the planetary, a perspective to which humans are incidental' (p. 67). Nevertheless, the vital problems of the planet, such as global warming, are treated by politics and business as issues of sustainable development. In essence, this means human-centred or capital-centred according to socio-political or economic desirability.

For Chakrabarty, 'The key term of planetary thinking that one could contrapose to the idea of sustainability in global thought is habitability' (p. 83). It does not only reference humans. 'Its central concern is life – complex multicellular life in general', and the central question is: 'What makes a planet friendly to complex life for hundreds of millions of years?' (p. 83). The 'relevant point is that humans are not central to the problem of habitability, but habitability is central to human existence' (p. 83).

Chakrabarty's position is not an ecocentric one in the strict sense. Rather, he seeks to think simultaneously 'human-centred and planet-centred' (p. 174). He is realistic in so far as he does not minimize the alterity of the planet, but still holds on to the goal of a life-friendly world: 'how hopelessly humancentric all our political and economic institutions still are' – 'the politics of human well-being has to be in conversation with the problem of "habitability" of this planet' (pp. 195–6). However, this also means that there is no way of avoiding a critique and revision of human centrism and exceptionalism. A 'Rethinking the Human in an Anthropocene World', according to theologian Norman Wirzba (cited in Chakrabarty, 2021, p. 252), is indispensable.

Decolonizing humans and earth

A soft reform of the deep-rooted anthropocentrism, as envisaged by Chakrabarty, disregards the fact that it is a centrepiece in the Eurocentric construct of modernity. It cannot be addressed unless one looks at the interplay of capitalism, racism, the Euro-centred colonial/modern world power, and also the associated androcentric gender relations that have been analysed in Latin American decolonial thought.

One of the starting points for this discourse is the work of the Peruvian sociologist Aníbal Quijano on the 'coloniality of power'. In an article written in 1989, he says: 'With the conquest of the societies and the cultures which inhabit what today is called Latin America, began the constitution of a new world order, culminating, five hundred years later, in a global power covering the whole planet' (Quijano, 2007, p. 168).

This means that the hegemonic order of a globalized capitalist society has as its prerequisite a coloniality of power that was first formed in the 'New World'. America was not discovered as it was – in all its multiplicity of cultures – but invented. This is, as Enrique Dussel (1995, p. 12) has expressed, a process that 'eclipsed whatever was non-European' and in the course of which Europe invents itself as a centre of power. In other words:

> The genocide of Amerindian peoples – the end of the world for them – was the beginning of the modern world for Europe: without the despoiling of the Americas, Europe would have never become more than the backyard of Eurasia ... No pillage of the Americas, no capitalism, no Industrial Revolution, thus perhaps no Anthropocene either. (Danowski and Viveiros de Castro, 2017, p. 107)

In this process, a specific power model of anthropocentrism is formed: by exalting (European) man and his attributes, indigenous people, women or other species could be categorized as 'subhuman' and dehumanized: 'The self-placement of Man at the Centre has allowed dislocations of nonhumans, "subhumans," and wild nature into the fringes of earthly landscapes and human mindscapes alike.' At the same time, it has 'disallowed a vantage point from which any need or desire for limiting human expansionism might be discerned' (Crist and Kopnina, 2014, pp. 388, 390).

Karina Ochoa Muñoz has examined this process by exploring topics that are linked to the theological debates in the sixteenth century constructed around the conquest. She identifies three elements 'responsible for configuring the patterns of power and domination that were to structure the modern colonial world system from then on': 'slavery (bestialization), racialization (of the colonized population) and the feminization of the Indigenous (which incorporates sexism and misogyny)' (Ochoa Muñoz, 2014, p. 106). Within this colonial triad, she emphasizes the conquered indigenous woman as the more immediate 'dominated-other'.

Intersectionality is a key for decolonial thinking, and includes not only racism, class domination, sexism and gender, but also the 'coloniality of nature'. For Catherine Walsh, it represents 'a pattern of power that occurs at the intersections of the cultural, ontological, existential, epistemic, territorial, cosmological and socio-spiritual' and that ultimately enforces a single dichotomous worldview of human (i.e. white, educated male) domination over nature (Walsh, 2015, p. 103). Since the Incas the Spanish colonial-imperial domination has been installing hierarchies and divisions based on the 'ideas' of race, gender, sexuality and nature, where previously gender relations were more 'dynamic, fluid, open and non-hierarchical' (p. 106).

The criticism of these dichotomies that still determine the world is shared by many thinkers and activists in the global South. Vandana Shiva (2023, pp. xi–xii) for example speaks of 'eco-apartheid' that goes hand in hand with anthropocentrism and has led to the current world situation: 'The multiple crisis and pandemics we face today ... are all rooted in a world view based on the illusions of separation and superiority which deny interconnectedness and oneness.' She names it 'eco-apartheid' because it is fundamentally based on the assumption 'that humans are separate from Nature, are her conquerors, masters, owners, and the denial of the fact that we are part of Nature, not separate from her. Apartheid is "apartness" or "separateness".'

From the perspective of intercultural philosophy, Raúl Fornet-Betancourt comes to a similar conclusion. For him, in the background of the hegemonic understanding of science is still the epistemological rupture at work that created in the history of the European mind a dichotomy of subject and object and the aggressive anthropocentrism of modernity, which understands the human being as detached from nature. 'With nature, which has been transformed into the other, into the "objective", we do not talk, we exploit it, we work it and we research it for the purpose of extracting its "riches"' (Fornet-Betancourt, 2017b, p. 28). The limitless extractivism that has become the ultimate model of development in Latin America bears witness to the consequences of such an 'epistemology of the hunter' (Panikkar, 1993, p. 30), which has transformed the human faculty of knowledge into an instrument for taking possession of the world's objects.

Diversity of liberation

How decolonization is perceived and lived depends very much on the context and the characteristics of oppression. Some examples: Fornet-Betancourt's intercultural philosophical approach is closely linked to demands for justice for the poor and marginalized cultures. In the face of the increasing scientific monopoly claim that disregards the diversity of forms of cognition and knowledge and which privileges industrial technoscience, he calls for responding with 'an uprising of the spiritual wisdom cultures of humanity' against 'the prevailing epistemic totalitarianism' (Fornet-Betancourt, 2017a, p. 14). However, the focus is not so much on the 'narrowing and impoverishment' of academic research. Rather, the 'rising' is 'linked to an ethical rebellion in favour of the dignity and rights of those that are humiliated by the hegemonic system' (p. 15) and its impacts.

As a postcolonial historian, Chakrabarty (2021, pp. 61–2) knows that the period of 'great acceleration' (roughly 1945–2015) not only reveals climate crisis and a 'sudden coming together' of human and earth history. He points out that the 'lurch into the Anthropocene' is also the 'period of great decolonisation in countries that had been dominated by European imperial powers' which has enabled an increase in social justice. Nevertheless, he insists on the necessity 'to look at the human world also from a nonhuman point of view' (p. 149). He poses the important question: 'Do we value the nonhuman for its own sake or because it is good for us?' (p. 64). On the other hand, he points to the forgotten 'culture of reverence on which all ancient, Indigenous, and even peasant religions were based' (p. 199).

For contemporaneous indigenous perspectives, the experiencing of coloniality is mostly the starting point. 'Decolonising ourselves means seeing reality with our own eyes and no longer with the eyes of the West', underscored Choquehuanca Céspedes (2020) in his inaugural speech as vice president of Bolivia. He also takes a stand on the Anthropocene debate and pleads for a 'cosmobiocene' and for 'geopolitics' instead of geopolitics of good living. Activists throughout the continent of Abya Yala are calling for such changes. To create an alternative to the environmental crisis, they are trying to recover the historical memory that has been denied and erased. Decolonizing for them means 'to restore human relationship with nature and life in order to connect with the spirituality and memory of the ancestors' (Arteta Melgarejo et al., 2021, p. 297).

The two aspects are inseparable: 'We must learn to live with the earth, not just from it and consume it. We liberate ourselves together with the earth,' states a declaration of the Nasa people in Colombia's Cauca Valley in 2004, entitled 'The Liberation of Mother Earth' (Escobar, 2020, p. 58). According to Walsh (2006, pp. 39–40), the '(re)creation of a collective sense of belonging ... that enters into an alliance with those who came before them' plays a particularly important role also for Afro communities in Ecuador and Colombia. In addition to the decolonization of power, knowledge and nature, this also involves a 'decolonisation of the self' (p. 41). 'Unlearning in order to learn again', is an important part of it, as Luis Macas, one of the founders of Ecuador's indigenous umbrella organization CONAIE, states: 'Experience and history have made us realize that we live a colonized interculturality, seen and created from a Western and colonial logic. We have, therefore, the great task of decolonizing interculturality, to dispose Eurocentrism, to de-monopolize life from our resistances and from our projects' (cited by Walsh, 2014, p. 75).

Building alliances of conviviality

The search for a 'coexistence of the human and the non-human in profound interrelation', of which Arturo Escobar (2020, p. 63) reports with impressive examples from Colombia, is not only underway there. Two-sided conviviality – between people and with earth – is a theme that Achille Mbembe is taking up from the African continent. In *The Earthly Community* Mbembe does so not only because the earth is our common place of origin, but because he comprehends earth history as a history of bio-symbiosis and mutuality (2022, p. 125). This way of reading the world is more than important to him since the Anthropocene as he understands it is a 'techno-libertarian age' that calls for new 'paradigms of liberation of the living' (p. 124). Liberation is required from technolatry – that is, from a 'technosphere which has become a structuring dimension of the biosphere' (p. 28), and from 'techno-molecular colonialism' which transforms 'life itself in a commodity to be replicated under the volatility of market consumption' (pp. 65–6).

Like Chakrabarty, Mbembe is addressing the 'questions of habitability' of the planet and of 'the interlacing of human history and the Earth's history' (Mbembe, 2022, p. 59). What sets him apart from his Indian colleague (both are postcolonial historians) is that he draws on the ancient archives of African tradition to 'imagine other ways of inhabiting the Earth, sharing it, repairing it, and taking care of it' (p. 124). For that:

> ... knowing how to make an alliance with the other vital forces is the surest way to participate in the realization of the Cosmos, that is to say, in the construction of a dwelling place open to all ... and in which everyone is called to become potential ancestors, segments in an uninterrupted chain of links. (Mbembe, 2022, pp. 122–3)

Rather than a return to earth, we should see this as a rediscovery of a kind of African 'ancestral future'. The search is not for what has been but, as Ernst Bloch would say, for what has not yet been realized: 'the last utopia of a possible earthly community ... a democracy of the living' (Mbembe, 2022, p. 84). That would be a project of earthly liberation, not of the human subject alone. 'The relationship between humans and the rest of the living world is therefore not based on a thirst for conquest and appropriation, but on the contrary on an ethic of misappropriation' (Mbembe, 2022, p. 123).

Mbembe's book is written in the spirit of Bloch's concrete utopian philosophy, but with a decolonial African direction of impact. A dawning of the future and hope for the unforeseen in history, as well as the 'advent of a universal and fraternal community' (Mbembe, 2021, p. 72), are important to both. Above all, they rely on what Bloch called the co-productivity of (non-human) nature. Obviously, he did not comment on the Anthropocene.

However, he recognized clearly that this Anthropos under capitalist auspices, with its techniques of domination, stands in nature 'like an army of occupation in enemy territory' (Bloch, 1986, p. 670). Long before the beginning of public debates on the ecological crisis, he took up the young Marx's perspective of a reconciliation between humans and nature and expressed it in the programmatic formula 'naturalisation of man, humanisation of nature' (Bloch, 1934, p. 188). Ten years later, when he wrote the chapter on the 'technical utopias' in *The Principle of Hope*, he further developed this idea with the concepts of an 'alliance with nature' and 'alliance technology'.

It is important to note that Bloch is not just concerned with a technology-based utopia. 'The capitalist concept of technology', he underlines, 'exhibits more domination than friendship, more of the slavedriver and the East India Company than the bosom of a friend' (Bloch, 1986, p. 670). Domination of nature is 'a manifestation of a violent society' (p. 696). Liberating processes have therefore to encompass 'the relation of people to people and to nature' (p. 286).

Bloch's proposal aims at re-embedding human practice in the web of nature and anticipates a possible alliance with nature which will be capable of freeing up 'the creative forces of a frozen nature' (Bloch, 1986, p. 690). This would presuppose a 'befriending' (p. 670) in the social relation to non-human nature, a sympoietic cooperation and definitely a 'technology without violation' (p. 691), contrasting with the violence of the modern appropriation of nature.

Bloch's 'co-productivity of nature' did not have much of an echo for a long time. It is only more recently that natural scientists such as Isabelle Stengers and Donna Haraway, but also social scientists such as Bruno

Latour, Tim Ingold and Jason Moore, have looked more closely at the agency of non-human actors. Haraway in particular emphasizes the formation of alliances and multi-species partnerships 'that can contribute to building a habitable world in sustained troubled times' (2016, p. 143). Her key words are sympoiesis ('making with') and symbiogenesis ('life making process'), for which she compiles a wide range of examples. These 'world making' processes require recognizing specificities. Therefore, 'a common liveable world must be composed, bit by bit' (p. 40).

In theology, these questions have been taken up above all by ecofeminist authors and – in so far as Bloch's alliance with nature is concerned – most notably by Leonardo Boff. A 'loss of the vital relationship with nature' was already being addressed in his book *Francis of Assisi* (Boff, 1982, p. 5). In an article published in 1995, he refers more to a new 'ecological age' that would bring a 'new alliance' with the earth, 'one of mutual respect and brother/sisterhood' (Boff, 1995, p. 70). Boff also raises the question of the emancipatory content of ecology: is it merely a truce that allows the domination and exclusion of people and nature to continue? (Boff, 1997, p. 7). What is therefore needed is 'a new use of science and technology with nature, on behalf of nature, never against nature' (p. 13).

All of this is not far away from Bloch, who was after all a strong source of inspiration for Boff and other liberation theologians (Martínez Andrade, 2019, pp. 30–4). For Boff, however, alliance-making has a great number of meanings, ranging from the new covenant with the earth that God made with Noah (Genesis 9.11–16), the symbiotic alliance of microbial collectives in biology and interdependencies in social ecology, the cosmological and spiritual meaning of a 'community of life' (Hathaway and Boff, 2009) to civil society and ethical alliances such as the Earth Charter Initiative which includes a governance project aiming at realizing Earth Democracy (Westra and Vilela, 2014).

If the web of life is threatened by capitalism and necropolitics, then a response-ability is called for that can only come from the very threads from which this web is woven. 'We can only counter necropolitics with biopolitics,' says Frei Betto. We can call this a 'deep solidarity' (Rieger, 2022, p. 51). This is not a 'cheap' solidarity or a repair shop for devastated nature. Alliance with nature is neither a sort of 'philanthropy for maltreated metals' (Bloch, 1986, p. 695) nor a solidarity 'with' nature, but one within nature, in the same sense as for Brazilian liberation theologians Leonardo Boff and Ivone Gebara ecofeminist work is deeply connected to poor people's movements (Rieger, 2022, pp. 39–40). This solidarity is not primarily a moral demand, but rooted in a reality that can be observed (p. 168). Theologically speaking: 'God is found not first of all in the world of ideas but in the tensions of life where alternative forms of production, reproduction, and agency – human and nonhuman – are emerging' (p. 53). Following this incarnating path, we should recognize 'that collaboration is real in the incredible diversity of the nonhuman world and its productive dynamics, which humans are still discovering' (p. 5).

In this way, a mutual adequacy and sympathetic cooperation can be achieved between the two, which will allow the earth to continue to be a home and dwelling place – and not only for humans. In fact, the earth's habitability and 'being indigenous to her' (Bloch, 1986, p. 671) are mutually dependent. But that demands to regain – instead of colonization – an upright gait that means social liberation, and an 'affinitive inhabitation in nature' (p. 671).

References

Agarwal, Anil and Narain, Sunita, 1991, *Global Warming in an Unequal World: A Case of Environmental Colonialism*, New Delhi: Centre for Science and Environment.

Altvater, Elmar, 2016, 'The Capitalocene, or, Geoengineering against Capitalism's Planetary Boundaries' in Jason W. Moore (ed.), *Anthropocene or Capitalocene? Nature, History, and the Crisis of Capitalism*, Oakland, CA: PM Press, pp. 138–53.

Bloch, Ernst, 1934 (1969), 'Nicht-Umsonst und Welt für uns. Ein Exercitium' in *Philosophische Aufsätze zur objektiven Phantasie*, Frankfurt a. M. 1969: Suhrkamp Verlag, pp. 184–9.

Bloch, Ernst, 1986, *The Principle of Hope*, vols I–III, trans. Neville Plaice, Stephen Plaice and Paul Knight, Cambridge, MA: MIT Press.

Boff, Leonardo, 1982, *Francis of Assisi: A Model for Human Liberation*, trans. John W. Diercksmeier, New York: Crossroad.

Boff, Leonardo, 1995, 'Liberation, Theology and Ecology: Alternative, Confrontation or Complementarity?', *Concilium* 31.5, pp. 67–77.

Boff, Leonardo, 1997, *Cry of the Earth, Cry of the Poor*, trans. Philipp Berryman, Maryknoll, NY: Orbis Books.

Bonneuil, Christophe, and Fressoz, Jean-Baptiste, 2016, *The Shock of the Anthropocene: The Earth, History and Us*, trans. David Fernbach, London and New York: Verso.

Buffon, Georges-Louis Leclerc de, 1778, *Histoire naturelle générale et particulière*, vol. 5, Paris: Imprimerie royale.

Chakrabarty, Dipesh, 2021, *The Climate of History in a Planetary Age*, Chicago, IL: University of Chicago Press.

Choquehuanca Céspedes, David, 2020, 'Speech of Assumption of the Vice Presidency of the Plurinational State of Bolivia', La Paz: Vicepresidency of the Plurinational State of Bolivia.

Crist, Eileen, 2016, 'On the Poverty of Our Nomenclature' in Jason W. Moore (ed.), *Anthropocene or Capitalocene? Nature, History, and the Crisis of Capitalism*, Oakland, CA: PM Press, pp. 14–33.

Crist, Eileen and Kopnina, Helen, 2014, 'Unsettling Anthropocentrism', *Dialectical Anthropology* 38, pp. 387–96.

Crutzen, Paul J., 2002, 'Geology of Mankind: The Anthropocene', *Nature* 415.

Crutzen, Paul J., and Schwägerl, Christian, 2011, 'Living in the Anthropocene: Toward a New Global Ethos', *Yale Environment 360*.

Crutzen, Paul J., and Stoermer, Eugene F., 2000, 'The "Anthropocene"', *IGBP Newsletter* 41.

Danowski, Déborah, and Viveiros de Castro, Eduardo, 2017, *The Ends of the World*, trans. Rodrigo Nunes, 2nd edn, New York: Polity Press.

Dietschy, Beat, 2023a, 'Toward a "Nature Alliance": Why Sustainability Must Be Rethought in Terms of Relationality' in Stephan Rist, Pattrick Bottazzi and Johanna Jacobi (eds), *Critical Sustainability Sciences: Intercultural and Emancipatory Perspectives*, London and New York: Routledge, pp. 119–45.

Dietschy, Beat, 2023b, 'Die Erde anders. Naturallianz aus interkultureller Perspektive', in Francesca Vidal and Manuel Theophil (eds), *Naturallianz in der Klimakrise. Zur Aktualität der Naturphilosophie Ernst Blochs*, Bloch-Jahrbuch 2022/23, Würzburg: Königshausen and Neumann, pp. 147–70.

Dussel, Enrique, 1995, *The Invention of the Americas: Eclipse of 'the Other' and the Myth of Modernity*, New York: Continuum.

Ellis, Erle, 2011, 'Anthropogenic Transformation of the Terrestrial Biosphere', *Philosophical Transactions of the Royal Society* 369, pp. 1010–35.

Escobar, Arturo, 2020, *Pluriversal Politics: The Real and the Possible*, Durham, NC: Duke University Press.

Fornet-Betancourt, Raúl, 2017a, 'Introduction' in Raúl Fornet-Betancourt (ed.), *Spiritualities and Religions: Their Contribution to Justice and Knowledge in the Global Society*, Aachen: Wissenschaftsverlag Mainz, pp. 13–16.

Fornet-Betancourt, Raúl, 2017b, *Elementos para una crítica intercultural de la ciencia hegemónica*, Aachen: Wissenschaftsverlag Mainz.

Fraser, Nancy, 2022, *Cannibal Capitalism: How Our System is Devouring Democracy, Care, and the Planet – and What We Can Do about It*, London and New York: Verso.

Ghosh, Amitav, 2021, *The Nutmeg's Curse: Parables for a Planet in Crisis*, Chicago, IL: University of Chicago Press.

Haraway, Donna J., 2016, *Staying with the Trouble: Making Kin in the Chthulucene*, Durham, NC and London: Duke University Press.

Hathaway, Mark, and Boff, Leonardo, 2009, *The Tao of Liberation: Exploring the Ecology of Transformation*, Maryknoll, NY: Orbis Books.

Hettinger, Ned, 2021, 'Age of Man Environmentalism and Respect for an Independent Nature', *Ethics, Policy & Environment* 24.1, pp. 75–87.

Keith, David, 2013, *A Case for Climate Engineering*, Cambridge, MA: MIT Press.

Lynas, Mark, 2011, *The God Species: Saving the Planet in the Age of Humans*, London: Fourth Estate.

Marris, Emma, 2011, *Rambunctious Garden: Saving Nature in a Post-wild World*, New York: Bloomsbury.
Martínez Andrade, Luis, 2019, *Ecología y teología de la liberación. Critica de la modernidad/colonialidad*, Barcelona: Herder.
Mbembe, Achille, 2021, *Out of the Dark Night: Essays on Decolonization*, New York: Columbia University Press.
Mbembe, Achille, 2022, *The Earthly Community: Reflections on the Last Utopia*, trans. Steven Corcoran, Rotterdam: V2_Publishing.
Melgarejo, Arteta et al., 2021, 'Colonialidad de la naturaleza: Aspectos decoloniales para el debate sobre el Desarrollo Sostenible', Encuentros, Revista de Ciencias Humanas, Teoría Social y Pensamiento Crítico, Maracaibo, Venezuela, pp. 288–300.
Moore, Jason W., 2017, 'The Capitalocene, Part I: On the Nature and Origins of our Ecological Crisis', *The Journal of Peasant Studies* 44.3, pp. 594–630.
Moore, Jason W., 2018, 'The Capitalocene, Part II: Accumulation by Appropriation and the Centrality of Unpaid Work/Energy', *The Journal of Peasant Studies* 45.2, pp. 237–79.
NSTC (National Science and Technology Council), 1999, 'Nanotechnology: Shaping the World Atom by Atom', Washington DC.
Ochoa Muñoz, Karina, 2014, 'El debate sobre las y los amerindios: entre el discurso de la bestialización, la feminización y la racialización' in Yuderkys Espinosa Miñoso et al. (eds), *Tejiendo de otro modo: Feminismo, epistemología y apuestas descoloniales en Abya Yala*, Popayán: Editorial Universidad del Cauca, pp. 105–18.
Panikkar, Raimon, 1993, 'La mística del diálogo', *Jahrbuch für kontextuelle Theologien* 1.
Quijano, Aníbal, 2007, 'Coloniality and Modernity/Rationality', *Cultural Studies* 21.2, pp. 168–78.
Rehmann, Jan, 2020, 'Ernst Bloch as a Philosopher of Praxis', *Praktyka Teoretyczna* 1.35, pp. 75–94.
Rieger, Joerg, 2022, *Theology in the Capitalocene: Ecology, Identity, Class, and Solidarity*, Minneapolis, MN: Fortress Press.
Shiva, Vandana, 2023, 'Foreword', in Stephan Rist, Pattrick Bottazzi and Johanna Jacobi (eds), *Critical Sustainability Sciences: Intercultural and Emancipatory Perspectives*, London and New York: Routledge, pp. x–xvi.
Steffen, Will et al., 2007, 'The Anthropocene: Are Humans Now Overwhelming the Great Forces of Nature?', *Ambio* 36.8, pp. 614–21.
Stengers, Isabelle, 2014, 'Penser à partir du ravage écologique' in Emilie Hache (ed.), *De l'Univers clos au monde infini*, Paris: Editions Dehors, pp. 147–90.
Walsh, Catherine, 2006, 'Interculturalidad y colonialidad del poder. Un pensamiento y posicionamiento otro desde la diferencia colonial' in C. Walsh et al. (eds), *Interculturalidad, descolonizacion del Estado y del conocimiento*, Buenos Aires: Ediciones del signo, pp. 21–70.
Walsh, Catherine, 2014, 'Decolonialidad, Interculturalidad, Vida desde el Abya Yala-Andino. Notas pedagógicas y senti-pensantes' in María Eugenia Borsani and Pablo Quintero (eds), *Los desafíos decoloniales de nuestros días*, Neuquén: Educo, pp. 47–78.

Walsh, Catherine, 2015, 'Life, Nature and Gender Otherwise: Feminist Reflections And Provocations from the Andes' in Wendy Harcourt and Ingrid L. Nelson (eds), *Practising Feminist Political Ecologies: Moving beyond the 'Green Economy'*, London: Zed Books, pp. 101-30.

Westra, Laura, and Vilela, Mirian (eds), 2014, *The Earth Charter, Ecological Integrity and Social Movements*, London and New York: Routledge.

8

'For the Life of the ... Animals': Christian Anthropology Revisited in Light of the Climate Crisis

NIKOLAOS ASPROULIS

Introduction

To talk about animals in the context of climate crisis might sound strange to many ears, those who still receive and interpret the surrounding reality by making use of premodern concepts and tools, being more or less accustomed with the Western Enlightenment and the resulting cultural development that recognizes a particular and dominant role to humanity. However, if we seriously take into account the various aspects of climate crisis as they are described today by environmentalists and other scientists, we will soon realize that things are quite different and at least more complex. Before, however, we explore the special position of animals in this regard, both as victims of climate crisis and as potential agents towards climate action, we briefly need to highlight aspects of climate crisis that concern the relationship between humans and animals.

Setting the scene: climate crisis and the 'Anthropocene'

One can clearly point to climate crisis (United Nations, 2023) as a global political, social and financial crisis, but primarily it is a spiritual (Ecumenical Patriarch Bartholomew, 2023) and moral crisis. Climate crisis happens everywhere, from north-western Europe with the increasing risk of river and coastal flooding, all the way to the Arctic, where temperature rises are much greater than the global average, as well as in the Mediterranean region, where one sees an expansion of habitats for southern disease vectors. Talking today about climate refugees (Climate Refugees, 2023) is not part of scientific fiction, but an unpleasant reality which gradually increases and affects various parts of the globe.

In more detail, climate crisis has been particularly defined in terms of CO_2 emissions, global warming, large-scale shifts in weather patterns, sea pollution from plastics, mega wildfires, and last but not least as closely related to meat production models and biodiversity loss which put in jeopardy animals of various species and in various ecosystems, but also humans.

It was only in 1967 that Lynn White, Jr (White, Jr, 1967, pp. 1203–7) published a very provocative article about the roots of the ecological crisis. Since then it has become clear that climate crisis is primarily caused by human-induced greenhouse gases in the atmosphere. Anthropogenic factors, human activity and the ensuing consumerist lifestyle causes this pollution, and it is a catastrophe not only to the planet but also to animals.

There is agreement today among scientists from various fields that we are living in the Anthropocene. The Anthropocene Epoch (Benner et al., 2021; Lamothe, 2021; Deane-Drummond, Bergmann and Vogt, 2017) is considered to be an unofficial unit of geologic time, used to describe the most recent period in the earth's history when human activity started to have a significant impact on the planet's climate and ecosystems. According to this perception, the history of the earth is divided into a hierarchical series of smaller chunks of time, referred to as the geologic timescale. These divisions, in descending length of time, are called eons, eras, periods, epochs and ages. These units are classified based on the earth's rock layers, or strata, and the fossils found within them. Officially, the current epoch is called the 'Holocene', which began 11,700 years after the last major Ice Age. What, then, of the Anthropocene?

In 2000, geologists Paul Crutzen and Eugene Stoermer (Crutzen and Stoermer, 2013, pp. 479–90) coined the word 'Anthropocene' to describe in a bold way a new epoch in the earth's history resulting from indiscriminate human overuse of natural resources, giving way to the destruction of ecosystems and human settlements. The word 'Anthropocene' itself is derived from the Greek words '*Anthropos*' for 'human' and '*Cene*' for 'new'. Scientists still debate whether the Anthropocene differs from the Holocene. Those who support the use of this new term argue that the beginning of the Anthropocene should be either the start of the industrial revolution or the first test of the atomic bomb (1945). Although not fully acceptable by all, Coudrain and colleagues (Coudrain, Le Duff and Mitja, 2022, pp. 1–18) argued that the scientific evidence and arguments supporting the Anthropocene amount to a 'paradigm shift' in Thomas Kuhn's understanding; this challenges not only scientists but also the wider public – and certainly religious leaders and theologians – to reconsider the broader ethical and philosophical perspectives on the role of human agency over planetary natural resources. Doubtless, Anthropocene is a child of our postmodern era where relativism, on the one hand, and eco-awareness or eco-activism, on the other, emerge in a very bold way, to address the catastrophic consequences of the human-caused climate crisis.

A glance at history: the rise of human exceptionalism

Today it has become clear that human beings played, and still play, the principal role in this difficult situation facing the planet. This has not come out of the blue but it was the result of a long development that took place in the course of history, especially after the spread of Christianity throughout the ancient world and a particular interpretation of the human identity – meaning the definition of the image of God in the human (imago Dei), which has prevailed since then. Looking through the long history of the Church from a theological point of view, it is not difficult for one to stress the strong rationalistic perception of the imago Dei, which ascribes ontological priority to reason over body, a mentality that led to the undervaluation of the materiality of creation which gradually, over the centuries, contributed to a clear anti-ecological orientation.

This particular understanding was evident in both Western and Eastern Christian traditions, though White (1967) focuses more on Western Christianity. Beginning with Origen (184–253), through Evagrius of Pontus (345–399) (Zizioulas, 2006, p. 21), and the subsequent whole monastic tradition recapitulated in the Philokalia spirituality (a collection of texts written between the fourth and the fifteenth centuries by spiritual masters of the Orthodox Christian tradition), a certain dichotomy between body and soul, a devaluation of the material aspect of the human and, by extension, of creation in its entirety, has been put forth in favour of the 'immortality of the soul' (despite its clear neo-Platonic connotations) and the participation in the spiritual world (like the Platonic ideas). In this light the human mind has been understood as the very link between God and creation, an attitude that led to an undervaluation of the dignity of the material world. A similar tendency appeared also in the West, where St Augustine pointed to the kingdom of God as the proper place for human souls only (Chryssavgis and Asproulis, 2021, p. 34). Thus, a certain metaphysic has been developed in later times, especially within Western Christianity with the mainstream scholastic tradition, where pure reason was considered as the proper means, perhaps the only means, and most important feature of the imago Dei by which humans are able to reflect the divine or participate in God's mind, while at the same time regulating their relationship with the cosmos in its entirety (considered as a sum of irrational and 'brute animals'; Salisbury, 2014, p. 80) as the first being in the chain of beings.

This development resulted further in a human-centred culture where the human is considered to be at the very centre of the world, with an alleged given privilege to dominate over the world and utilize it according to its own desires. In this vein, René Descartes's '*cogito ergo sum*' ('I think, therefore I am') (Newman, 2015, pp. 128–35) has been a natural outcome, whereby nature and creation were perceived as simply a means towards the fulfilment of an individualist cause, the unquenchable pleasure (eudemonism) of humans, leading to the present scientific boost and technological revolution (e.g. artificial intelligence). A whole chain of modern Western thinkers, from Immanuel Kant (1724–1804) to Emmanuel Levinas (1906–95) and others, appear to have adopted this long theological, philosophical – and in general spiritual – tradition where a predominant focus on human reason or morality (based on 'pure reason') comes first – and sometimes in opposition to the rest of the world or despite any real concern for it. This development of the human independently from the body and senses, as well as in opposition to its natural environment, is best reflected in a famous statement by René Descartes (1596–1650). In his *Discours de la Méthode*, he argues that:

> We can reach knowledge that would be very useful in life and we could find a practical method, whereby the force and energies inherent in fire, water, air, the stars, celestial and all other bodies that surround us might be used in the same manner in all suitable applications, and so we may become masters and possessors of nature [*maîtres et possesseurs de la nature*]. (Descartes, 1824, Chryssavgis and Asproulis, 2021, pp. 65, 190)

In this perception of the non-human creation, no place for animals (one could hardly find a place for humans too!) has been preserved, since they do not meet the rational skills, cognitive capacities and moral standards of humans.

If that is the case, what can we say or do with regard to animals? What does theology have to say about the role and position of animals in the wider divine plan? If theology deals principally with life and death matters (i.e. ontology), then creation itself in its entirety should be given proper attention. The current Postlapsarian conflict between nature and humans, evident in the increasing environmental crisis, challenges the traditional anthropological teaching of the Church, which often understands humanity as that power that denies, disables and enslaves creation in its entirety so as to spread its authoritarian influence and utilitarian wealth. It goes without saying that humans, at least according to the biblical account of the creation of the world, play a significant role in the divine plan. But what about animals? Do they have a future in the kingdom of God? Do they contribute somehow to the salvation of the entire cosmos, to the so-called theosis (deification)? If the answer to these questions is affirmative, a more inclusive and embedded understanding of humans is then desperately needed, in order to reverse the more or less monistic approaches that devalue non-human animals, thus going beyond the still predominant human exceptionalism. In order to move in this direction, one needs to revisit one of the central assumptions of Christian theological anthropology – namely, the imago Dei – so as to liberate it from its long negative perception through the lens of reason and superiority over the rest of creation. By adopting such a liberating theological perspective, by no means does one have to abandon the traditional doctrine of the Church. Instead, what is required is to revisit the imago Dei tradition by bringing to the fore certain neglected elements which can address and meet the new and unforeseen challenges.

The present challenges in relation to animals

Speaking about challenges with regard to the relationship between humans and animals, one should primarily point to the biodiversity loss. When using this term (Rafferty, 2023) one describes a decrease in biodiversity within a certain species, a local or a wider ecosystem, a given geographic area, or earth as a whole – which tends to be the case nowadays. In principle, biodiversity as a term refers to the number of genes, species and individual organisms within a given species, and biological communities within a defined geographic area, ranging from the smallest ecosystem to the global biosphere. To this end, biodiversity loss describes the decline in the number, genetic variability and variety of species, and the biological communities in a given area, which is considered to be one of the major factors contributing to climate crisis. This loss in the variety of life can seriously affect, in various ways, the functioning of the ecosystem and its sustainability. This is so because an ecosystem (National Geographic, 2023) is understood as a geographic area where a variety of plants, animals and other organisms, as well as weather and landscapes (humans included), work more or less together to form a sort of bubble of life. This understanding of an ecosystem highlights the close interdependence among the various organisms and parts of the system. In more theological terms, this amounts to a sort of Trinitarian ecosystem, where the divine Trinitarian persons participate in the one common substance, forming in this way a divine bubble of life. At the same time, this biodiversity evident in an earthly ecosystem can also be understood in the light of the absolute personal otherness of the Trinitarian persons, who commune with one another and share in the one divine substance in a Trinitarian play of life.

To return to the loss of biodiversity, this is caused by a number of things – reasons such as the habitat loss and degradation that reduces or eliminates the food resources and living space for most species; the invasive species that try to dominate the domestic ones; the human over-exploitation and pollution of air and water and everything around them, as well as climate change associated with global warming – meaning the modification of the earth's climate that is the result of the use of fossil fuels.

The effects of biodiversity loss are crucial and numerous not only for animals but also for humans. Biodiversity loss clearly affects the human economic systems and societies of both developing and developed countries. From the very beginning of their existence, humans have relied on various plants, animals and other organisms for food, building materials, as well as medicines, and their availability as commodities is important in many cultures. If we take into account the Covid-19 pandemic (Asproulis and Wood, 2020), its impact on the life of the whole planet but also its relationship with the climate crisis, the loss of biodiversity among these critical natural resources puts in jeopardy global food security (Werner and Geglitza, 2016), and the development of new pharmaceuticals to deal with future diseases.

Another challenge related to our discussion about the role and position of animals in our life – but also in the divine plan – has to do with so-called animal rights. Animal rights are considered to be moral principles grounded in the belief that non-human animals deserve the right to live as they wish, without being subjected to the desires of – or abuse by – human beings. At the core of animal rights' theory is autonomy: the right of animals to self-define themselves as animals and not beings in relation to – or under the guidance and dominion of – humans. Despite the ambivalent status of the reception of human rights in many countries today, they are still considered a major achievement in the modern history of humanity as they seek to protect certain freedoms, such as the right to expression, freedom from torture, and access to democracy, for all people – but especially for minorities and people in all kinds of need. It is true that these choices vary depending on social locations such as race, class and gender, but generally speaking human rights tend to secure and justify the minimum tenets of what makes human lives worth living. In this same direction, the discussion today about animal rights points to the establishment of a similar framework, where non-human animals can have access to certain basic rights that recognize their own dignity, value and otherness.

One can refer here to certain examples of animal rights laws from recent history. In 2021 the government in the United Kingdom introduced the Animal Welfare (Sentience) Bill. This Bill sought to enshrine in law that animals are, in fact, sentient beings and they deserve humane treatment by humans. Although the law that came into being – Animals Welfare (Sentience) Act 2022 – did not afford animals full autonomy, it was a watershed in the movement towards the protection of animals, which officially recognizes animals' capacity in feeling and suffering, distinguishing them from inanimate objects. An important result of years of campaigning in the United Kingdom, the Act includes in its definition of animals not only 'any other (animal) than homo sapiens' but 'also any cephalopod mollusk, and any decapod crustacean'.

Much further back in time, the United States had already passed the Animal Welfare Act (AWA) in 1966. There is no doubt this was an important piece of federal legislation addressing the treatment of animals. However, its scope is somehow limited, as it excludes various species, including farmed animals, which for the United States is a topic with a specific economic dimension. The law does establish, though, specific guidelines for the sale, transport and handling of animals such as dogs, cats, rabbits, non-human primates, guinea pigs and hamsters. The Act also protects the psychological welfare of animals who are used in lab experiments, and prohibits the violent practices of dogfighting and cockfighting. This aspect is of particular importance as it directly or indirectly recognizes a degree of moral dignity to animals as 'individuals' who experience suffering and pain. Again, however, this law does not recognize the autonomy of animals.

Taking into account the above cases, one realizes how important it is for the welfare of animals to accord them further rights. This would gradually form a specific legal framework which could recognize a set of rights to animals such as the following measures: animals may not be hunted; the habitats of animals must be protected to allow them to live according to their choosing. From a theological perspective, the major right that must be given to animals should be the capacity to participate in the kingdom of God, to share in theosis, as the major goal of the divine plan and life in Christ which affects creation in its entirety.

A forgotten, but still relevant, debate for the animal rights discussion

In his 'Conjectural beginning of human history' (Kant, 2007, pp. 163–75), Immanuel Kant provides an interesting interpretation of the Genesis account (chapters 1–3), focusing on the special role attributed to human beings due to their capacity of reason. In this light, a human gradually becomes 'conscious of … reason as a faculty that can extend itself beyond the limits within which all animals are held' (p. 165), pointing out humans' superiority over all other creatures, as with reason, human 'elevates … entirely above the society of animals' (p. 167). According to Kant:

> The first time (human) he said to the sheep: Nature has given you the skin you wear not for you but for me, then it took it off the sheep and put it on himself (Gen. 3.21) he became aware of a prerogative that he had by his nature over all animals, which he now no longer regarded as his fellow creatures, but rather as means and instruments … (Kant, 2007, p. 167)

We have already seen that Kant belongs to a wide chain of thinkers who one way or another contributed to the rise of human exceptionalism. In this understanding, any discussion about rights or dignity accorded to non-human animals is fully rejected as meaningless. To this end it is also important to stress the role played by a particular interpretation of the biblical narrative which amounts to the historical roots of climate crisis.

On the contrary, in his *An Introduction to the Principles of Morals and Legislation* (1789; 2000, pp. 227ff), Jeremy Bentham (1748–1832), an English philosopher, jurist and social reformer, the founder of modern utilitarianism, strongly criticizes Kant's opinion by asking a very critical question in relation to the animal's condition: the question is not whether animals can reason, nor whether they can speak, but whether they can suffer? The critical moment for animals is not if they can participate in the 'kingdom of ends' (in Kantian terms) but if they can experience pain and pleasure. It is, then, quite relevant how important this Kant–Bentham debate is for the discussion about animal rights; this is especially so from a theological perspective, which deals not only with the welfare of a being but with its eternal life, its eternal being.

Revisiting imago Dei in terms of communion

Returning to the more theological discussion of the relationship between humans and non-human beings, and especially to the need of a new definition of the imago Dei, one should clearly distinguish between two basic ontological-philosophical views. It is not my intention here to survey their long history, but only to facilitate our perspective. These two perspectives are the *personalist* and the *substantialist* ontology. For one familiar with the history of ideas in Western culture, the distinction might sound from the outset both relevant and promising for our discussion.

The substantialist view, which resulted from the encounter of the early Church with Greek thought and was determined by the special attention given to nature, was considerably developed, especially throughout the Middle Ages. It had become clear by then that a human can be properly understood through the lens of its own intellectual – or, rather, natural – capacities as if it were an 'objectified substance' characterized by certain and measurable qualities that distinguished it from all other creatures.

In contrast, a personalist ontology, where the relationship between persons and beings has priority over a self-defined constitution of an individual, seeks to overcome the fixed dichotomy between the human and the world, between humanity and nature. The present climate crisis, as well as the increasing loss of biodiversity we all face – primarily as a result of a conception of the human who receives creation in terms of superiority, possession and dominion – makes it clear that certain aspects of the mainstream understanding of human identity from the point of view of Christian theology and our common ecclesiastical tradition constitute part of the problem and not its solution. By saying this, I do not mean to dismiss altogether the long tradition of the Church. In contrast, by stressing the need to reconsider certain aspects of this tradition, I intend to bring to the fore some neglected points. The communal understanding of the imago Dei, in terms of the common ontological (creaturely or animal) ground shared by all creatures of God, can be considered as one of these neglected aspects.

We have been familiarized for many centuries now with a lifestyle that justifies an inevitable break between human and nature, both in terms of practice and theory. If that is true, and in order to address the present climate crisis, a new model of anthropology is required. This new model needs to go beyond any dated human exceptionalism or narrow anthropocentrism, where more attention should be given to those elements of the imago Dei that link the human to the rest of creation (e.g. animality), and not to those elements that deepen or stress their discontinuity, giving priority to the human over all other creatures of God. By redefining the image of God in a more holistic and inclusive way through the lens of 'dinivanimality' (Moore, 2014), theology can provide an all-embracing anthropological view that accounts for the proper place and reception of animals not only in our discourse, but also in our practice.

In this vein, if one defines the human from the point of view of a personalist ontology, then the human cannot be understood without a clear reference to a You, and an It that is without a close dependence on the other (either humans, world, or God). This relational/communal understanding of humanity can serve as the background of a new ethos that can be expressed in the following phrase: 'Every part of creation matters' (Nieuwerth, Pavlovic and Shaw, 2022), or, put another way, every creature of God matters. If this is the case, the human can be seen through the lens of its priestly role, meaning that one needs to be responsible by offering the whole of creation to God so as to survive eternally. This is not just a moral task, but a new way of life that takes seriously into account creation in all its aspects as an ontological component of the imago Dei. This was at least the understanding of the Greek Fathers of the Church, like Irenaeus (second century) or Gregory Palamas (fourteenth century) when they argued that the imago Dei is incomplete unless the whole of creation is recognized as being a constitutive part of it (Palamas, 1970, p. 488). If the image of God in humans cannot fully manifest without taking into account the whole variety of creatures, this clearly means that animals do share in the salvation of the whole of creation, and that they do go to heaven. After all, this is the goal of the definite divine plan as it was finally manifested in Christ through the paschal mystery, the salvation of the entire world, not only of humans. According to the Gospel of John (1.1) 'the Word became flesh,' not just human, or angel or anything else. The term 'flesh' points to the animalhood that all living organisms share in common, as the creaturely substratum of their constitution through God's original fiat. Christ assumed, then, 'animality' so as to save the world in its entirety, not just humanity. Otherwise, the non-human creation and animals would have been created in vain.

It is widely accepted by all Christian traditions and churches that the goal of life in Christ is deification, theosis; in other words, our adoption by God the Father in Christ through the Spirit (Asproulis, 2021, pp. 29–57). It is clear, then, that theosis is a gift of God. At the same time, though, theosis is a result of the human ascetic struggle in history against the various forms of evil, a synergy with the grace of God towards the transfiguration of our nature, the sacrifice of our fallen nature with our self-indulgent sinful passions and an offering of the creation to the hands of the Creator. In saying this, one cannot continue to ignore the 'rights' of all the creatures of God in this salvation plan. Non-human animals have also the right to deification, to the degree that theosis acquires a clear cosmological dimension, concerning the salvation of the entire earth and not only of humanity. Indeed, in the mainstream currents of Christian tradition humans are favoured over non-human animals. This is a result of the rationality and cognitive skills of the former. Undoubtedly such a view led to the profound irreversible catastrophe of our planet. This does not mean, though, that humanity should be deprived of its central, albeit compassionate, role. Things, however, completely changed after Darwin and Freud. What really matters now is to bring to the fore the communion element which accounts for the interdependence between all animals, be they humans or non-humans. This is perhaps the only way to overcome all the historical impasses or failures and build an inclusive anthropology – namely, a new perception of the imago Dei.

Following the major landmarks in modern science since Darwinism, theological anthropology should also adopt this more inclusive perception of the human since any difference among the creatures of God is considered to be one of degree, not of kind. This latent proximity, however, between humans and non-human animals should not be overestimated to the point of reducing the former's responsibility for the survival of the earth. Although it is indisputable that the imago Dei has been endowed to humanity alone, following the above analysis, where communion gains an ontological priority over any substantialist perception of humanity (meaning a self-defined, self-referent perception of human identity) should also include all creatures due to their deep ontological connection, as well as to their share in the common animalhood. In other words, and based on this encompassing interpretation of the image, could one speak here of the animals as part of the imago Dei? In view of the present discussion, I think this is possible as otherwise this image cannot be complete; this means that the salvation of the whole of creation indeed will be realized in the eschaton if nothing is left behind (eschatological 'just transition'). This is the goal of the divine plan. Although it is true that Christ himself became human, and not an angel or any other creature, this should not be understood in terms of human exceptionalism. On the contrary, it should be seen through the lens of an emphasis on the creaturely, animal character of this assumed nature. Such a move would both affirm the traditional doctrine of the incarnation but also address current ecological challenges.

Conclusion

Can we still define the human being in terms of reason, morality or even freedom against the results provided by modern science about the status of the non-human creatures, the animals? Can we continue to treat the non-human creation as an irrational or even inferior part of God's plan to be used for the endless satisfaction of human needs? I think that the present ecological crisis and the debate about loss diversity and animal rights have convinced us that such a model of life can no longer be sustainable. In order to reverse this unpleasant condition, a new understanding of the human is required that will take into account as a sine qua non condition the whole range of non-human animals, so as to save not only biodiversity, a necessary aspect of our very life, but the earth itself, which groans in suffering (Romans 8.2). If the imago Dei means *capax infiniti*, then only as *imago mundi* that is a 'corporate animality' (Johnson, 1942) can humans contribute to the divine plan for the salvation of the world, the theosis of the entire world and not only humans.

References

Asproulis, Nikolaos, 2021, 'Eucharistic Personhood: Deification in Orthodox Tradition' in Ortiz Jared (ed.), *With All the Fullness of God: Deification in Christian Traditions*, Lanham, MD: Lexington Books/Fortress Academic.
Asproulis, Nikolaos and Wood, Nathaniel (eds), 2020, *Time for Action: Orthodoxy Facing Covid-19 Pandemic*, Volos: Volos Academy Publications.
Benner, Susanne et al., 2021, *Paul J. Crutzen and the Anthropocene: A New Epoch in Earth's History*, Cham, Switzerland: Springer Publishing.

Bentham, Jeremy, 2000, *An Introduction to the Principles of Morals and Legislation*, Kitchener, Ontario: Batoche Books.
Chryssavgis, John and Asproulis, Nikolaos (eds), 2021, *Priests of Creation: Zizioulas on Discerning an Ecological Ethos*, London/New York: T&T Clark.
Climate Refugees, 2023, https://www.climate-refugees.org/ (accessed 7.12.2023).
Coudrain, Anne, Le Duff, Matthieu, and Mitja, Danielle, 2022, 'The Anthropocene Is Shifting the Paradigm of Geosciences and Science', Comptes Rendus, *Géoscience* 355.1, pp. 1–18.
Crutzen, Paul J., and Stoermer, Eugene F., 2013, 'The "Anthropocene (2000)"' in Libby Robin, Sverker Sörlin and Paul Warde (eds), *The Future of Nature: Documents of Global Change*, New Haven, CT: Yale University Press, pp. 479–90.
Deane-Drummond, Celia, Bergmann, Sigurd, and Vogt, Markus, 2017, *Religion in the Anthropocene*, Eugene, OR: Cascade Books.
Descartes, René, 1824, *Discours de la méthode*, texte établi par Victor Cousin, tome I, sixième partie, Levrault.
Ecumenical Patriarch Bartholomew, 2023, 'Address', https://ec-patr.org/toward-an-ecological-worldview-address-by-his-all-holiness-ecumenical-patriarch-bartholomew-monaco-october-19-2023/ (accessed 7.12.2023)
Johnson, A. R., 1942, *The One and the Many in the Israelite Conception of God*, Cardiff: University of Wales Press.
Kant, Immanuel, 2007, 'Conjectural Beginning of Human History' in Gunter Zoller-Robert Luden (ed.), *Anthropology, History and Education*, Cambridge: Cambridge University Press, pp. 163–75.
Lamothe, Ryan, 2021, *A Radical Political Theology for the Anthropocene Era*, Eugene, OR: Cascade Books.
Moore, Stephen (ed.), 2014, *Divinanimality: Animal Theory, Creaturely Theology*, New York: Fordham University Press.
National Geographic, 2023, 'Ecosystem', *National Geographic*, https://education.nationalgeographic.org/resource/ecosystem (accessed 7. 12.2023).
Newman, L., 2015, 'Cogito Ergo Sum', in L. Nolan (ed.), *The Cambridge Descartes Lexicon*, Cambridge: Cambridge University Press, pp. 128–35.
Nieuwerth, Kees, Pavlovic, Peter, and Shaw, Adrian, 2022, *Every Part of Creation Matters: A Discussion Paper*, Geneva: Globethics.net.
Palamas, Gregory, 1970, 'Against Akindynos', 7, 11, 36.25-8, Pan. Chrystou (ed.), vol. 3, Thessaloniki.
Rafferty, John P., 2023, 'Biodiversity loss', *Encyclopedia Britannica*, 11 November.
Salisbury, Joyce, 2014, 'Do Animals Go to Heaven? Medieval Philosophers Contemplate Heavenly Human Exceptionalism', *Athens Journal of Humanities & Arts* 1.1, pp. 79–86.
United Nations, 2023, 'Climate Change', *United Nations*, https://www.un.org/en/climatechange/what-is-climate-change (accessed 7.12.2023).
Werner, Dietrich, and Geglitza, Elizabeth (eds), 2016, *Ecotheology, Climate Justice and Food Security*, Geneva: Globethics.net.
White, Jr, Lynn, 1967, 'The Historical Roots of Our Ecologic Crisis', *Science* 155.3767, pp. 1203–7.
Zizioulas, John, 2006, *Communion & Otherness. Further Studies in Personhood and the Church*, London/New York: T&T Clark.

UK legislation, 2022, https://www.legislation.gov.uk/ukpga/2022/22/enacted (accessed 7.12.2023).
USDA legislation, https://www.nal.usda.gov/animal-health-and-welfare/animal-welfare-act (accessed 7.12.2023).
'Biodiversity loss', *Encyclopaedia Britannica*, https://www.britannica.com/science/biodiversity-loss (accessed 7.12.2023).

PART 3

Voices from the Global South

9

Ecojustice in Abya Yala: Decolonization and the Practice of 'Good Living'

YENNY DELGADO

The links between climate change and the use of carbon-based fuels are undeniable and are leading to disastrous ramifications across the planet. One of the root causes of the current climate crisis can be linked to implications of colonization and the ongoing ecocide in Abya Yala. Indeed, reflecting on ecojustice in Abya Yala is a prophetic action still being viewed with suspicion. The ecocide actions suffered on the continent are not new but instead began with an abrupt period in the history of colonization, which started the systematic destruction of the natural world, for both those who inhabited it and Mother Nature itself, throughout the continent.

A key part of this chapter is using a decolonial lens to understand and describe the process that has taken place in the environment, with a particular focus on the continent and using the term Abya Yala. Abya Yala's name comes from the Guna language, 'land in full maturity and land of vital blood'. The Guna people inhabit the North and South meeting points geographically, and utilizing their word for the land represents the connectivity and unity of the continent called America during colonization. In the 1970s, Abya Yala was adopted as the name instead of North America, which was inhabited primarily by English speakers, and Latin America, inhabited mainly by Spanish and Portuguese speakers; these are names that perpetuate Eurocentric and colonial divisions (Delgado and Ramirez, 2022, p. 18).

The freedom to live in a natural environment was seen as a Motherland to all the continent's inhabitants. The impact of the colonization of Abya Yala, with the arrival of Europeans in 1492, caused a catastrophic destruction of our Motherland. The deforestation of ancient trees, the imposition of monoculture farming processes, the use of chemical fertilizers on the land, the contamination of the water through the extraction of minerals, and the genocide of the native population through all this contamination and poisoning has led to immense loss. The unquenchable thirst for natural products such as gold and copper, and now oil, to satisfy the demands first of colonizers and then the global economy has had terrible consequences in Abya Yala. Reflecting on this situation based on context and historical review shows the oppressive and destructive colonizing process that now affects those who continue to live on the land.

Often, the continent and the process of colonization are divided succinctly between the different colonizing forces from Europe; however, for this chapter and reflection, as opposed to focusing heavily on linguistic and cultural differences in the impact of colonization, I focus on the consequences of the colonization system implemented that shared many things in common whether from Spanish, Portuguese, French or English colonizers. From this vantage point, it becomes clearer that, overall, the implications of colonization were ultimately disastrous and shows how both native populations and the environment suffered as a result of these encounters. Indeed, ecojustice in Abya Yala is a critical reflection on liberation and embraces a truly theological decolonized approach that can allow us to carry out actions of justice in terms of protection and conservation of the land, the trees, the animals, and everything we relate to in this world as part of the vast cosmos in which we cohabit as human beings.

Historical approach under a decolonization review

The invasion of Abya Yala from European kingdoms in 1492 was motivated by the possibility of possessing, controlling and owning a new land, what Europeans called the beginning of the 'new world'. For thousands of years, the native peoples of Abya Yala lived well and prospered through practices that provided a good living and unity between a naturalistic cosmology and spirituality. But today, what was presented as conquest, civilization and Christianization has led to significant challenges for native peoples in their efforts to maintain traditional ways of life. Occupation and forced enslavement of the native population drastically changed the lives of thousands and, not surprisingly, it was the result of the 'intense competition for control among the European powers' (Stephanson, 1995, p. 25). Christian countries such as Spain,

Portugal and England forced native populations to forget their cultures, languages and beliefs, fearing that their traditions could be dangerous or lead them into rebellion against their new rulers.

Developing a vision of the land as being 'unproductive' (Dunbar-Ortiz, 2014, p. 30), European colonizers claimed ownership of vast territories through treaties, massacres and military force, dividing the continent into pieces. This often resulted in disposing of native communities from their ancestral lands, separating communities, and breaking the ways of living and caring for territories that communities had developed. Control of the land and food from it played a pivotal role in the interactions and subjects of supremacists.

The European colonizers introduced in Abya Yala the concept of private land ownership, which was alien to many communities with regard to land rights. Without taking the time to understand the laws and ways of ruling in the communities of the original population, the colonizers controlled the land to satisfy personal ambitions and feed the demands of a Europe that was moving from a medieval and barbaric age to the beginning of modernity. Indeed, Dussel writes:

> But modernity as such was 'born' when Europe was in a position to pose itself against another, when, in other words, Europe could constitute itself as a unified ego exploring, conquering, colonizing an alterity that gave back its image of itself. This other, in other words, was not 'dis-covered' or admitted, as such, but concealed, or 'covered up' as the same as what Europe assumed it had always been. So, suppose 1492 is the moment of the 'birth' of modernity as a concept. In that case, the moment of origin of a very particular myth of sacrificial violence, it also marks the origin of a process of concealment or misrecognition of the non-European. (Dussel, 1993, p. 66)

In order to live in modernity, others had to live in darkness, between chains and violence. With this process, we can understand how Abya Yala was subject to hungry oppression in the modern era of the 'old European world'. The rape of the Motherland by colonizers is viewed clearly in the southern part of the continent through forced labour systems to exploit the newly acquired lands and resources, such as the *encomienda* system in Spanish colonies. In the *encomienda* system, native populations were forced to work on lands for the benefit of colonizers without regard for their well-being or their existing practice. Native people were coerced into working on plantations, mines and other agricultural enterprises, leading to the exploitation of their labour and often harsh living conditions. Native agriculture and food-gathering practices were marginalized or replaced by European-style farming, ranching and forced labour. The supremacist relationship that ruled the new system brought injustice and destruction. As Brazilian theologian Ivone Gebara writes in her book *Longing for Running Water*:

> This hierarchical worldview justifies not only the ascendancy of male human beings, but also the power of one ethnic group over another, of one religion over another, of one social group over another, and of one sex over another. It is, in a certain sense, an accomplice to the present situation of destruction that affects many peoples as well as the planet Earth itself. (Gebara, 1999, p. 81)

Despite the challenges, many native communities resisted colonization and attempted to maintain control over their lands and sources of food. Some groups adapted to the new agricultural practices and selectively incorporated and introduced crops into their diets while preserving their traditional knowledge of local food resources. As a result of colonization, agricultural and mining practices were often developed primarily for commercial purposes; as such, balanced agricultural practices were abandoned for staple crops such as tobacco, sugar, and cotton. This occurred a great deal throughout the southern part of the United States (cotton/tobacco) and throughout the Caribbean (sugar); extractive processes for precious metals were most heavily utilized in the Andean region (gold and silver); while timber and cacao were harvested from the Amazon region. The colonial administration divisions, originally called viceroyalties and colonies, continue in what are today the republics without major changes to the conditions of the original population and how the land and nature were treated until now.

Modernity in Europe was not only achieved through the process of stealing land but also through the stealing of people. The enslavement of individuals, Africans as well as native people, was utilized to increase profits and control. Unpaid labour was needed to turn a profit in the new world. Native populations went from keepers of the land to forced servitude without rights of freedom, and this marked the beginning of what today is the impoverished and injustice situation of native communities. Centuries later the descendants of the native populations in many countries remain the most impoverished and under-resourced throughout all of Abya Yala. In the words of Gustavo Gutiérrez, the father of liberation theology in the 1970s:

> We must pay special attention to the words we use. The term poor might seem not only vague and churchy, but also somewhat sentimental and aseptic. The 'poor' person today is the oppressed one, the one marginalized from society, the member of the proletariat struggling for his most basic rights; he is the exploited and plundered social class, the country struggling for its liberation. In today's world the solidarity and protest of which we are speaking have an evident and inevitable 'political' character insofar as they imply liberation. To be with the oppressed is to be against the oppressor. In our times and on our continent to be in solidarity with the 'poor,' understood in this way, means to run personal risks. (Gutiérrez, 1973, p. 301)

This reflection was prescient for its time but neglects to categorically state who were the poor and the ultimate beneficiaries of the impoverishment. In this reflection, we find a system that has subjected the land and the communities, and which has not honoured how the land was cared for and how we lived in the community. Up to this point, we can see that the colonial process has been baked into the current lived reality in Abya Yala. Not considering it would be a betrayal of the memories and resistance struggles of the people and, as a theologian descended from the original population, I would not be loyal to my ancestors, part of the original people, to ignore the practices that peasant grandmothers who lived and suffered these conditions of oppression had to endure. Such colonization facts as these many today want to erase.

However, the resistance is not only in epistemological reflections, but some are living through the good practices of the people who can teach us to resume this form of ecojustice for Mother Earth. This deeply spiritual practice honoured the land as 'Mother', and the community as a way to live in harmony.

Destruction of nature, seeds, plants and water

Five centuries after the destructive encounter of colonization, Abya Yala is still known for its rich biodiversity, vast rainforests, diverse plant life, and abundant water resources. However, degradation risks the lives of the new generations who still practise and care for the land. Large-scale deforestation for agriculture, logging, mining, water pollution and urban expansion has been a significant driver of environmental destruction in areas rich in biodiversity. Rapid urbanization in many areas has converted natural areas into concrete jungles, further contributing to crowded and noisy cities, which are stressful as a result of noise pollution. The use of oil, the creation of waste and plastics, and the pollution of water sources, have all brought unfortunate and irreparable consequences. This description undoubtedly falls within what we currently call ecocide, that which is caused by human actions. The destructive impacts in Abya Yala are directly linked to colonial thinking that seeks to take everything possible from the earth. What can we do in response to this reflection of ecojustice in Abya Yala?

A key component of both the plantation systems in the North and the *encomienda* in the South was to ensure that individuals working the land, whether enslaved or deeply indentured, did not have access to means of escape from this economic and social oppression. Today, though the systems are no longer in place, aspects of modern corporate farming have led to similar forms of debt for farmers throughout the continent. One clear example of colonial oppression of the land and the people in modern agribusiness is the agricultural company Monsanto, which developed genetically modified seeds that are essentially sterile. The use of selected harvesting and cross-pollination has been standard practice in agriculture for millennia. Abya Yala is well known for its biodiversity due to the ingenious farmers who developed thousands of varieties of potatoes and other crops. Indeed, throughout human existence we have modified seeds and animals to increase yields and productivity to provide a better life for all. However, Monsanto utilized genetics to develop essentially sterile seeds, so that every year farmers would need to buy from them once again to plant their crops instead of retaining a part of the harvest to reseed their land. Essentially through corporate manipulation, there has been a technological murder of the fullness of the land and its produce. It is clear that colonial control continues; the seeds that have been kept for centuries and belong to the native communities are in the hands of multinational corporations.

The colonial power structures now operate in more 'modern' ways but still feed the same people who started the company. Though farmers increasingly resist these new practices, many governments are allowing multinational corporate interventions to impact food security. For those of us who have farming families, we know what seeds mean – so let's consider where they come from and the ancestral process.

As daughters of the corn, we know what the process involves. After the corn is harvested, it is dried, saved and stored for the next year of planting. In contrast, terminator seeds are genocide as they are modified to only last one generation to ensure farmers have to purchase new seeds from the organization. Apart from the expenditure involved in this process, this method poses an environmental concern, being that it significantly reduces crop diversity and monopolizes the production of food through the privatization of seeds. From the base communities, we find a deep sense of knowing among the people about how to take care of Mother Earth and protect our animal brothers and sisters, the rivers and the mountains. It is understood that the interrelation that we have is a cosmos-felt existence, in which we are part of an existence with nature's ancestral symbols, such as the corn that nourished for centuries and continues to this day to feed people. As such, quinoa and other products are a vital force, but we face destruction when the means to reproduce are privatized and crops are no longer available. Thus, we look for ways to resurrect in theological code.

In these communities, we find reflections of a painful colonial history that continues to bring profound reflections to new generations; many phrases resonate with the last years of the social movements with regard to decolonization: 'They Tried to Bury Us, They Didn't Know We Were Seeds' is a famous refrain from the Popol Vuh (Sacred Book of the Mayans). 'They plucked our fruits, they cut our branches, they burned our logs. But they couldn't kill our roots.'

The consequences of colonialism, as illuminated in the sacred texts of the Mayans, manifest a desire to erase, render invisible and annihilate all elements associated with native peoples – their environment, memories and cultural fabric. Despite enduring resistance and an ongoing quest for liberation, the pervasive impact of a system rooted in continuous destruction is evident, particularly in the Amazon region. Incidents of widespread fires, often resulting from misappropriation policies and corruption, have been alarmingly high, with 33,116 illegal fire hotspots recorded in August 2022, marking the highest level in 12 years. This escalating threat jeopardizes the rainforest, indigenous and traditional communities, the unparalleled biodiversity of the region, and the global climate; all these demand genuine, sustainable solutions (Greenberg, 2022, pp. 8–10).

Furthermore, heinous acts such as the targeted murders of native leaders and activists, exemplified by the assassination of Bertha Cáceres, a Honduran environmental activist, and the persistent harassment faced by Maxima Acuña, a Peruvian indigenous activist, underscore the perilous conditions faced by those advocating for environmental preservation. The Global Witness report puts Brazil in the lead for total documented killings of environmental defenders, with 342 lethal attacks between 2012 and 2021. One-third of the victims were Indigenous people or Afro-descendants, and 85 per cent of these crimes took place within the Brazilian Amazon region (Fernandez, 2023, pp. 57–60).

Notably, the wanton destruction of land, crops and ancient trees is intertwined with the targeted assassinations of native leaders who bravely speak out against ecocide. This disturbing correlation underscores the urgency for government policies that prioritize the well-being of native populations, recognizing the intrinsic connection between safeguarding lives and preserving the ecology of crucial global regions. The Amazon, often referred to as the 'lungs of the world', serves as a poignant reminder of this inseparable relationship:

> The Amazon forest provides valuable ecosystem services in terms of maintaining biodiversity, recycling water needed to maintain rainfall in the Amazon and in south-eastern and central Brazil, as well as in neighbouring countries, and in avoiding global warming through its storage of carbon. In this context, the Amazon has a value for society that is much greater than the profits that a landholder can reap by destroying the forest. However, and crucially, progress has been slow in converting this value into payments for ecosystem services that would use this value as an incentive to keep the forests standing. (Carvalho et al., 2019, pp. 122–30)

Native communities with indigenous practices intricately engage with the care of the Motherland. This responsibility often transforms into a defensive stance, as they protect lands, territories and communities against encroachments by corporations and governments. The resistance extends to countering extractive projects that contaminate the water and air in search of mineral wealth. Indigenous communities experience routine violations of their individual and collective rights, including land theft, displacement, cultural repression, contamination and physical assaults.

Ecojustice and the embrace of decolonization practices

In response to the recent antecedents of ecocide, there has been a heightened mobilization of actions by civil society, churches and government entities, all aiming to actively participate in the care process. It is crucial to recognize and re-evaluate the long-standing practices of environmental stewardship that indigenous communities have imparted and practised for centuries.

The imperative to conserve and protect Mother Earth, with whom we coexist, underscores the need to revive sustainable practices. This revival involves embracing the indigenous wisdom that has fostered a harmonious relationship with the environment. In this context, we envision a relational and cosmo existence where all beings are honoured. The '*Sumak kawsay*', a Quechua language phrase that translates into English as 'good living', is a principle observed in native communities in Abya Yala. The phrase emphasizes the understanding that everyone deserves to live well in harmony, with access to essential resources such as food and clean water, a commitment to nature conservation, and the freedom to practise their spiritual beliefs. It is the understanding that the environment does not need us to live, but rather *we* need nature, and it is this relationship that leads us to respect it, care for it, and be in communion with it.

The concept of 'good living' transcends individual well-being; it is a communal notion that extends to encompass the entire social group and the natural world. Living well, therefore, necessitates fostering a healthy relationship between peoples, creation, and all aspects of nature. The historical experiences of native populations subjected to European 'Christian' influence were marked by control and imposition, resulting in profound consequences. Living under oppressive and impoverished conditions, driven by inequality and colonization, not only jeopardized the well-being of indigenous communities but also posed a significant threat to the delicate balance of nature itself.

For this reason, we need to return to a time of a full bond with the cosmos. Theologians such as Sofía Chipana from the Aymaran nation of Bolivia speaks to this when she wrote:

> It is a time of healing that seeks to restore balance and harmony in the inhabited cosmos, to continue awakening to the various knowledge and wisdom from the cosmic consciousness, since there are realities and situations that are not understood only from human Feeling-thinking the relationship of mutuality, of listening and observing the rhythm of others and other beings of the Ayllu (community) is required. (Chipana Quispe, 2022b, pp. 36–9)

From this work, the Church has sought to generate a dialogue to value these practices so that this relationship is preserved, the environment is cared for, and value and ecojustice are redefined. In the document written for the Synod of Bishops' special assembly for the pan-Amazonian region, we can read, 'It is a matter of living in harmony with oneself, with nature, with human beings, and with the Supreme Being, since there is intercommunication throughout the cosmos; here there are neither exclusions nor those who exclude, and here a full life for all can be projected.' However, in a society with a colonial past and the remnants of thought of control towards native peoples, it is necessary to see the situations of oppression to which they continue to be subjected.

To address the ramifications of colonization, we need to develop and embrace a theological perspective that integrates the recognition of the population and nature from the same context as Abya Yala. For this to be possible for the emergence of a new way of thinking, a heart from the same land then makes a challenge that requires a prophetic and bold voice. It is necessary to embrace from theological thought and faith to enter into a process of liberation. As the theologian Leonardo Boff wrote:

> We are not the focal point of creation. We are not, as it were, its landlord, adopting the attitude of Adam, who gave all things their names and thus possessed them. We are here to serve as shepherds and custodians of other beings, and we are responsible for their integrity. We can use them, therefore, solely for our needs which, as those of human beings, always contain a measure of superabundance and gratuitousness. (Boff, 1995, p. 86)

In the context of the relationship between the land, their children and all creation, Abya Yala refers to a land that is alive, mature, and of vital blood (Delgado and Ramírez, 2022, pp. 2–3). This terminology implies two things in need of interpretation. First, native peoples maintain ways of understanding the world holistically; our land is not just a reservoir of resources to be used but a Motherland, more mature and of greater wisdom; second, on the other hand, the vitality of the blood of the land courses between all her peoples and through the generations; this implies that the descendants of native peoples who still suffer from colonization will never wholly assimilate into the European-derived culture established to erase all our ways to connect with our ancestors.

We persist within the framework of an anthropocentric and patriarchal model, inflicting significant harm upon the shared home we inhabit. It is imperative that we shift towards embracing the wisdom inherent in Mother Earth and recognize the pivotal role played by women, the nurturers and caretakers of our environment. By doing so, we can actively contribute to the restoration of equilibrium.

The theological implications of this conception of Abya Yala invites us to reflect on where we are, both in terms of our geographical location and in terms of our historical context. This is a process that reflects and considers the experience of receiving the Christian message through the lens of European colonizers. Through reflecting and disconnecting the truth of the message of 'the Hope' from the hands of the oppressor.

So, from the point of view of ecocide, it is to see not only the past colonizing process but today's continued destruction of nature, the murders of community leaders and activists as a crucifix. The constant crucifixion and suffering as a result of the ongoing colonial desire and ambition to take over resources is in symbolic form, the crucifixions of the people of the land of Abya Yala who thirst for justice and seek liberation.

Here we are, native people and their descendants who have been crucified for centuries under colonization, control, oppression, genocide and ecocide; today, we witness our Motherland's resurrection and hear God's good news to all her children as believers of the message. The Jesuit priest Jon Sobrino provides some insight on this interpretation of the resurrection – that it brings Hope for the crucified – which is a new interpretation for us:

> If what has been said so far is taken seriously, it follows, not from a fundamentalist reading of the texts, but from a profound honesty towards them, that the resurrection of Jesus is Hope in the first place for the crucified. God raised a crucified, and since then, there is Hope for the crucified of history. (Sobrino, 1995, p. 239)

Sobrino's reading needs to be adapted to respond to our own context. However, it confirms that natives and their descendants in Abya Yala are under God's protection and recipients of God's Hope. This God is the one who resurrects and liberates us from a long process of colonization and oppression.

From a biblical and theological reflection, the assassination of native activists is not overlooked. There is a call to face the events, and we seek to keep present the voices of those who have been murdered, and reporting these crimes is an act of justice. Passages like the one we find in Genesis show us that it is our job to warn against continuous murders. In Genesis 4.10, we read, 'The Lord said, "What have you done? Listen! Your brother's blood cries out to me from the ground."' It is then that ecojustice becomes more than a necessary issue to reflect; it is a critical action of justice; resuming ancestral practices of care and protection and not abusing the resources causing so much damage will be a step towards generating and recovering lands devastated, and creating that much-needed healing. In the words of Leonardo Boff:

> The environment has its rights, and there is such a thing as ecological justice. Everything has the right to continue to exist within the ecological balance. This right produces a corresponding duty in human beings to preserve and defend the existence of every being in creation. Today, we call this the dignity of the Earth, seen as a whole. (Boff, 1995, p. 87)

Conclusion

Abya Yala is a land rich in biodiversity, with the original population that continues to strive to protect and persevere with regard to the environment, trees, water and nature. Abya Yala has experienced ecocide, expropriation and territorial division as a result of colonization. Despite this scar tissue, the deep-rooted connection of native peoples to the land remains strong and is evident as they continue to fight against the destruction of nature even if their own governments are silent. Native populations have the wisdom of taking care of their environment with their lives. This modern crucifixion is an act that should call us as a Church to actively participate in stopping this destruction and promoting a process of liberation that allows the good life of all peoples who inhabit the continent today.

For a sustainable and harmonious future, a call to action in an honest decolonization process is necessary in history and theology. Acknowledging and rectifying past injustices is vital for building a society where the spiritual practices of 'Good Living' can flourish for all inhabitants of Abya Yala.

This decolonization process should encompass governments, churches and other institutions that have played significant roles in the continent's history. These entities must engage in diverse, honest conversations and approaches to welcome and respect native practices, spiritual beliefs and traditional knowledge. These conversations and dialogues are a first step, but our actions and efforts must not stop in the reflective space or 'book clubs'; instead, they must lead to a transformative change in liturgical practices and the relationship with our community.

Embracing native practices and knowledge can offer valuable insights and solutions to the ecological challenges faced by Abya Yala and beyond. The deep understanding of the land and its biodiversity held by native communities can contribute to more sustainable and respectful ways of interacting with the environment. It is a step towards acknowledging past mistakes and embracing a collective responsibility. Abya Yala can move towards a future where the principles of 'Good Living' can be embraced and practised by everyone, leading to a more harmonious and sustainable coexistence with nature.

References

Boff, Leonardo, 1995, *Ecology & Liberation: A New Paradigm*, New York: Orbis Books.

Carvalho, William D. et al., 2019, 'Deforestation Control in the Brazilian Amazon: A Conservation Struggle Being Lost as Agreements and Regulations are Subverted and Bypassed', *Perspectives in Ecology and Conservation* 17.3, pp. 122–30.

Chipana Quispe, Sofía, 2022a, 'El restablecimiento del equilibrio y armonía desde la cosmovisión Andina', *Publica Theology*, https://publicatheology.org/2022/05/23/el-restablecimiento-del-equilibrio-y-armonia-desde-la-cosmovision-andina/ (accessed 3.01.2025).

Chipana Quispe, Sofía, 2022b, 'Cosmovivencias nutridas en las fuentes ancestrales', *Publica Theology*, https://publicatheology.org/2022/04/22/cosmovivencias-nutridas-en-las-fuentes-ancestrales/ (accessed 3.01.2025).

Delgado, Yenny and Ramírez, Claudio, 2022, 'Abya Yala Theology', *Publica Theology*, https://publicatheology.org/2022/04/06/abya-yala-theology/ (accessed 3.01.2025).

Delgado, Yenny, and Ramirez, Claudio, 2023, 'Abya Yala Theology: Decolonizing the Christian Message from a Native Perspective', *Ecumenical Trends* 52.2, March/April, Graymoor Ecumenical & Interreligious Institute.

Dunbar-Ortiz, Roxanne, 2014, *An Indigenous Peoples History of the United States*, Boston, MA: Beacon Press.

Dussel, Enrique, 1993, 'Eurocentric and Modernity', *Boundary* 2, Autumn, 20.3, The Postmodernism Debate in Latin America, Durham, NC: Duke University Press, pp. 65–76.

Fernandez, Belen, 2023 'The Murders of Indigenous Activists Mark the Death of the Planet', Aljazeera https://www.aljazeera.com/opinions/2023/8/9/the-murders-of-indigenous-activists-mark-the-death-of-the-planet (accessed 15.02.2025).

Gebara, Ivone, 1999, *Longing for Running Water: Ecofeminist and Liberation*, Minneapolis, MN: Augsburg Fortress Press.

Greenberg, Chris, 2022, 'Amazon Rainforest Fires 2022: Facts, Causes, and Climate Impacts', *Greenpeace*, https://www.greenpeace.org/international/story/55533/amazon-rainforest-fires-2022-brazil-causes-climate/ (accessed 3.01.2025).

Gutiérrez, Gustavo, 1973, *A Theology of Liberation: History, Politics, and Salvation*, New York: Orbis Books.

Sobrino, Jon, 1995, *Jesús en América Latina. Su significado para la fe y la cristología*, Santander: Sal Terrae.

Stephanson, Anders, 1995, *Manifest Destiny: American Expansion and the Empire of Right*, New York: Hill & Wang.

Synod of Bishops Special Assembly for the Pan Amazonian Region, 2019,, 'The Amazon: New Paths for the Church and for an Integral Ecology', *Vatican*, https://www.vatican.va/roman_curia/synod/documents/rc_synod_doc_20191026_sinodo-amazzonia_en.html# (accessed 3.01.2025).

10

Sustainable Anthropocene and Ecological Justice: Perspectives from the Ethos of the United Congregational Church of Southern Africa (UCCSA)

REVD XOLANI MASEKO AND
THANDI SOKO-DE JONG

Introduction

This chapter explores the concepts of sustainable Anthropocene and ecological justice and their missiological implications for the Church in the twenty-first century. These are not just concerns for the Church, but for all humanity. This chapter builds on the author's and co-author's recent article on the theme 'traditional religion: reclaiming sustainable Anthropocene' (ASEAN *Journal of Religious and Cultural Research* 5(1)). The article will serve as the foundation of this chapter, and lessons will be gleaned from the arguably 'rich Congregational ethos' that is practised in the United Congregational Church of Southern Africa (UCCSA). The author, an adherent of Congregational ecclesiology, draws inspiration from, and finds value in, UCCSA's Congregational ethos.

The argument presented in this chapter is based on the theoretical framework of 'value-oriented ethics of the environment' and 'intrinsic value discourse', which can be supported by biblical principles. This discussion lies at the intersection of liberation, public theology and ecclesiology. Here we will begin by defining sustainable Anthropocene and ecological justice, followed by a brief discussion of the author and co-author's previous work on sustainable Anthropocene. Finally, it explores the ethos and values of Congregationalism that could play a significant role in achieving sustainable Anthropocene and ecological justice. This chapter hypothesizes that the agency of local communities can foster a sustainable Anthropocene, and adopting certain beliefs and practices from the UCCSA may aid local communities, particularly those in Southern Africa, in this endeavour.

Ecological and environmental justice

There are significant negative effects of ecological and environmental justice, whether on the physical ecosystems or the atmospheric environment. It has been argued that a world that is treated fairly by humans will provide a good environment for human habitation and social and economic development. Conversely, if humanity continues to treat nature unjustly, the earth will suffer. Uncontrolled activities such as the burning of trees and forests, continuing to emit toxic gases into the atmosphere, causing injury to the earth through unregulated and illicit mining, will result in increased environmental disasters such as earthquakes and cyclones. This will, in turn, affect livelihoods as the environment becomes uninhabitable.

In Southern Africa, which provides the context of this chapter, it has been argued that countries like Zimbabwe face instances of injustice to creation. An environmental management agency (EMA) was created to fight against injustices to the environment inter alia. A common seasonal activity in Zimbabwe is the burning of forests. According to the Environmental Management Authority in Zimbabwe (EMA, 2015), burning forests have emerged as one of the greatest environmental challenges. Trees provide food and shelter, but they also help to reduce the force and speed of winds. They are critically important because they release oxygen, which is necessary for the well-being of life on earth. This is already a reality as southern Africa experiences drought, harsh weather and the extinction of some animal species.

Conceptual framework

Ecology deals with all living organisms and their relationship with one another and the environment. It includes humans, marine life, rocks and ecosystems. Many societies have argued for the value of creation based on the worth that humans ascribe to it. This is called the anthropocentric ethics of non-human creation (Kronlid and Öhman, 2012, p. 4). This may be argued to have resulted in the negative effects on ecology as human activity and dominance proceed from a utility point of view. The philosophy of this chapter is based on the belief in the intrinsic value of non-human creation (ecology); even if one may not see any value in it, it is worthy because the Creator chose to bring it into being (Kronlid and Öhman, 2012, pp. 4, 8). From the perspective of the Abrahamic faiths, a critical look at scriptures such as the Genesis account of creation, even with its symbolic and sometimes mythical implications, reveals the goodness of creation in God's sight. God saw it as good and beautiful – even without the presence of humans at the time (see Genesis 1.4, 10, 12, 18, 21, 25).

Sustainable Anthropocene

Though the Anthropocene is sometimes used to describe a time when humans have a negative effect on the planet and/or creation, in this chapter it is used to mean the dominating effect of humans on the environment or planet earth for their ends and habitation (Soko-de Jong and Maseko, 2022). By implication, 'Anthropocene' refers to the negative effects of this dominance. However, when one refers to it as sustainable, as is argued in this chapter, this includes factors such as intrinsic value-oriented ethics, indigenous knowledge and wisdom and, in the case of this chapter, the philosophy of Congregationalism, which is Christian in orientation.

According to Paulo R. Mourao and Vítor D. Martinho (2021, pp. 4680–92), in his *Laudato Si'*, Pope Francis calls for what may be called sustainable Anthropocene by pointing to the 'dominant technocratic paradigm' as the root of the crisis of ecological injustice as a result of the way humanity relates with the non-human creation. The world in the hands of unethical humans with massive technocratic advances only results in negative Anthropocene. The same conclusions can be reached when one considers Thandi Soko-de Jong and Xolani Maseko whose summary argument is captured in the following words:

The isiZulu proverb '*Uma uluma ngokungakhethi, ugcina udla umsila wakho*' (When you bite indiscriminately, you end up eating your own tail) provides a framework for acting sustainably on the environment. The proverb can be taken to mean that when we are reckless with nature, we will be left homeless. Paying closer attention to spiritualities at the margins, such as indigenous African spiritualities, and their pro-environmental characteristics and agency, helps inform a 'positive Anthropocene'. Furthermore, such frameworks provide us with indigenous wisdom that is useful in challenging and decentring monolithic narratives about the impact of religions on the environment (Meziane, 2021, p. 6, paraphrased).

In this argument, it can be seen that reclaiming an approach to nature that decentres humans as super predators can help humans embrace nature's potential to restore and heal them as it restores itself. There is no need to romanticize spirituality but communities can nonetheless adopt the practice of setting apart water bodies, forests and other natural environments to allow them to replenish themselves, knowing that their health will improve climate health. Additionally, adopting such practices is a helpful reminder that human options go beyond simply 'need' versus 'greed' but extend to others such as the sustainability of natural resources. Prioritizing sustainability keeps communities mindful of the finite nature of the planet's resources and therefore the need to safeguard them sustainably.

Ecological justice

Ecology is the study of all living things, including marine life and its relationship with the environment. It studies ecosystems that are destroyed by wildfires, deforestations, injury to the earth caused by mining, pollution and the use of natural resources for the extreme ends of humans, which are mostly as a result of greed and capitalistic development. It was in the realization of the harmful Anthropocene that scholars like Leonardo Boff called for the liberation of creation along with humanity (Boff, 1995, p. 70). He argues that the world has been made poor by humanity who is also in a poor state; hence, the Church has the social responsibility to participate in the ecojustice struggle.

The UCCSA has been reflecting on the need for eco-theology and has argued that 'it is clear that the congestion of cities, the destruction of living creatures, the plunder of fuel and minerals and the erosion of soil hold out frightening possibilities for the future unless we are prepared to curb excess, manage on less and use the earth resources to promote the health of all'. Ecology is therefore a concern of the Church because nature and the environment are created by God and have value; therefore they must be cared for. If this is done properly, humanity will enjoy a good and habitable environment.

Perspectives from the UCCSA's theology and ministry

The UCCSA is Congregational in terms of ecclesiology and polity. It is part of the reformed tradition. It is a united, transnational and multi-ethnic Church that spans seven countries, primarily in Southern Africa and partly in Central Africa. Its ethos if to be a welcoming Church that believes its calling is mission and service for the building of the kingdom of God on earth. The heritage of the UCCSA, like most Congregational churches, draws from three strands of theology: (a) John Wycliffe, who taught that the Bible is the ultimate court of appeal in all matters of doctrine, conduct and government; (b) that there is such a thing as private judgement in doctrinal matters; (c) that the Church in grasping temporal power sacrifices its true authority – John Calvin taught sole sufficiency for Scripture for ecclesiastical polity and the Radical Reformers emphasized the self-governance of each congregation (Forsyth, 1912/1995, p. 13).

It is the emphasis on the primacy of the local congregation in Congregationalism that centres mission in the local church. Hendriks (2004, p. 3) argues that the local congregation is the first and foremost manifestation of the Church; the local church is a complete church in which the fullness of Christ dwells. If congregations fail, little hope can be found elsewhere. The same logic applies to local and extended families, which form a tribe or community that, in turn, forms a society and a nation. Christian families, faith communities and congregations are the first manifestations of the Church. The local church with its local people in local communities are central in the mission story. Rein Brouwer (2009, p. 4) argues that 'ecologies differ according to their geographical location, degree of urbanisation, regional economic situation, political culture, religious diversity, etc.'. Therefore:

> Where there is only one faith community, such as in a small village, there is no biodiversity. In vital ecologies, with great biodiversity in a rich (nutritious) environment, there are different active faith communities that both compete with and/or support each other. Communities of faith therefore form a religious population within an ecology that is continually changing and evolving. (Brouwer, 2009, p. 4)

Many ecological and climate conventions may be described as products of elites converging in hotels and places that are symbols of affluence. This leaves the struggle for ecological justice as an academic matter and never owned by the local people who must be key stakeholders of the mitigation strategies for ecological justice. The UCCSA's theological understanding and practice that puts the local church in the prime position of ecclesiology and doing mission is ideal because it is in the local areas that we find indigenous knowledge systems, some of which are pro-environment. Soko-de Jong and Maseko argue in this light by stating that, 'For centuries, African spiritualities – generally described as African Traditional Religions (hereafter, ATR) – integrated nature into their belief systems' (2022, p. 6). This had pro-environment implications, 'as ATR shaped both individual and collective stances and conduct toward nature'. Other sustainable Anthropocene around the world is similarly based in localized, indigenous spiritualities.

A good example of indigenous wisdom in Africa, particularly in Southern Africa, is that there are people whose surnames and totems are linked with certain trees and animals; hence, they would protect those trees and animals as they are considered sacred according to their beliefs (Taringa, 2014, p. 53). It is the argument of this chapter that such an attitude towards the environment will result in a sustainable or positive Anthropocene.

Related to the argument for the local church and local context as the locus of mission – and as a motivation for contextual ecological interventions in the local context – is the belief of the UCCSA in the priesthood of all believers. This theological doctrine states that it is the duty of all baptized members in a local church to be responsible for the work of ministry and mission – in other words, not just the clergy. Scriptures such as Exodus 19.5–6, 1 Peter 2.9, Revelation 5.9–10 and 1 Corinthians 12.12–13 are used to argue for this theological principle (Maseko, 2021, p. 111). This principle could be used to inspire the participation of all citizens of the community in strategies for sustainable Anthropocene and ecological justice. This must not be left only to civic groups, ecumenical church organizations and the non-governmental organizations, as is often the case.

The UCCSA prides itself on being a 'covenant church'. This is one aspect at the centre of any Congregational church. D. Roy Briggs, in his book *A Covenant Church* (1996) where he discusses the ecclesiology of the UCCSA, argues that the 'covenant' in the UCCSA comprises three parts – namely, 'to worship, work and witness' together in the fellowship of the church, for the building of the body of Christ and the manifestation of the kingdom of God on earth. The covenant and kingdom of God are aspects fundamental to ecojustice.

In the Old Testament, when the covenant was made or cut, an animal was sacrificed, thereby bringing animals as part of creation into the picture. Similarly, the covenant promised certain benefits, which in many cases included the protection of the land that the lesser party owned, thereby bringing natural resources (creation) into the picture. This may be learnt in Scripture concerning covenants, especially in the Old Testament: Abraham and Abimelech (Genesis 21.27); Abraham and the Amorites (Genesis 14.13); and Laban and Jacob (Genesis 31.44) (see von Rad, 1975, p. 129). Examples of covenants between Yahweh and individuals are: God and Noah (Genesis 9.13), with the rainbow as a symbol of agreement; God and Abraham, with circumcision as a seal (Genesis 15.18–21; 17.4–14). There were also covenants that God made with the people, such as with Israel on Mount Sinai (Deuteronomy 29.1f). If one follows this theological reading of the covenant, and grapples with the ecclesial description and identity of the UCCSA as a covenant church, the issue of ecological justice is placed at the centre of church and mission.

Still on the theology of the covenant, the same idea is seen in the New Testament when it comes to the theology of the Eucharist. Briggs quotes from *A Book of Services and Prayers*, stating that, 'at no point in the public worship are things local and universal brought more closely together than at holy communion. Here the Saviour of the world gives himself to particular persons as each receives bread and wine' (Briggs, 1996, p. 164). Bread comes from plants and hence the soil is involved; wine comes from vine trees. Hence, vegetation is brought to the fore. In UCCSA, which adheres to the Congregational tradition, the sacraments are signs of the Church along with the preaching of the gospel. It is therefore correct to argue that the earth and vegetation, which are part of ecological life, are important to the UCCSA's mission. In his commentary on Pope Francis' *Laudato Si'*, Paul McPartlan (2024) argues that:

> At the Last Supper Jesus took bread and wine into His hands, and all of the accounts tell us that He gave thanks to God for them. Unlike human beings, who take things without any thankfulness to God, He was full of thanks and praise, and the bread and wine were transformed by His act of thankfulness. They became His own body and blood. Instead of groaning, they rejoiced. They were fulfilled in His hands. Pope Francis says that in the Eucharist 'all that has been created finds its greatest exaltation ... Joined to the incarnate Son, present in the Eucharist, the whole cosmos gives thanks to God. Indeed, the Eucharist is itself an act of cosmic love' (*Laudato Si'*, no. 236). Jesus said to His disciples, 'Do this in memory of me.' Do we ever think that among the many lessons He was teaching us at that moment one of

them was how to treat creation? Handle it with love and thanksgiving, not with violence and greed!

The UCCSA's concept of the kingdom of God informs all ministry and activities of the Church. This is one of the distinguishing marks of churches in the reformed tradition: the establishment of God's kingdom is understood to be the main objective of mission. The UCCSA Covenant as recited by members in all executive meetings and assemblies prescribes that: '... we covenant to worship, work and witness together in the fellowship of this church, for the building up of the body of Christ, and the manifesting of the Kingdom of God on Earth' (Briggs, 1996, p. 23).

This kingdom of God is not seen as a futuristic, eschatological reality but involves a socio-economic and political transformation in the here and now. It is in agreement with this concept of the kingdom of God that the UCCSA understands care as stewardship of creation to be one of the marks of mission. Writing about this relationship between ecology and mission, the UCCSA (2019, p. 19) states that, 'mission is about caring for creation. There was a time when climate could be predictable along the seasons. But today it is not always possible because of global warming. Global warming is a result of injury that human beings inflicted on mother earth. According to the Old Testament scriptures, humans were created and put in a position of caring for the rest of creation.'

Therefore, the argument of this chapter is that a sustainable Anthropocene may be possible when humanity and the Church take seriously their missional mandate and work for the establishment of the kingdom of God through the responsible stewardship of creation along with other missional interventions, as stated in the teachings of the UCCSA.

The UCCSA understands itself as a Justice Church. This is not just a slogan but a theological imperative born out of biblical reflection and seeking to understand the purpose of the Church. The concept of justice not only speaks of social, economic and political systems but also ecological justice. When ecology and climate are injured by human agency and are hostile to humanity, it affects the fullness of life. The UCCSA, which espouses a missional ecclesiology, describes its commitment to mission as, '... re-reading the Bible in the light of our experience and mission; Journeying together in the search for transformation of the systems that deny justice, equality and human rights'.

This confession by the UCCSA is aimed at justice for all people and indeed their environment (creation), which impacts their daily experiences. As a missional Church, the UCCSA believes that it is called to answer to the contextual challenges, and at the present moment the issue of ecological justice is an urgent imperative if the dream for a sustainable Anthropocene is to be realized.

The concept of justice has the potential to bring revolution to the care of creation not only by the Church but by the entire world – by applying the environmental ethic of recognizing the intrinsic worth of non-human creation. The creation accounts in Genesis, despite their symbolic nature, give humanity a missiological responsibility to care for the environment. With regard to justice and the environment, the World Council of Churches in 'Towards a Just, Participatory and Sustainable Society' (Nairobi Assembly of the WCC, 1975) and 'Justice, Peace and the Integrity of Creation' (Vancouver Assembly of the WCC, 1983) outlined the core aspects of the social responsibility of the Church as 'economic justice and environmental sustainability' (Bailey, 2020, p. 13). Leonardo Boff is of the same opinion: that the non-human environment has intrinsic worth, yet it is impoverished and oppressed by human exploitation (Boff, 1995, p.70). The efforts of all, including the Church, can help reverse the damage and ensure a sustainable impact of humanity on earth (Anthropocene).

The UCCSA's charge for the struggle for a sustainable Anthropocene is evident in the resolutions from the UCCSA 41st Assembly in 2022, which was endorsed by the 2023 UCCSA March Executive. These august meetings resolved, among other things:

1 To encourage all local churches to observe September as the month of creation in line with the World Council of Churches initiative on the climate crisis.
2 To set aside a Sunday during this month to bring the missional dimension of climate change to the worship and witness of the Church.
3 To provide support in the form of liturgy, Bible study and sermon guides to local churches and ministers to ensure this concern is addressed robustly.
4 To request the Theological Commission to draft a document on Environmental Theology to elicit discussions in the Church among ministerial fraternities.
5 To encourage local churches to consider ways of reducing their carbon footprint by implementing alternative forms of electricity generation and by initiating methods of 'reduce, reuse and recycle'.
6 To encourage the local churches to motivate each member to plant a Spekboom tree (*Portulacaria afra*) in order to contribute to reducing carbon dioxide in the atmosphere.

7 That all churches are to report through their Mission Councils on the progress made in an attempt to plant 500,000 Spekboom (*Portulacaria afra*) trees before the next Assembly.

Strategies such as planting trees and recycling may lead to a sustainable Anthropocene. This is in line with what Howard A. Snyder and Joel A. Scandrett (2011, p. 3) argue, that 'salvation means creation healed'. The disease of alienation between humanity and God goes along with the alienation of humanity from the rest of creation.

'Rest' and the oikos

Oikos

It is critical to note that there are alternative ways to contribute to a sustainable Anthropocene, in addition to action-oriented strategies such as planting trees. One such way is to provide the environment with ample opportunities to rest and rejuvenate. Theologian Steve de Gruchy referred to the earth as our 'home' and used the theological term 'oikos' to describe it. De Gruchy was not only a prominent South African theologian but also a member of the UCCSA. His theological contributions focused on the intersection of theology and development, addressing issues that affect both society and the environment. His insights on ecology complement the range of the UCCSA's contributions by highlighting, among others, the concept of oikos.

In 'An Olive Agenda: First Thoughts on a Metaphorical Theology of Development', de Gruchy argues that economic pursuits and ecology are interconnected in that they both have to do with the concept of oikos as 'the earth, our home' (de Gruchy, 2010, p. 1). Oikos, meaning 'home' in ancient Greek, comprises part of the two words: economy (*oikos-nomos*), which concerns 'the rules that should govern the way we run our home' (p. 1), and ecology (*oikos-logos*), the 'wisdom of how our home functions' (p. 1). He adds that ecology, as *oikos-logos*, was how humans in diverse times and places built their economic life in ways that respected their relationship to the ecological boundaries they experienced (p. 1). This, as opposed to taking the earth and dissecting it into profitable natural resources, 'and then – with new forms of power – pummelling it into shape as commodities to serve the market for such goods' (pp. 1–2).

The coherence between economic pursuits and ecology is a reminder that both dictate how our home, the earth, functions. De Gruchy adds, 'given that we inhabit only one earth as our home, our economy or household-rules should be rooted in ecology, our household-wisdom' (de Gruchy, 2010, p. 1). In other words, our economic pursuits have a direct and undeniable impact on the physical environment; therefore, they ought to be rooted in ecological principles that help sustain our only home/oikos. A significant part of those principles is the recognition that while planting trees and engaging in other sustainable activities is vital, it is equally critical to allow the environment to rest from our consumption needs to enable its replenishment.

Rest

Rest, concerning the environment, is a practice with direct theological connotations. According to Madipoane Masenya, 'Just as there is a human need to sleep and rest the body, the land, needs to be rested' (Masenya, 2015, p. 431). This is also applicable to the rest of the physical environment including water sources facing overfishing and pollution. Thus, in a time where there is an economic demand for increasingly more production and profit, rest is a reminder that neither humans nor nature is infinite. Masenya's call to acknowledge the importance of rest is also a reminder of life's rhythms and cycles, without which restoration comes at a very high cost. The concept of rest is also recognizable in Bible passages such as Leviticus 25.4 (seventh year as a sabbath year for the land), alongside Exodus 20.8–10a (honouring the Sabbath as a day of rest from work).

The UCCSA's environmental justice advocacy

Land and ownership

The UCCSA has constantly been in the struggle for environmental justice and participates in conversations relating to land and ownership. Issues relating to land ownership in Southern Africa include the reality that in South Africa the majority of the land is privately owned by individuals and corporations. In 2009, through the South African Council of Churches, a tool for Bible studies addressing mitigation and intervention strategies was produced titled *Climate Change: A Challenge to Churches in South Africa*. Through this book, the Church in South Africa acknowledges its role in ecological justice and the need to be an active participant. In Botswana, the majority of the land is privately owned by the state and the Roman Catholic Church. In countries like Zimbabwe, where land redistribution has taken place, the state retains ownership and leases out plots of land and farmland. Some private companies retain their interest in land, especially where they own mining concessions and/or operate safari tours.

Veld fires

Furthermore, the UCCSA has spoken out against veld fires, which are commonly used to prepare land for seasonal cultivation. For example, on 13 October 2022, they wrote in a Pastoral Statement that 'we implore all citizens to respect nature and the environment and desist from creating veld fires and the destruction of mother earth. We are called to be stewards of this beautiful earth. Let us all take care of the environment because our carelessness costs the lives of our loved ones' (paraphrased).

Artisanal mining

The UCCSA Synod of Zimbabwe, through its leadership, has constantly been in mediation with illegal, violent artisanal miners who constantly cause unsustainable damage to the environment. Their mining activity is not regulated and, as such, they dig and often leave open holes in the ground, to the detriment of people and animals. In the same vein, the UCCSA is active in Zimbabwe through its participation in the Zimbabwe Council of Churches Commission on Land and Environment. The Church is actively engaged in a struggle for ecological justice in Zimbabwe. It is the argument in this chapter that if these efforts were to be extensively localized in every Synod, then a sustainable Anthropocene is possible.

Conclusion

It is the thesis of this chapter that a 'sustainable Anthropocene' is possible not only for the sub-region of Southern Africa but for the whole world. It is argued here that a sustainable Anthropocene requires embracing principles such as returning to and valuing indigenous knowledge systems. Additionally, the Church ought to prioritize theologizing and preaching the gospel of pro-ecological justice alongside enacting practical interventions and mitigation measures against global warming such as promoting recycling, the planting of trees, and stopping pollution. Through these and other interventions, the Church also ought to preach awareness of the dangers of harmful activities such as veld fires and wanton injury to creation. The UCCSA, in its ecclesiology and polity, has principles and points of departure that are helpful in the struggle for ecological justice. These include the UCCSA's understanding of mission as establishing the kingdom of God, focusing on the centrality of the local context, and emphasizing the role of the laity in mission and witness. These, this chapter has argued, can help shift the Anthropocene narrative towards one of a sustainable relationship with nature and the sustainable use of natural resources.

References

Bailey, Jerome E., 2020, 'Poverty, Wealth and Ecology: A Critical Analysis of a World Council of Churches Project (2006–2013)', MA thesis, University of the Western Cape.
Boff, Leonardo, 1995, *Ecology and Liberation*, Maryknoll, NY: Orbis Books.
Briggs, D. Roy, 1996, *A Covenant Church: Studies in the Polity of the United Congregational Church of Southern Africa in Terms of Its Covenant*, Gaborone: Pula Press.
Brouwer, Rein, 2009, 'Missional Church and Local Constraints: A Dutch Perspective', *Verbum et Ecclesia* 30.2, pp. 1–5, doi: 10.4102/ ve.v30i2.329.
de Gruchy, Steve, 2010, 'An Olive Agenda: First Thoughts on a Metaphorical Theology of Development', *The Green Times*, https://thegreentimes.co.za/wp content/uploads/2020/11/DeGruchy_An_Olive_Agenda.pdf (accessed 28.11.2023).
EMA (Environmental Management Agency), 2015, 'Fighting the Veld Fire Scourge', www.ema.co.zw/index.php/136 (accessed 28.07.2023).
Forsyth, Peter T., 1912/1995, *Faith, Freedom and the Future*, London: Independent Press.
Hendriks, Jurgens, 2004, *Studying Congregations in Africa*, Wellington: Lux Verbi.
Kronlid, David O. and Öhman, Johan, 2012, 'An Environmental Ethical Conceptual Framework for Research on Sustainability and Environmental Education', *Environmental Education Research* 19.1, pp. 1–24.
Maseko, Xolani, 2021, 'The Relevance of the Calvinistic Understanding of Ordination within the Current Zimbabwean Context', doctoral dissertation, University of Pretoria.
Masenya, Madipoane, 2015, 'In the Ant's School of Wisdom: A Holistic African-South African Reading of Proverbs 6:6–11', *Old Testament Essays* 28.2, pp. 421–32. https://dx.doi.org/10.17159/2312-3621/2015/V28N2A11.
McPartlan, Paul, 2024, 'Eucharist and Ecology: Deep Down, the Ecological Crisis is a Spiritual Crisis, and the Mass is the Key to our Response as Catholics', Simply Catholic. Available at: https://www.simplycatholic.com/eucharist-and-ecology/ (accessed 12.04.2023). This was a summary of McPartlan's 2023 article, 'Euchar-

ist and Ecology', *International Journal of Evangelization and Catechetics*, 4(1), pp. 5–29, doi.org/10.1353/jec.2023.a912018.

Meziane, Mohamad A., 2021, 'Is There a Secularocene?' *Political Theology Network*, https://politicaltheology.com/is-there-a-secularocene/ (accessed 30.09.2021).

Mourao, Paulo R., and Martinho, Vítor D., 2021, 'Discussing a Challenging Document Focused on Land Use: The First Bibliometric Analysis of *Laudato Si*", *Land Degradation & Development* 32.16, pp. 4680–92.

Snyder, Howard A. and Scandrett, Joel Alan, 2011, *Salvation Means Creation Healed: The Ecology of Sin and Grace: Overcoming the Divorce between Earth and Heaven*, Eugene, OR: Wipf and Stock Publishers.

Soko-de Jong, Thandi, and Maseko, Xolani, 2022, 'African Traditional Religion: Reclaiming the Sustainable Anthropocenes', *ASEAN Journal of Religious and Cultural Research* 5.1, pp. 6–10.

South African Council of Churches, 2009, *Climate Change – A Challenge to the Churches in South Africa*, Marshall Town: South African Council of Churches.

Taringa, Nisbert T., 2014, 'Towards an African Christian Environmental Ethic', *Bible in Africa Studies* 13, Bamberg: University of Bamberg Press.

UCCSA (United Congregational Church of Southern Africa), 2019, *Tell Me the Old, Old Story*, Brixton, Johannesburg: UCCSA.

von Rad, Gerhard, 1975, *Old Testament Theology*, vol. 1, London: SCM Press.

11

Out of the Closet and Out of the Tomb of Ecological Sins

SUZANA MOREIRA

Introduction

Dear reader, welcome to a reflection based on a theology that has been incarnating in my life through my academic experience and professional work, permeated by my lived experiences with the Latin American grassroots communities that dedicate themselves to care for creation and narrative liberation theology. I am a witness to my own integral liberation process and that of the Roman Catholic Church[1] and also a witness to how slow that process is. I have no intention of being 'academically sound' here, but rather to share my personal theological diary on the reflections I've been making as I've been living these past few years through crying, cumming, and hoping for a better future.

In my studies and research on eco-theology, I started noticing that 'ecological sins' can be a strategic turning point in helping Roman Catholics to go into a process of ecological conversion – that is, to change their lifestyles, their hearts and their minds to better care for our common home. One of the reasons for that is because those who are fond of the dualistic and moralist approach to Roman Catholicism are drawn to the concept of sin being like a fetish. Bringing to these people the notion of ecological sins disturbs their reality but attracts them to the conversation. Their first reaction might be apprehensive, but they can't stop themselves talking about sins. I started realizing this through a Lent campaign in 2023 whose theme was 'Moving away from ecological sins and into ecological conversion'. While this Lent campaign was happening, in my personal life I was reading Ana Ester's recently published book *Os Dezmandamentos: teologia lésbico-queer-feminista* and also at the same time I was working on the translation of Luís Corrêa Lima's book *Teologia e os LGBT+: Perspectiva histórica e desafios contemporâneos*, soon to be published in English. Reflecting on these two queer-focused theology books, along with that Lent campaign, was when I started thinking about how Roman Catholic eco-theology still reproduces gender and sexual injustices and, therefore, is still far from a true integral ecological conversion.

As I mentioned, the reflection I will bring here is also a personal theological diary, and this in itself is part of the methods I have been learning with both narrative liberation theology and queer theology. Therefore, as part of this section of my chapter I must also introduce myself to you. I am a Brazilian lay and nomadic theologian, lover of the arts, who plays the acoustic guitar and ukulele to calm the soul and dances with stilts to always remember the need for balance and lightness in life. I was born and raised a Roman Catholic, in a line of several generations of Roman Catholic families. I grew up moving around cities in Brazil, Argentina and the United States. Since 2017, I've been advocating for socio-environmental justice.

I have a Master's degree in Systematic Pastoral Theology from the Pontifical Catholic University of Rio de Janeiro, Brazil, where I researched on theologies of the body from the perspective of Latin American liberation theologies, including feminist theology, Black theology, indigenous theology and decolonial theology. Since 2019, I have been working for a movement whose mission is to inspire and mobilize the Catholic community worldwide to care for our common home and achieve climate and ecological justice, in collaboration with all people of good will. Most of the work I do involves eco-spirituality and eco-theology, with a special concern for multiculturality and the complexity of minority groups who most suffer the consequences of the climate and ecological crises.

Because my work is remote, I choose to be a nomad so I can set foot in the realities of the people I love and the people I am called to love. Apart from the paid work I do, I'm also an *educadora popular* (grassroots educator) of *Escuelita Bendita Mezcla*, a grassroots formation on narrative liberation theology especially for Ecclesial Base Communities across Latin America and the Caribbean. I also participate in the interfaith Movement of Liberating Spiritualities currently preparing for the 3rd National Encounter of Youth and Liberating Spiritualities that will take place in 2024 in Bahia, Brazil; and I'm a member of the Madalena group of the National Network of LGBT Catholic Groups in Brazil.

With this personal context in mind, the reflection I seek to bring here is to contemplate the connection between overcoming ecological sins and embracing the gift of LGBT+ people as part of creation and as part of the solution for the socio-environmental crisis. The queer worldview and theology have much to offer Roman Catholic eco-theology in overcoming its limitations. Going through a journey from the concepts of ecological sins and ecological conversion to the methods of narrative liberation theology and queer theology, I dare us all to come out of the closet and out of the tomb of ecological sins, to come into the Good News for the whole cosmos.

The Roman Catholic (closeted) theology on ecological sins

In 2015, Pope Francis published the first-ever pontifical document focused exclusively on ecology. This document was called *Laudato si': on the care for our common home'*, one of the longest encyclical letters in the history of the Roman Catholic Church, much inspired by the example and spirituality of St Francis of Assisi who used the expression *Laudato si'* (praised be) to praise God for the elements of nature and for our Sister Mother Earth in his famous Canticle of the Creatures. *Laudato si'* immediately became one of the most controversial documents from the Roman Catholic Social Doctrine, given that the right-wing and fundamentalist sectors of the Roman Catholic Church and society were predictably sceptical about its content.

Already in its first paragraphs, Pope Francis introduces the notion that failing to properly care for our common home and harming the natural environment is a sin against ourselves and against God. He mentions this by quoting the Orthodox Ecumenical Patriarch Bartholomew of Constantinople, who remarkably has been developing theological reflections on this front for several decades. However, Pope Francis does not dedicate further reflection to this dimension of sin. What arose later as one of the many fruits from *Laudato si'* was a synod by the Roman Catholic Church focused on the Pan-Amazonian region, a synod in which for the first time in Vatican history the term 'ecological sin' was adopted by Roman Catholic bishops. Albeit not yet fully officially recognized and taught as part of Roman Catholic doctrine, the concept of ecological sin sets the stage for a wider process of deeper understanding of how our individual actions and actions as a collective group impact the well-being of the earth and of our most vulnerable sisters and brothers. I will first give an overview of how the Roman Catholic Church understands sin, to then present the concept of ecological sins and ecological conversion.

The *Catechism of the Catholic Church* states that the definition of sin is 'an offense against reason, truth, and right conscience; it is failure in genuine love for God and neighbor caused by a perverse attachment to certain goods. It wounds the nature of man [sic] and injures human solidarity' (Catholic Church, 1993, n. 1849–1850). This understanding means that any type of offence against God is a sin. In this sense, any human initiative, whether action, intention, thought, etc., that is not in tune with the love intended and carried out by God in their creation, hurts their divine design. For this reason, there is a multiplicity of sins diversified in their form and object, which may include, for example, the lack of action or omission in the face of injustice (cf. Catholic Church, 1993, n. 1853). Any damage to the reality created and willed by God is an offence to God.

The concept of original sin and its consequences for humanity and the cosmos can be understood better in this light. The divine creative act established creation in communion, thus creating an interdependence of creatures (cf. Catholic Church, 1993, n. 340). All created reality and the diversity of beings and complexity of the cosmos was created for the order and harmony that reflect the infinite beauty of the creator (cf. Catholic Church, 1993, n. 341). Original sin, therefore, is a rupture with this communion of interdependence and solidarity of the human being with God and with all creation because it breaks the deep bond that unites humanity to God (cf. Catholic Church, 1993, n. 386).

As much as the definition of sin by the Roman Catholic Church already contains what would be needed to denounce actions against the proper care for our common home, the Pan-Amazonian Synod in 2019 recognized the need to name this properly. The synod bishops declared:

> We propose to define ecological sin as an action or omission against God, against one's neighbor, the community and the environment. It is sin against future generations, and it is committed in acts and habits of pollution and destruction of the harmony of the environment. These are transgressions against the principles of interdependence, and they destroy networks of solidarity among creatures (cf. Catholic Church, 1993, n. 340–344) and violate the virtue of justice. (Synod of Bishops, 2019, n. 82)

The proposal of the Pan-Amazonian Synod bishops is only possible to be made and understood in the reading key of integral ecology exposed by Pope Francis in *Laudato si'*. The definition of ecological sin in the Final Document of the Pan-Amazonian Synod restores an integral vision of humanity as a creature in communion with other creatures, thus recalling that any and all disrespect or rupture with this communion is an offence to God.

Pope Francis in his ecological encyclical repeatedly reinforces this understanding: 'The harmony between the creator, humanity and creation as a whole was disrupted by our presuming to take the place of God and refusing to acknowledge our creaturely limitations' (Pope Francis, 2015, n. 66). For this reason, the ecological crisis in which we find ourselves is the 'sign of the ethical, cultural and spiritual crisis of modernity', of a humanity that has broken and forgotten all its fundamental human relationships (Pope Francis, 2015, n. 119). The concept of ecological sin is found in the lack of gratitude and lack of recognition of the gift of creation.

This is where the notion of 'ecological conversion' becomes essential for the needed process of recognizing our shortcomings in the care for creation. The word 'conversion' in the Christian context is charged with many negative complexities. Being from a country that was colonized by a European Catholic crown, I'm aware of how an abusive understanding of conversion was used to justify the oppression and annihilation of the original peoples of this territory we now call Brazil, and that can still be seen in several contexts today that continue to oppress and annihilate BIPOC people. This is not the concept of conversion that the Roman Catholic Church has been using to develop the awareness of ecological conversion. The concept does not refer to evangelization, much less proselytism, but rather to a personal and collective process that arises as a result of the personal encounter with Jesus.

Pope John Paul II was the first pope to coin the expression, saying that we must encourage and support ecological conversion which has been helping humanity understand the catastrophic future we are causing to ourselves. Despite giving a positive step towards recognizing the importance of an ecological awareness, he does not deepen nor explain what he means by 'ecological conversion' and continues to reproduce conservative and androcentric approaches as he was known for through his whole pontificate. After mentioning the expression, he goes on to say that 'Man is no longer the Creator's "steward", but an autonomous despot, who is finally beginning to understand that he must stop at the edge of the abyss' (Pope John Paul II, 2001). Pope Francis is the one who takes up this expression once again in *Laudato si'*, dedicating six paragraphs in the encyclical precisely to provide a better bearing as to what 'ecological conversion' is and how it is intrinsically connected to the very essence of Christian faith. Different from John Paul II, Francis intentionally avoids using the gender male as a general term for humans or humanity.

In his perspective, there are two fundamental aspects to the understanding of what ecological conversion is: the personal encounter with

Jesus, and its community dimension. He expresses that all Christians need this ecological conversion, 'whereby the effects of their encounter with Jesus Christ become evident in their relationship with the world around them' (Pope Francis, 2015, n. 217). This conversion is a change of that which results from the encounter with Jesus and that reflects on how the Christian relates to the earth, and so it is essential to the Christian life and part of the Christian vocation. This also calls for a recognition of the social problems that can only be addressed as a community. Therefore, 'the ecological conversion needed to bring about lasting change is also a community conversion (Pope Francis, 2015, n. 219).

What the Roman Catholic Church continues to fail to recognize is how within this social dimension of the environmental crisis that we have caused there is also a gender and sexual crisis underpinned and caused by the androcentric, Eurocentric, white and cisheteronormative worldview. If we are to truly go into an integral process of ecological conversion, we must also recognize how this worldview is the one that shaped the unsustainable development of society and its abusive relationship with the earth. When Pope Francis says that the ecological crisis in which we find ourselves is a 'sign of the ethical, cultural and spiritual crisis of modernity' (Pope Francis, 2015, n. 119), we should recognize how this crisis of modernity is also a crisis of the male. The male patriarchal way of understanding itself as superior to all other creatures, including women, and excluding any possibility of gender or sexual diversity, shapes how the Roman Catholic Church reflects on ecology. There is still a long way to go in the process of recognizing how ecological sins are also connected to sins against diversity.

The encounter with queer (uncloseted) theology

I first heard about queer theology sometime around 2015, when I started paying more attention to feminist theology as part of my studies into Latin American liberation theology. That was the same year when Pope Francis released *Laudato si'*. It was also the same year that I broke up with a boyfriend and started my process of coming out of the closet and loving myself for being bisexual. As Pope Francis says: 'Everything is connected' (Pope Francis, 2015, n. 91 and n. 117), and as Marcella Althaus-Reid says: 'Every theology is always a sexual theology' (Althaus-Reid, 2006, p. 67). So right from the beginning, my reflections and actions based on *Laudato si'* were permeated by my bisexual way of thinking, being and existing.

My involvement with grassroots communities while I was deepening my work and commitment to creation care led me to a deep experience of narrative liberation theology in El Salvador in 2022. Leonardo Boff defines the narrative liberation theology as:

> Meterse profundamente dentro del mundo de los condenados de la Tierra, de los invisibles, para escuchar sus historias y testimonios … escuchar y de nuevo escuchar lo que ellos nos testimonian. Y más que todo, notar en estas narrativas la revelación del Crucificado y del Dios que sostiene sus vidas y sus esperanzas.[2] (Boff, 2020, p. 8)

This personal encounter with narrative liberation theology in the lived experience with Ecclesial Base Communities in San Salvador, the capital of that Central American country, was a life-changing turn for me.

Escuelita Bendita Mezcla was what brought me to El Salvador, a grassroots school for theological formation directed towards youth from Latin America and the Caribbean. Narrative liberation theology is an expression that has risen in this school experience, an experience rooted in Latin American liberation theology and Paulo Freire's thought. Paulo Freire was a world-renowned Brazilian educator and philosopher, crucial to the development of critical pedagogy and known for his work *Pedagogy of the Oppressed*. One of the pillars of Paulo Freire's pedagogical methodologies is knowing that knowledge is built collectively. Those who society usually views as lesser educated – the minorities oppressed and that lack access to conventional education – have just as much to bring to educating as any person with higher education qualifications. Therefore, my role there as an *educadora popular* was also to be an active listener and learner. The community and the individuals in the community teach the educator at the same time that the educator shares any knowledge they may have. Education becomes, then, an ongoing process of shared lived experiences. My encounter with this theological and pedagogical methodology happened at the same time as I was deepening my studies into feminist, ecofeminist and queer theologies.

Similar to this narrative liberation theology, queer theology is a first-person and autobiographical theology. Narrative is key. The first happens mostly through a shared community experience of *fazer memória* (to account for the memories); however, as a result of the predominance of closeted theologies – and the heterosexual economy as Marcella Althaus-Reid puts it – the need for the latter becomes fundamental. Alas, as Marcella reminds us, 'Queering theology … is no longer simply one option among others … [it] is the path of God's own liberation, apart from ours, and as such it constitutes a critique to what Heterosexual Theology has done with God by closeting the divine' (Althaus-Reid, 2003, p. 4). So if a narrative liberation theology is to authentically dive into the reality of those who have been excluded and condemned, it must enter into the LGBT+ diaspora too.

The people and communities I was able to listen to and learn from in El Salvador were all conscious of the injustices and violences they suffered as a result of the government's unlawful prolonged state of exception, rooted in the complex historical process of El Salvador's genocidal dictatorships. Many accounted for the gender and sexual violences present in this horrific process but lacked the narrative methodological tools and languages to break from the cisheteronormative way of expressing reality and be able to denounce these violences in a decolonized way. If narrative is key, language is fundamental. And language is always a field in dispute.

Mother Earth bears witness to our unsustainable lifestyles and progress, and she also bears witness to the spilled blood of human violence and oppression. The cries of Mother Earth are deafening along with the cries of transgender victims of transphobia, women victims of misogyny, child victims of paedophilia, BIPOC people victims of environmental racism, and poor people victims of aporophobia. The tomb is the reality of socio-environmental injustice that the white cishetero-male Eurocentric approach caused in Western society with its impacts against the whole world.

But recognizing this tomb – this death place where socio-environmental injustice reigns – is not enough as a result of the androcentric cisheteronormative influences that still shape whatever capacities we have to remove the stone from the tomb and step closer into the garden of life in abundance for everyone. Along with the tomb, there is also a closet holding us back from the Good News to all creation. If Roman Catholic eco-theology is to continue deepening the notion of ecological sins, ecological conversion and creation, it must urgently liberate the very notion of what creation is. An integral non-cisheteronormative perspective of creation would naturally recognize LGBT+ and other than human creatures as beloved and essential parts of creation. Therefore, saying that we must care for creation would also mean to care for the LGBT+, to care for other than human creatures. Not only that, but also LGBT+ and other than human creatures themselves have different ways of expressing and caring for the whole cosmos.

I must confess that my knowledge of eco-theology is much deeper than of queer theology. The more I dwell in my own reflections and lived experiences of eco-theology and queer theology, the more I realize I still have a long way to go in learning about these fields. However, I realize that what I used to call my own 'out of the box' theology is queer theology. Being bisexual gives me a different life experience and cosmovision that directly resounds in the way I do and express theology. Every time I read Marcella Althaus-Reid and her explanations about what queer theology and indecent theologians are, I find descriptions of myself. Marcella Althaus-Reid explains the experience of the queer theologian as someone who holds several passports, being able to transit different spaces, which has literally been my life experience. Our theology is a nomadic theology because we don't have a fixed place. I live in transit, occupying different spaces, and this applies both to my life in the symbolic sense of the social and theological circles I travel through, and to my nomadic life moving around cities and countries.

As I commit to my own process of integral ecological conversion, I recognize that I must work continuously in my own process of liberation and decolonization. I was born and raised to be Roman Catholic and, unfortunately, the Roman Catholic eco-theology is predominantly white, Eurocentric, androcentric, cisheteronormative, monogamous and monoaffective. As much as it seeks to bring forth the perspective of integral ecology and to use interdisciplinary approaches recognizing the diversity of life and methods for reflection, this eco-theology does not yet include gender and sexual diversities into the mix. In great part, the reason for this is that eco-theology was born and still takes place from the discourse of hegemonic and homogeneous Western Christianity.

It is sad to think about how much this discourse oppresses our capacities for affection. Roman Catholics might easily show compassion for creation as they 'become painfully aware' (Pope Francis, 2015, n. 19) of the loss of biodiversity, species that are becoming extinct, natural catastrophes and forced migration that are direct results of climate change, but they still see other than human creatures as inferior; they still don't recognize LGBT+ people as 'normal'; they still begrudge the sight of two men holding hands in their parish, or a child with two mothers, or a transgender person getting baptized; they still grumble at Christians who actively work to promote the care for creation. News about Brazil being the country that most kills transgenders in the world, or that Brazil is one of the countries that most kills environment activists, barely make a dent in hearts shaped by this blind Roman Catholicism worldview. Roman Catholics' capacity for affection ends up restrained to a limited comprehension of the cosmos and the intrinsic dignity of all beings who exist in it.

I've come out of the closet in my personal life, but in theology I'm still afraid to come out completely. At this point in my life, the time is coming as I plan to start a PhD precisely on eco-theology from the queer perspective. Queer people are everywhere, including in the grassroots communities I share experiences with, and in the movement where I currently work. Among those 'claiming against the destruction of nations and individual lives, including the environment, are people still talking about gay or bisexual rights and orgasms and God' (Althaus-Reid, 2003, p. 4). But there is a silent fear that oppresses the capacity to feel free to share LGBT+ stories and experiences. I personally live constantly feeling as if I need to measure myself, to justify the way I think, my words, my actions, what I do with my body publicly, and what I post on my social media, as I try to navigate these cisheteronormative spaces that at any moment can decide to 'invite' me to leave or ask me to be less outspoken on my bisexuality, just because Roman Catholicism isn't quite OK with it yet (only if I abstain from the 'sinful ways and tendencies', as many say …).

What soon becomes a key point for eco-theology as I try to lead it into a queering process is the very notion of creation. The first three chapters of Genesis have been used as justification for subjugating women, nature, and denying any possibilities of sexual or gender diversities. Just as an example, John Paul II who first talked about ecological conversion was also the first pope to talk about a 'theology of the body', which he developed under the perspective that 'man and woman He created them' (cf. Genesis. 1.27), and which has been increasingly used by right-wing and fundamentalist Roman Catholics as justification against the LGBT+ community. The androcentric cisheteronormative worldview of religion and ecology determined the diaspora that queer people live in today, and from which they engage in activism for LGBT+ rights and advocacy for the care of our common home. In this way, the ecological crisis in which we live today, caused by the ecological sins of 'civilized' society, is also fruit of the patriarchy.

Coming out of the closet and out of the tomb of ecological sins

I mentioned at the beginning that I am witness to my own integral liberation process and that of the Roman Catholic Church as well, and also a witness to how slow this process is. The more I understand how complex, problematic and difficult my liberation is, the more I understand that it's even worse for the Roman Catholic Church because it is an institution, a government state, and made up of millions of other people just as complex. People often ask me why I still consider myself Catholic and sometimes I wonder that as well. But when I try to consider 'leaving' the Roman Catholic Church, I have a very clear understanding that the Roman Catholic Church way of thinking won't ever really leave me. It has shaped my life and identity in ways that, if I chose to throw it all away, I would be also denying my very own history and existence. Instead, what I have been trying to choose is to stand and occupy this faulty ground of Roman Catholicism, advocating for a more inclusive and decolonized Church, even if that is not possible in the ideal way I and others would hope for.

Being realistic, I don't think the Roman Catholic Church is anywhere near a process of coming out of the closet and out of the tomb of ecological sins. Two events at the end of 2023 represent well the paradox of its capacity for a true liberation process. The first was Pope Francis' release of the apostolic exhortation *Laudate Deum* (Praise God), a pontifical document of lesser importance than an encyclical, advertised as a second part to *Laudato si'*, with a focus on climate justice only, especially in the context ahead of COP28 in Dubai. When I first heard about his decision to release *Laudate Deum*, my only hope was that he would use more references from women as the basis for his reflections, something that was clearly lacking in *Laudato si'*. The only reference to women that made it into *Laudato si'* were not for grounding content, but rather to use the example of the life of saints (namely, Thérèse of Liseux and Mary as Queen of Creation). Although he does not advance much in the deconstruction of his own patriarchal point of view and references in *Laudate Deum*, to my great surprise he did in fact use a reference from a woman – and not just any woman.

'God has united us to all his creatures. Nonetheless, the technocratic paradigm can isolate us from the world that surrounds us and deceive us by making us forget that the entire world is a "contact zone"' (Pope Francis, 2023b, n. 66). This short sentence that made it into the apostolic exhortation refers to the concept of 'contact zone' developed by Donna Jeanne Haraway, a feminist biologist and philosopher from the USA, who uses an interdisciplinary approach in her studies, with a special focus on the debate about the Anthropocene, post-humanism and intersectional feminisms, and the multi-species relationships found in the frontiers between nature and culture. At the same time that this is a huge step for a pope to be referencing a feminist thinker, it also leaves much to be desired given that he does not dwell in the concept nor explores the possibilities of how this would imply different ways to talk about ecology and eco-theology in the Roman Catholic Church.

The second event at the end of 2023 was that during a meeting with members of the International Theological Commission at the Vatican, Pope Francis noticed there were few women present and made an impromptu statement about that. This speech instantly went viral on social media, with many praising him for being so sensitive to the need for including more women in the Church. But if we take a closer and attentive look at his address, it's clear to see the still patriarchal and binary way of thinking:

> The Church is woman. And if we do not know what a woman is, what the theology of a woman is, we will never understand what the Church is. One of the great sins we have had is to 'masculinize' the Church. And this is not solved by the ministerial path; that is something else. It is resolved in the mystical way, the real way ... And you will ask me: where does this discussion lead? Not only to tell you that you should have more women here – that is one thing – but to help reflect. The Church as woman, the Church as a bride. And this is a task that I ask of you, please. To make the Church less masculine. (Pope Francis, 2023a)

Truly, it is remarkable to hear a pope saying that the Church needs to *desmaculinizar* (become less masculine). However, the examples he uses to justify this are all grounded in a binary and stereotypical notion of what a woman is, which is also how the Roman Catholic Church historically has viewed women. Connecting the female with the 'mystical way' and 'bride' are typical patriarchal ways of defining what makes women unique. Furthermore, despite it not being mentioned here, these typical patriarchal views of the Roman Catholic Church on women are often also connected with the notion of 'mother' and 'the one that gives life', which is also dismissive of the reality of transwomen and other women who do not have the capacity to bear life nor give birth.

Coming out of the tomb and out of the closet of ecological sins is recognizing the androcentric, patriarchal and cisheteronormative worldviews that monopolized the development of Western society and caused the current socio-ecological crisis that affects the whole world. It is also an act of resistance and resilience: to share our stories, to share our sins, to sow cross-cultures within our communities. The miracle of life is solidarity and communion among diversity. Mother Earth survives by itself, despite all human nocive action, because it thrives in diversity, diverse species, diverse biomes, diverse ecosystems, all in tension and in harmony, interconnected and interdependent. This communion of diversity should be the compass for the Roman Catholic Church in its process of integral liberation and ecological conversion.

To change the reality of the Roman Catholic Church from the ground up we must recognize that the ecological crisis is fruit of patriarchy, a patriarchy shaped by the white cisheteronormative and Eurocentric worldview. We must denounce violence and listen to the eco-human cry of women, queer people, Mother Earth, and more than human creatures. We must get rid of the systemic injustices that keep coming from the top. We must advocate for a life of ecological conversion, not conversion therapy. If we affirm God as creator and creation as gift, we must be consistent in recognizing the gifts of all creation, including queer people. This is how I challenge myself and invite all of us to come out of the closet and leave the tomb of ecological sins, so that we can enter together into the Good News for all of creation, for the whole cosmos.

'The entire material universe speaks of God's love, his boundless affection for us. Soil, water, mountains: everything is, as it were, a caress of God' (Pope Francis, 2015, n. 84). And so are LGBT+ people.

Notes

1 I would like to acknowledge that, in Brazil, I never specify my religious experience as Roman Catholic when I say that I am Catholic, given that historically it has been a predominantly Roman Catholic country. However, as Hugo Córdova Quero explains in his book *Sin Tabú: Religiones y diversidad sexual en América Latina*, the Roman Catholic Church is one among many other Catholic churches, and if I keep using the term 'Catholic' as a generalization when I'm just referring to the Roman Catholic Church I end up serving to its power of hegemonizing (read: colonizing) the notion of what Catholicism is.

2 English translation: 'Go deep into the world of the damned on earth, the invisible, to listen to their stories and testimonies ... listen and listen again to what they testify to us. And most of all, notice in these narratives the revelation of the Crucified and of the God who sustains their lives and their hopes.'

References

Althaus-Reid, Marcella, 2003, *The Queer God*, London: Routledge.
Althaus-Reid, Marcella, 2006, '*De la teologia de la liberación feminista a la teologia torcida*' in Nancy Cardoso, and André Musskopf (org.), *A graça do mundo transforma Deus: diálogos latino-americanos com a IX Assembleia do CMI*, Porto Alegre: Editora Universitária Metodista, pp. 64–9.

Boff, Leonardo, 2020, 'Prólogo' in *Bendita Mezcla: Hermanxs escuchadorxs, comunidades palabreras*, Fundación Amerindia: Montevideo, https://www.amerindiaenlared.org/uploads/adjuntos/202103/1615463805_N6Spr37k.pdf (accessed 4.03.2025).

Catholic Church, 1993, *Catechism of the Catholic Church*, Vatican City: Libreria Editrice Vaticana, https://www.vatican.va/archive/ENG0015/_INDEX.HTM (accessed 4.03.2025).

Córdova Quero, Hugo, 2018, *Sin Tabú: Religiones y diversidad sexual en América Latina*, REDLAD/GEMRIP: Bogotá/Santiago de Chile.

Pope Francis, 2015, *Encyclical letter Laudato si' on the care for our common home*, 24 May, Vatican City: Libreria Editrice Vaticana, http://w2.vatican.va/content/francesco/en/encyclicals/documents/papa-francesco_20150524_enciclica-laudato-si.html (accessed 4.03.2025).

Pope Francis, 2023a, *Address of His Holiness Pope Francis to the members of the International Theological Commission*, 30 November, Vatican City: Libreria Editrice Vaticana, https://www.vatican.va/content/francesco/en/speeches/2023/november/documents/20231130-cti.html (accessed 4.03.2025).

Pope Francis, 2023b, *Apostolic exhortation Laudate Deum to all people of good will on the climate crisis*, 30 November, Vatican City: Libreria Editrice Vaticana, https://www.vatican.va/content/francesco/en/apost_exhortations/documents/20231004-laudate-deum.html (accessed 4.03.2025).

Pope John Paul II, 2001, *General Audience*, Vatican City: Libreria Editrice Vaticana, 17 January, https://www.vatican.va/content/john-paul-ii/en/audiences/2001/documents/hf_jp-ii_aud_20010117.html (accessed 4.03.2025).

Synod of Bishops, 2019, *Final Document: The Amazon: New Paths for the Church and for an Integral Ecology*, General Secretariat of the Synod of Bishops, http://secretariat.synod.va/content/sinodoamazonico/en/documents/final-document-of-the-amazon-synod.html (accessed 4.03.2025).

Epilogue
Facing Climate Collapse: Ecology, Theology and Capitalocene

JOERG RIEGER

Mentioning the geological age of the Capitalocene in the title of a book when most scholars still talk about the Anthropocene is a bold step in the right direction for various important reasons. While the geological age of the Holocene, which refers to the past 11,000 years since the last Ice Age and marks the emergence of human civilizations, is commonly acknowledged, there is disagreement about naming the geological age in which we find ourselves, and this disagreement is foundational for the study of religion and theology, as we will see.

Many now argue that we find ourselves in the Anthropocene, the age in which humanity supposedly has taken over the planet. To be sure, the impact of a population of 8 billion people is significant for the globe, and virtually no space on the globe remains untouched by some form of human presence and activity. However, naming the present age the Anthropocene also covers up the profound reality that some parts of humanity are shaping the fate of the planet substantially more than others. That 81 billionaires now own as much wealth as half the population of the planet has consequences that must be addressed because wealth and power go hand in hand (Mlaba, 2023). As some have the means to effectively reshape the face of planet earth in their image and dream of eventually leaving earth behind, many others continue to live in some form of harmony with the planet, not for idealistic reasons but because their survival depends on it. Largely ignoring these constellations, when some proponents of the Anthropocene note some of the challenges of neocolonialism, militarism and capitalism, these appear to be secondary matters.

Those who argue that we find ourselves in the Capitalocene reject the notion of the Anthropocene for various reasons. They question the universalism of the notion of the Anthropocene, for instance, failing to account for the stark differences among humans. In addition, they emphasize the flows of power that profoundly determine human existence under the conditions of global capitalism. More specifically, they note that the point of the Capitalocene is not merely the fairly obvious observation that some humans are more powerful and wealthier than others, but that there are systemic pressures that determine the flows of power and shape how humans relate to one another as well as to the planet. At the heart of the problem, therefore, are not greedy individuals or power-hungry dictators, as is often assumed, but regimes of exploitation and extraction that have deep roots and long histories that date back centuries. This can be illustrated, for instance, by the requirement for CEOs to work for the benefit of stockholders (and some stakeholders, like customers, a recently expanded version of capitalism in the United States) but never for the benefit of workers. A CEO who refuses to comply will not be in office for long.

For the study of theology and religion, these debates are foundational, as both the Anthropocene and the Capitalocene have implications beyond economy, politics and ecology. Scholars of theology and religion adopting the notion of the Anthropocene have few options but to blame humanity in general for the deterioration of the conditions of life and related distortions of theology and religion. Not surprisingly, variations of the charge of 'anthropocentrism' are still among the most common arguments in ecological theology, coupled with the assumption that things would be fine if humanity were less anthropocentric and more caring for, and concerned about, the environment as related to the things of God.

These arguments take many forms, starting with romantic notions of indigenous traditions that are supposedly less anthropocentric and therefore presented as the solution and recognitions of God as closely tied to nature in pantheism and panentheism. Other examples of seeking to address the problems of the perceived Anthropocene include somewhat romantic ideas of economic degrowth (including population degrowth) and of 'small is beautiful'.

By contrast, scholars of theology and religion engaging the notion of the Capitalocene have more options for developing a clearer sense of 'what we are up against', a quest I often present when engaging with students in the classroom and in collaborations with other scholars. What if the core problem is not anthropocentrism – as the majority of scholars in the humanities have assumed ever since Lynn White's paradigm-shifting article in the late 1960s (White, Jr, 1967) – but specific relationships of exploitation and extraction for the benefit of the few, whose influence also tends to determine religious imaginations and practices, often by default? This requires some (intersectional) class analysis, a topic from which many academics shy away – especially in the United States – but which makes it clearer where the fault lines of our geological age might be located, with dire consequences for the planet. In this perspective, even religious traditions that pay more attention to other-than-human nature as related to the Divine, and are therefore less anthropocentric and otherworldly, are not off the hook but have to be examined in terms of the bigger flows of power of which they are a part.

This development has profound consequences for how scholars and communities of faith engage with ecological challenges. Proponents of the Anthropocene typically argue for what some Christian religious communities are calling 'creation care', or 'stewardship of creation', based on the assumption that engaging with other-than-human concerns and being more emphatic and caring for the environment as God's creation is what it takes to rectify the situation. Likewise, well-meaning efforts to decentre humanity in relation to other-than-human nature and the Divine are often based on limited understandings of what kind of humanity is at the centre of our age. Clearly, it is not hard to show that blaming all human beings is misdirected, but even some of the more pointed critiques of parts of humanity (like 'Westerners' or 'citizens of the modern world' or 'settlers' or the 'middle class' or 'consumers') still tend to lack clarity about what we are up against. This is not to say that settler colonialists or middle-class consumers are not part of the problem, but in both cases what really drives colonialism and capitalist expansionism largely disappears, in particular the interests of the respective ruling classes.

This does not mean that mentioning the Capitalocene automatically takes care of all the oversights of the Anthropocene. Theological and religious engagements of the Capitalocene are only at their beginning and much remains to be done, although this edited volume is an exciting part of the work. Unfortunately, even critiques of capitalism and ecology often fail to deal with the deeper problems. Take, for example, typical critiques of 'consumerism' and 'greed', which tend to misdirect blame to hapless individuals who are often more victims than perpetrators of an economic-cultural climate in which consumption and acquisitiveness are driven and expertly manipulated by the interests of corporate investors and their mandates. Or take generic critiques of progress and growth, which fail to engage the engines of those dynamics and blame those who are in a desperate search for a better life. Common moral critiques, which blame individual actors or bemoan the lack of people's willpower, often tend to cover up what is at the heart of the Capitalocene: systematic relationships of exploitation and extraction.

What might be the solutions? Some of the chapters in this book emphasize conviviality and solidarity, including references to my notion of deep solidarity. This is the flip side of the pressures of the Capitalocene: that which exploits and extracts also welds together what is exploited and extracted. Solidarity, therefore, is not a moral appeal to well-meaning individuals or communities; solidarity is what emerges among those who realize that they are not in control and that the only way to change anything is work alongside all those who find themselves in the same boat. This solidarity includes, first of all, those most exploited such as indigenous and other minority communities, but even the middle class in the United States and elsewhere might wake up and realize that the Capitalocene's motto of 'winner takes all' does not apply to them. All this has consequences for how we imagine God's involvement as well, as operating not from the top down but being at work alongside movements of liberation and sustainability, as generations of liberation theologies have argued.

Once this is clear, perhaps more positive notions of the Anthropocene can be developed, as suggested by some of the authors in the book, which include more profound understandings of sin, as another author suggests, as well as related processes of salvation. What matters here is agency and the labour of human and other-than-human actors, without which none of us would be alive. At the heart is reproductive labour, often relegated to minorities as well as women and other-than-human nature, which takes us back to the land and the commons in new ways that will yet have to be explored.[1] All other labour and creativity is built on it, possibly including the Divine's own labour and creativity, and the most effective resistance movements are rooted here, including the Landless Movement, the increasing organizing of working people in the formal and informal sectors of labour, worker cooperative movements, and those ecological justice movements that are linked to it all. If another world is possible, it will have to engage these questions with renewed seriousness and this book provides one of the steps in the right direction.

Note

1 In Joerg Rieger, *Theology in the Capitalocene: Ecology, Identity, Class, and Solidarity* (Minneapolis, MN: Fortress Press, 2022), chapter 3, I am arguing that reproductive and productive labour defines what theologian Paul Tillich called the 'ultimate concern', i.e., that which is genuinely theological because it is a matter of being and non-being.

References

Mlaba, Khanyi, 2023, 'The Richest 1 Percent Own Almost Half of the World's Wealth and Nine Other Mind-Blowing Facts', *Global Citizen*, 19 January, https://www.globalcitizen.org/en/content/wealth-inequality-oxfam-billionaires-elon-musk/#:~:text=81%20billionaires%20have%20more%20wealth,is%20not%20even%20a%20thing (accessed 6.01.2025).

Rieger, Joerg, 2022, *Theology in the Capitalocene: Ecology, Identity, Class and Solidarity*, Minneapolis, MN: Fortress Press.

White, Jr, Lynn, 1967, 'The Historical Roots of Our Ecological Crisis', *Science* 155.3767, 10 March.

Index of Names and Subjects

Abya Yala
  destruction of nature 139–42
  ecojustice 142–6
  invasion and colonization 136–9
  sustainable and harmonious future 146–7
  see also Canada; Latin America; Mexico; United States
Acuña, Maxima 141
Adorno, Theodor W.
  Dialectics of Enlightenment (with Horkheimer) 7–8, 10–11
Afghanistan
  'shock and awe' tactics 42
Africa
  'ancestral future' 112–13
  artisanal mining 160
  context for salvation 60–1
  earth-centred liturgy 64–6
  environmental degradation 57
  Kariba dam 61–2
  land ownership 159–60
  people stolen from 138
  veld fires 160
African Traditional Religions 154
Agarwal, Anil 107
agency
  humans and the environment 27
agriculture
  changes in Hawai'i 45–6
  chemical-intensive 74
  chemical poisoning and 136
  colonial 137–8
  current social oppression 140
  Day of the Lord 77–8
  exploited indigenous labour 137–8
  seeds and Monsanto 140–1

Shiva's seed conservation 90
  Tayal people in Taiwan 95–6
Alexander, M. Jacqui 52–3
Althaus-Reid, Marcella 168, 169–70, 171
Altvater, Elmar
  on Crutzen's Anthropocene 105
  politics and geophysics 107
Amazonia
  Pan-Amazonian Synod 166
  threats to rainforest 141–2
Amerindians
  colonial treatment of 109
Amos, Book of
  Day of the Lord 78–9
animals
  biodiversity loss 123–4
  climate change and 119
  human exceptionalism and 127–30
  Kant-Bentham debate 126–7
  rights of 124–7
'An Olive Agenda: First Thoughts on a Metaphorical Theology of Development' (de Gruchy) 158–9
Anthropocene
  adoption of term 120–1
  Boff on 19
  building alliances 112–15
  Capitalocene and 14–15, 177–9
  as colonial discourse 26–7
  concept of 1, 7, 23–5
  controversies about 22–3
  cosmobiocene 111
  as ideology 13–15
  Militarycene and 47, 53–4
  naming the epoch 103–6
  onset of 13

paradigm shift 120-1
politically sterilized 18
Rapley on 22
social structures and agency 25-6
start of 103
sustainable 151-2, 160-1
term proposed by Crutzen 103-6
theology and 28-36, 32-3
'Who is Anthropos?' 107
whose? 33
'The Anthropocene as Colonial Discourse' (Simpson) 26-7
Anthropocene: A Very Short Introduction (Ellis) 22-4
'Anthropocene or Global Coloniality? A Decolonial Theological Reflection' (Sadje) 22-36
'Anthropocentrism More than Just a Misunderstood Problem' (Kopina et al.) 24-5
Anthropocene or Capitalocene? (Moore) 25-6
The Arcades Project (Benjamin) 12
ASEAN *Journal of Religious and Cultural Research* 149
Asproulis, Nikolaos 3
'For the Life of the ... Animals' 119-30
Atheism in Christianity (Münster) 11
St Augustine of Hippo
human souls 121-2

Bachofen, Johann 12
Bangladesh, flooding in 74
Bantu concepts 60-1
Barros, Marcelo 18
Bartholomew, Patriarch of Constantinople 165
Beigi, Tina 43
Beltráne-Barrera, Yilson 16
Benjamin, Walter
On the Concept of History 11-12
critique of modernity 11-12
Bentham, Jeremy
An Introduction to the Principles of Morals and Legislation 126-7

Berry, Thomas
'Ecozoic Age' 106
Betto, Frei 18, 114
The Birth of the Anthropocene (Davies) 25
Bloch, Ernst
The Principle of Hope 11, 113
technical utopia 113
Boff, Leonardo 1-2, 157
alliance with nature 114
on the Anthropocene 19
on the Capitalocene 76
eco-socialism 18
eco-theology in Brazil 10
justice for environment 146
liberation theology 169
'noosphere' 8
role of human beings 144
Botswana, land ownership 159-60
Brazil
Boff and 10
Landless Workers' Movement 10
oppression in 171
seringeurios 2
threats to environment 141-2
Briggs, D. Roy
A Covenant Church 154-6
Britain
Animal Welfare Bill 125
colonization of Abya Yala 136-9
wars in Persian Gulf 42-3
Brouwer, Rein 153
Brueggemann, Walter
Prophetic Imagination 79
Brumley, Albert 59
Buffon, Georges-Louis Leclerc de 103

Cáceres, Bertha 141
Cajigas-Totundo, Juan Camilo 15-16
Calvin, John 153
Cambodia, Agent Orange and 48
capitalism
colonization and 16-18
Critical Theory and 7-8
ecocidal logic of 10-13
exploiting the Earth 105-6
global institutions 48

INDEX OF NAMES AND SUBJECTS

Klein on disasters and 46
neoliberal domination 17
war and disasters 51
Capitalism, Nature, Socialism.
 A Journal of Socialist Ecology 18
Capitalocene
 billionaires as gods 73
 concept of 1
 as critique of Anthropocene 25–6
 Day of the Lord 76
 ecofeminism and 89–90, 92–6, 100
 gardens *versus* nature 71–5
 nature as a capital asset 105–6
 Necrocene 72
 Shiva on eco-imperialism 73–5
 theology and 177–8
Capra, Fritjof 75
Cardoso, Nancy 10
Caribbean plantation economy
 16–17
Carroll, Seforosa 1–3
Carvalho, William D. 142
Centro Intercultural de
 Documentacíon 18
Céspedes, Choquehuanca 111
Chakrabarty, Dipesh
 'The Climate of History: Four
 Theses' 24
 decolonization 111
 two kinds of 'now' 107–8
Chang Pei-Lun 88
China, Republic of: Han viewpoint
 99
Chipana Quispe, Sofía 143
Chipko movement 9
Christianity
 Anthropocene and 179
 Bible as authority 153
 colonization of Americas 136–9
 communion 155
 creation and 58
 Day of the Lord 69, 75–81
 decolonization and 143–5
 earth-centred liturgy 61–4
 ecological reformation of 64–7
 ecology 57–61
 as exploiting nature 56
 hope in resurrection 145

human exceptionalism 121–3
 imago Dei 121–3, 127–30
 salvation 57–61
Church and Climate Justice (Wesley)
 9
Cirakayan (Amis) people 97–9
cities and urban development
 artificial systems of 70–5
 factors of ecological crisis 73–4
climate change
 concept of Anthropocene 7
 decolonial perspective 32
 evidence of crisis 119–21
 human responsibility 24
 human solidarity and 34
 rising temperatures 74
 as symptom, not cause 34
 urgency of issue 33
 web of life 75
 see also Anthropocene; Capitalocene
Climate Change: A Challenge to
 Churches in South Africa (South
 African Council of Churches)
 159–60
'The Climate of History: Four Theses'
 (Chakrabarty) 24
Club of Rome reports 8
Colombia
 co-existence with Earth 112–13
 decolonization 111
 Nasa people 2, 111
colonialism and imperialism
 Abya Yala/North America 135–47
 Anthropocene as Eurocentric 26–7
 coloniality of nature 109–10
 as commercial enterprise 73
 decolonization 30–3, 35, 110–12
 decolonizing humans and Earth
 108–10
 ecojustice 142–6
 interconnectedness of systems 32
 liberation 110–12
 modernity project and 15–18
 'New World' 109
 not a Western canon of thought 32
 Othering 32
 plantation economy 16
 recent anthropology and 29–30

Taiwan's indigenous people
  87–100
 theology and 28–30
'Conjectural beginning of human
  history' (Kant) 126–7
Connell, R. W. 51
Conradie, Ernst 64–5
Corrêra Lima, Luís
 Teologia e os LGBT+ 163
Coudrain, Anne 120–1
Council for World Missions (CWM)
  2
 DARE programme xiii
 liberation theologies xiii
Cou (Tsou) people 89
A Covenant Church (Briggs) 154–6
'Covid, Capitalism, Climate: The
  Way Forward' (Shiva, podcast)
  73–5
Covid-19 pandemic 73
Crist, Eileen 106, 109
Critical Theory
 anticolonial 18
 on capitalist modernity 7–8
Crosby, Alfred W.
 Ecological Imperialism 14
Crutzen, Paul J.
 proposes 'Anthropocene' 13,
  103–6, 120

Daneel, Marthinus L.
 ecological liturgy 63, 65
Danowski, Déborah 109
Dark Ecology 1
Darwin, Charles
 human and non-human 129–30
Davies, Jeremy
 The Birth of the Anthropocene 25
death
 resisting 50–3
 state sovereignty and 48–54
*Decolonizing the Anthropocene:
 Disobedience via Plural
 Constitutions* (Jackson) 29–30
De Gruchy, Steve
 'An Olive Agenda' 158–9
De La Torre, Miguel
 Christianity and empire 30

Delgado, Yenny 3
 'Ecojustice in Abya Yala' 135–47
dependency theories 13
Descartes, Rene
 'cogito ergo sum' 122
 Discours de la Méthode 122
Dialectic of Enlightenment
 (Horkheimer and Adorno) 7–8,
  10–11
Dietschy, Beat 3
 'Upright Walk on a Habitable Earth
  in Anthropocene' 103–15
Discernment and Radical
 Engagement (DARE)
 Programme xiii, 2
Discours de la Méthode
 (Descartes) 122
Dryzek, John 70–1
Dussel, Enrique
 European modernity 137
 Europe in the Americas 109

Earth
 biodiversity loss 123–4
 see ecology; environment
Earth Charter Initiative 114
The Earthly Community
 (Mbembe) 112–13
d'Eaubonne, Françoise 89
ecofeminism
 anti-war and military 41
 contextualist ethics 96
 indigenous in Taiwan 87–8
 indigenous literature 91–6
 key concepts of 89–90
 in the Militarycene 47–54
'Ecojustice in Abya Yala:
 Decolonization and the Practice of
 "Good Living"' (Delgado) 135–47
Ecological Imperialism (Crosby) 14
ecology 3
 all living organisms 150–1
 artificial human systems 70–5
 facing collapse 177–9
 forest systems 70
 Pope Francis on 28
 sinning against 165–8
 and socialism 13

economics
  the plantation 16
  see also Capitalocene
Ecuador, decolonization of 111–12
education 169
Elizabeth I, colonialism of 73
Ellis, Erle Christopher
  Anthropocene: A Very Short Introduction 22–4
Engel, Mary Potter 66
Enloe, Cynthia 52
environment
  military and war damage 40–54
  oikos 158–9
  shock of war 42–4
  'slow violence' 45
  solidarity and 180
Ergen, Mustafa 72
Escobar, Arturo 15, 112
Ester, Ana
  Os dezmandamentos 163
Esteva, Gustavo 14
ethics and values
  anthropocentrism of non-human creation 150–1
Europe
  colonialism and Anthropocene 13
  colonizer ideas of 'subhumans' 109
  Eurocene 47
Evagrius of Pontus 121
externalization, Lessenich and 12
Extinction, Sixth Mass 69

'Facing Climate Collapse: Ecology, Theology and Capitalocene' (Rieger) 177–80
Fanon, Frantz 35
Fensham, Charles J. 62, 63
forests and trees
  deforestation 135–6
  Nürnberger on deforestation 63–4
  self-sustaining 70
  war and military actions 41
'A Forgotten Body of War' (Pae) 40–54
Fornet-Betancourt, Raúl
  decolonization 110–11
  human detachment from nature 110

'"For the Life of the ... Animals": Christian Anthropology Revisited in the Light of the Climate Crisis' (Asproulis) 119–30
fossil fuels, Anthropocene and 13
Foucault, Michel 49
Fourel, Christophe 18
Francis, Pope
  the Church is a woman 174
  entire material universe 175
  Laudate Deum 173
  Laudato si' 28, 151, 155–6, 165–8, 173
Fraser, Nancy
  cannibalistic over-exploitation 105–6
Freire, Paulo
  Pedagogy of the Oppressed 169
Frère, Bruno 10–11
Freud, Sigmund 129

'The "Garden on Fire": An Ecological Reading of the Day of the Lord in the Old Testament' (Nokcharenla) 69–81
gardens, artificial systems of 70–5
Gaza war
  Christmas and 54
Gebara, Ivone 10
  ecofeminist theology 48, 50–1, 51–2, 53
  'interrelationality' 41
  Longing for Running Water 138
  poor people's movements 114
Genesis, Book of
  all creation 151
  animals and 126
  covenants 155
  creation and good 59
  earth-centred liturgy and 62
  ecological understanding 67
  Noah's covenant with God 114
  subduing the earth 73
  warns against murders 145
Ghosh, Amitav
  The Great Derangement 26
  'Nutmeg's Curse: Parables for a Planet in Crisis' 106

religious attention to climate 35
Global Witness 141
God in Creation (Moltmann) 8
good living 143
Gorz, André 18
The Great Derangement: Climate Change and the Unthinkable (Ghosh) 26
greenhouse gases
  'clouds of darkness' 78
  war and military emissions 43
Gressmann, Hugo 76
Grove, Jairus 47
Guan Dawei 96-7
Guna people 135
Gunkel, Hermann 76
Gutiérrez, Gustavo 138-9

Hartley, Daniel 25-6
Harvey, David 17
Hawai'ian Islands 45-6
Hayward, Tim 24-5
Hendriks, Jurgens 153
Hettinger, Ned
  Age of Man Environmentalism 104
  anthropocentric narcissism 106
'The Historical Roots of Our Ecological Crisis' (White) 28-9
History and Class Consciousness (Lukacs) 11
Hölderlin, Friedrich 12
Homeland of the Mountain Cherry Blossoms (Rimuy Aki) 94-6, 99-100
Honneth, Axel
  A Struggle for Recognition 12
Horkheimer, Max
  Dialectics of Enlightenment (with Adorno) 7-8, 10-11
Hsieh Jolan 97-9
human beings
  activities towards crisis 69
  animal rights and 124-7
  anthropocentric ethics 150
  artificial systems of 71-5
  as citizens, not conquerors 80
  eco-apartheid 110
  engagement with nature 81
  exceptionalism 121-3, 127-30
  and geophysical time 107-8
  hope and 81
  ideas of 'subhumans' 109
  imago Dei 121-3, 127-30
  responsibility for climate change 24
  solidarity against catastrophe 34
  ways of inhabiting Earth 112-15
  see also Anthropocene; Capitalocene

Illich, Ivan
  Centro 18
Inca people 110
Indigenous Knowledge Systems and Practices (IKSPs) 33
indigenous people
  anti-colonialism 17-18
  colonizer ideas of 'subhumans' 109
  decolonization 110-12
  exploitation of labour 137-8
  female knowledge 96-100
  IKSPs and non-Western ideas 32-3
  intercultural philosophy 110
  knowledge systems 88-9
  literature in Taiwan 91-6
  recognizing wisdom of 80-1
  Taiwan's social structure 87-8, 97
  women in Taiwan 88
intersectionality 109
An Introduction to the Principles of Morals and Legislation (Bentham) 126-7
Iraq
  Gulf Wars in 42-3
  'shock and awe' tactics 42
Israel, Gaza war and 54

Jackson, Mark
  Decolonizing the Anthropocene 29-30
Jayath, Mathew
  ecological understanding 67
  salvation 58
Jesus Christ
  hope for crucified 145
  the Last Supper 155-6
Jewish people and Judaism 12
  Yom YHWH 76

Joel, Book of 77–8
John, Gospel of
  'flesh' as animalhood 128–9
John Paul II, Pope 167, 172
justice
  ecojustice for Abya Yala 136
  eco-liturgy towards 61–2
  Old Testament and 75
  southern Africa and 150
  UCCSA and 156–8
  UCCSA and eco-theology 152–8

Kant, Immanuel 122
  'Conjectural beginning of human history' 126–7
King Jr, Martin Luther 77
Klein, Naomi 46
Kopnina, Helen 109
  'Anthropocentrism More than Just a Misunderstood Problem' (et al.) 24–5
Korea, South
  napalm and Agent Orange 43–4
  'shock and awe' tactics 42
  wartime chemicals 43–5
  Yongsan garrison pollution 44–5
Kreike, Emmanuel
  'environcide' 42
Kuhn, Thomas 121

land and ownership
  UCCSA and 159–60
Landless Workers' Movement, Brazil 10, 17
Landron, Oliver 8
Laos, Agent Orange and 48
Latin America
  capitalism and modernity 15
  capitalist modernity and 8
  'epistemology of the hunter' 110
  see also Abya Yala
Latour, Bruno 1
Laudate Deum (Pope Francis) 173
Laudato si' (Pope Francis) 151, 173
  Moreira's reflections on 165–8
Lawyers for a Demographic Society, Korea 44
Le Duff, Matthieu 120–1

Leff, Enrique 17–18
Leopold, Aldo
  human as citizen, not conqueror 80
Lessenich, Stephan
  externalization 12–13
Levinas, Emmanuel 122
liberation theology 163–5
  Boff on 169
  ecology and 1–2
  education and 169
  LGBT+ 169–72
  rebuilding foundations 66
Liglav A-wu 93, 94
Lin Wan Jou 3
  'Taiwan Indigenous Women and Ecofeminism' 87–100
Lin Yu-hsin 94
literature, indigenous, in Taiwan 91–6
Longing for Running Water (Gebara) 138
Löwy, Michael 12
Lukacs, Georg
  History and Class Consciousness 11
Lyiking Yuma 93
Lynas, Mark
  humans over Nature 106

McBrien, J.
  Capitalocene as Necrocene 72
McNeill, John R. 14
McParlan, Paul
  on communion and Pope Francis 155–6
Malachi, Book of
  Day of the Lord 80
Malm, Andreas 7, 13
Mann, Charles 14
Marris, Emma 104
Martínez Alier, Joan 14
  environmentalism of the poor 2, 18
Martínez Andrade, Luis 1–3
  'Theology and Anticolonial Critical Theory in "Capitalocene"' 7–18
Martinho, Vitor D. 151
Marx, Karl 17
masculinity, military and patriarchy 51–2

Maseko, Revd Xolani 3
  integrated belief systems 154
  'Sustainable Anthropocene and Ecological Justice' (with Soko-De Jong) 149–61
Masenya, Madipoane
  rest 159
Mayan people
  Popol Vuh 141
  'they tried to bury us' 141
Mbembe, Achille
  decolonization project 27
  The Earthly Community 112–13
  sovereignty and killing 49
Melgarejo, Arteta 111
Mendes, Chico 2
Méndez Arceo, Bishop Sergio 18
Mendoza, Lily 28–9
Mexico
  neo-Zapatistas 2, 17
  see also Abya Yala
Mies, Maria 92
  capitalist patriarchy 100
Mignolo, Walter 12, 31
Militarycene
  Agent Orange 48–9
  Anthropocene and 53–4
  ecofeminism 47–54
mining
  artisanal 160
  colonial exploitation 16
Mintz, Sidney W.
  plantation economy 16–17
Mitja, Danielle
  paradigm shift of 'Anthropocene' 120–1
modernity
  European 137
Moe-Lobeda, Cynthia 9
Moltmann, Jürgen
  God in Creation 8
Monsanto
  Agent Orange and 50
  seeds policy 140–1
Moore, Jason W. 7, 13, 103–4
  Anthropocene or Capitalocene? 25–6
  cheap nature 105

Moreira, Suzana Regina 3
  'Out of the Closet' 163–74
Morton, Timothy
  Dark Ecology 1
Mourao, Paulo R. 151
Münster, Arno
  Atheism in Christianity 11
Müntzer, Thomas 103

Narain, Sunita
  global warming and inequality 107
Narodniks 14
Nasa people
  Liberation of Mother Earth 111
natural disasters
  capitalist views of 51
  Day of the Lord 80
  human focus of 81
  hyper-natural 80
  KwaZulu Natal flooding 57–8
  New Orleans and Katrina 46
  types of loss and 56–7
  urban design and flooding 74
  'wrath of God' and 57–8
nature
  alliance with 113–15
  as a capital asset 105–6
  capitalism and resources 61–2
  colonial destruction of 139–42
  eco-apartheid 110
  Frankfurt School and 11
Ndlovu-Gatsheni, Sabelo J.
  colonial power structures 30–2
New, Charlee 28
Nixon, Rob
  slow violence 45, 47
Nokcharenla 3
  'The "Garden on Fire"' 69–81
Norgaard, Richard B. 14
Northcott, Michael
  eco-salvation 63
Nothwehr, Dawn M. 75
Nürnberger, Klaus
  on deforestation 63–4
'Nutmeg's Curse: Parables for a Planet in Crisis' (Ghosh) 106

Ochoa Muñoz, Karina 109

O'Connor, James
Capitalism, Nature, Socialism. A Journal of Socialist Ecology 18
Oikos: Our Common Home (Zachariah) 14–15
oil spills
 in war 43–4
On the Concept of History (Benjamin) 11–12, 12
Oregon and Agent Orange 49–50
Origen
 human exceptionalism 121
Orthodox Christianity
 human exceptionalism 121
'Out of the Closet and Out of the Tomb of Ecological Sins' (Moreira) 163–74

Pae, Keun-Joo Christine 3
'A Forgotten Body of War' 40–54
Palamas, Gregory
 imago Dei 128
Palermo, Angel 14
Palestinians
 Gaza war 54
Pedagogy of the Oppressed (Freire) 169
The People vs. Agent Orange (documentary film) 49–50
Persian Gulf
 shock and awe in wars 42–3
Peru
 political ecology and Marxism 18
Picard, Michael
 on Persian Gulf wars 43
Piccolo, John
 'Anthropocentrism More than Just a Misunderstood Problem' (et al.) 24–5
Pierron, Jean-Philippe 1
Plato
 immortality of the soul 121
Plumwood, Val 92
 philosophical animism 90–1
pollution
 agent Orange 43–4
 agriculture and 74
 military poisons 48–50

napalm 43–4
 'slow violence' 44–6
 transport and 74
 war and military actions 43
 Yongsan Children's Garden 44–5
Portugal
 colonization of Abya Yala 136–9
Powell, Samuel
 salvation and creation 58
power relations
 decolonialization 108–10
 war and 48–50
 see also colonialism and imperialism
The Principle of Hope (Bloch) 11, 113
Prophetic Imagination (Brueggemann) 79
Psalms, Book of
 earth-centred liturgy and 62
Puar, Jasib
 'right to maim' 49

Quechua people
 Sumak kawsay/good living 143
Quijano, Aníbal
 coloniality of power 108–9

Rapley, Professor Chris
 on the Anthropocene 22
refugees, climate 120
Reiger, Joerg 3
rest 159
Rieger, Joerg 13
 Capitalocene 14
 concept of 'Capitalocene' 7
 'Facing Climate Collapse' 177–80
 on gardens 71
 Theology in the Capitalocene 34
Rimuy Aki
 Homeland of the Mountain Cherry Blossoms 94–6, 99–100
Rognon, Frédèric
 Protestant ecology 8–9
Roman Catholic Church
 ecological sin(s) 165–8, 172–5
 Moreira's personal context 3–5
 out of the closet 172–5

Pan-Amazonian Synod 166
Romans, Letter to
  Earth groans 130
Rosenzweig, Franz 12
Rowley, H. H.
  on Day of the Lord 76
Ruether, R.
  eco-salvation 63

Sadje, Hadje Cresencio 3
  'Anthropocene or Global
    Coloniality?' 22–36
Sakupapa, Chalwe, Teddy 60–1
salvation
  African context 60–1
  ecological view of 57–61
  'Salvation and Liturgy Reimagined
    through Earth-centered Worship
    in the Age of Anthropocene'
    (Siwila) 56–67
Sayre, Robert 12
Scandrett, Joel A. 158
Schwägerl, Christian
  humans and nature 104
sexuality
  military and 51
Shiva, Vandana 92
  capitalist patriarchy 100
  'Covid, Capitalism, Climate' 73–5
  decolonizing ecofeminism 90
  eco-apartheid 110
  seed conservation and small farms
    90, 91
Simpson, Michael
  Anthropocene as colonial discourse
    31
  'The Anthropocene as Colonial
    Discourse' 26–7
Siwila, Lilian Cheelo 3
  'Salvation and Liturgy Reimagined'
    56–67
Sixth Mass Extinction 69
slave labour
  the plantation 16
Smith, John M. P.
  on Day of the Lord 76
Smith, Linda Tuhiwai
  indigenous research 88–9

Snyder, Howard A. 60, 158
Sobrino, Jon 145
social justice
  web of life 75
social structures
  environmental problems 25
  global institutions 48
Soko-De Jong, Thandi 3
  integrated belief systems 154
  'Sustainable Anthropocene and
    Ecological Justice' (with Maseko)
    149–61
solidarity
  Rieger on 34
de Sousa Santos, Boaventura 32
South Africa
  KwaZulu Natal flooding 57–8
  see also United Congregational
    Church of Southern Africa
    (UCCSA)
Spain
  colonization of Abya Yala 136–9
Stengers, Isabelle
  on the Anthropocene 107
Stoermer, Eugene F.
  'Anthropocene' term 103
  coins 'Anthropocene' 120
A Struggle for Recognition (Honneth)
  12
'Sustainable Anthropocene and
  Ecological Justice: Perspectives
  from the Ethos of the UCCSA'
  (Maseko and Soko-De Jong)
  149–61

Taiwan
  changes for indigenous people
    87–8
  Cirakayan (Amis) people 97–9
  ecofeminist literature 91–6
  female indigenous knowledge
    96–100
  socio-economic structures of 87–9
  Tayal people 94–6
  Traditional Ecological Knowledge
    96
  'Taiwan Indigenous Women and
    Ecofeminism' (Lin) 87–100

INDEX OF NAMES AND SUBJECTS

Tassinari, Aidée
  capitalism and colonialism 17
Taylor, Bron
  'Anthropocentrism More than Just a Misunderstood Problem' (et al.) 24–5
technology
  Bloch's 'technical utopia' 113
  indigenous knowledge and 80–1
  nanotechnology 104
Teilhard de Chardin, Pierre 8
theology 3
  Anthropocene and 28–9
  attention to climate 34–6
  Boff on alliance with nature 114
  Capitalocene and 177–8
  colonialism and 28–30
  ecological repositioning 8–10
  human exceptionalism/imago Dei 121–3, 127–30
  interconnectedness 51
  liberation 163–5
  neoliberal mindset and 32–3
  not one-size-fits-all 32
  queer 163–5, 168–72
  'Theology and Anticolonial Critical Theory in "Capitalocene"' (Martínez Andrade) 7–18
Theology in the Capitalocene: Ecology, Identity, Class and Solidarity (Rieger) 34
Thistlethwaite, Susan Brooks
  liberation theology 66
Tonga people
  Kariba dam disaster 61–2
tourism
  environmental effects 46
Travis, Sarah 62
  earth-centred liturgy 63

United Congregational Church of Southern Africa (UCCSA) 160–1
  advocacy in environmental justice 160–1
  eco-theology 152–8
  as justice church 156–8
  land and ownership 159–60
  oikos 158–9

  values and environment 149–50
United Nations Geosphere-Biosphere Programme
  Crutzen proposes 'Anthropocene' 103–6
United States
  Abya Yala 135–47
  Animal Welfare Act 125
  on climate change threat 40
  damage to Hawai'i 45–6
  Militarycene 47
  New Orleans and Katrina 46
  Oregon and herbicides 49–50
  pollution of Yongsan garrison 45
  Vietnam and Agent Orange 48–9
  wars in Persian Gulf 42–3
United States National Science and Technology Council
  'Nanotechnology: Shaping the World Atom by Atom' 104
UNOSAT Flood Monitoring 74
'Upright Walk on a Habitable Earth in Anthropocene' (Dietschy) 103–15
uranium
  war and military actions 41

Vayayana, Tibsunungu 'e
  Cou knowledge systems 89
Vega Cantor, Renán 7, 13
Vietnam
  Agent Orange 48–9
  'shock and awe' tactics 42
Viveiros de Castro, Eduardo 109
von Rad, Gerhard
  on Day of the Lord 76

Wallerstein, Immanuel 12
Walsh, Catherine
  coloniality of nature 109–10
  decolonization 111–12
Waltke, Bruce
  Day of the Lord 79
war and military actions
  chemical weapons 43
  deforestation 41
  'Militarycene' 40–54
  shock tactics 42–6

'slow violence' 44–6
Warren, Karen 96
Washington, Hayden
  'Anthropocentrism More than Just a Misunderstood Problem' (et al.) 24–5
water
  agriculture and 74
wealth and poverty
  Day of the Lord 78–9
  environmentalism and 1
Wesley, Vinod
  Church and Climate Justice 9
White Jr, Lynn
  exploitation of Earth 178–9
  'The Historical Roots of Our Ecological Crisis' 28–9
  human cause of climate change 120
wildfires
  veld fires 160
Wirzba, Norman 108

The Work of Art in the Age of Mechanical Reproduction (Benjamin) 12
World Bank
  Kariba Dam and 61–2
World Council of Churches 157
Wycliffe, John 153

Yang Tsui 94

Zachariah, George
  Christianity and ecology 28–9
  Oikos: Our Common Home 14–15
Zambia, Tonga people 61–2
Zimbabwe
  artisanal mining 160
  environmental injustice 150
  Environmental Management Authority 150
  land ownership 160
  tree-planting eucharist 63

www.ingramcontent.com/pod-product-compliance
Lightning Source LLC
Chambersburg PA
CBHW032337300426
44109CB00041B/1121